PRAISE FOR *LOTUS GIRL*

"Other books have told us, engagingly, of how West began to meet East in the 1960s and beyond. But none I have read cuts through every illusion and projection with the warmth, the clarity, the unflinching self-awareness of Helen Tworkov's indispensable memoir. She takes us, exhilaratingly, to Kyoto, Saigon, and Kathmandu and she offers us fond, indelible portraits of some of the seminal figures of our time. But the great gift of *Lotus Girl* is to share with every reader a wise, undeluded, deeply searching enquiry into mind and how we can start to transform it."

—**Pico Iyer,** bestselling author and journalist

"When the history of Buddhism in America is one day chronicled, this book—brutally honest and beautifully written—will form an essential chapter."

—**Donald S. Lopez, Jr.,** Arthur E. Link Distinguished university professor of Buddhist and Tibetan Studies at the University of Michigan

"*Lotus Girl* is not only a beautiful memoir of one strong, Buddhist woman's journey through the social and political upheavals of the 1960s until now, it is also one of the most powerful and compelling accounts I've read of how Buddhist practices found their way into American culture. Readers will be grateful for this gift of her hard-won spiritual insights, knowledge, personal experience, and wisdom."

—**Charles Johnson**, author of the National Book Award–winning novel, *Middle Passage*

"[A] terrific book. I could not put it down. It's the book I've been waiting for and gives so many answers to how we unfold and become who we are. Gorgeously written. In her story, I also discover myself."

—**Natalie Goldberg**, author of *Writing Down the Bone*s and *Three Simple Lines*

"Brilliant writer Helen Tworkov shares the splendid details of a life lived fully. Her discerning sensibility shines through in her captivating, delightful, and wondrous telling of tales that would be enough for several ordinary lifetimes. An extraordinary treat."

—**Daniel Goleman**, psychologist and
New York Times bestselling author of *Emotional Intelligence*

"Helen takes us on a great ride! *Lotus Girl* is a fabulous description of being right in the creative middle of the Dharma flowering in the West. Honest and poignant, engaging and deep, both touching and enlightening, leaving us with a smile and a tear."

—**Jack Kornfield,** author of *A Path With Heart*

"A vivid account of an amazing, lifelong spiritual odyssey by a woman who never took no for an answer."

—**Lawrence Shainberg**, author of
Ambivalent Zen and *Four Men Shaking*

"*Lotus Girl* is at once the most unsullied and compellingly unsentimental memoir I've read in years. Her journey speaks generously of our perpetual struggle to reach a truth and compassion that is so urgently needed now. It's a must-read for all walks of life."

—**Phong H. Bui**, publisher and artistic director, *The Brooklyn Rail*

"It's a journey I loved and learned from through this wonderful new book by one of the pioneer women of American Buddhism."

—**Mirabai Bush**, author with Ram Dass of *Walking Each Other Home*

"This rich and unique memoir has value for any reader interested in the possibilities of positive change."

—**Philip Glass**, composer

LOTUS GIRL

My Life at the Crossroads of Buddhism and America

· · · · · · · · · · · · · · · · · ·

Helen Tworkov

ST. MARTIN'S
ESSENTIALS
NEW YORK

First published in the United States by St. Martin's Essentials,
an imprint of St. Martin's Publishing Group

www.stmartins.com

Library of Congress Cataloging-in-Publication Data

Names: Tworkov, Helen, author.
Title: Lotus girl : my life at the crossroads of Buddhism and America / Helen Tworkov.
Description: First. | New York : St. Martin's Essentials, 2024.
Identifiers: LCCN 2023038225 | ISBN 9781250321558 (hardcover) |
    ISBN 9781250321541 (ebook)
Subjects: LCSH: Tworkov, Helen. | Buddhist women—United States—Biography. |
    Buddhist converts—United States—Biography. | Buddhism—United States.
Classification: LCC BQ990.W67 A3 2024 | DDC 294.3092 [B]—dc23/eng/20231002
LC record available at https://lccn.loc.gov/2023038225

Our books may be purchased in bulk for promotional, educational, or business use.
Please contact your local bookseller or the Macmillan Corporate and
Premium Sales Department at 1-800-221-7945, extension 5442, or
by email at MacmillanSpecialMarkets@macmillan.com.

First Edition: 2024

10 9 8 7 6 5 4 3 2 1

With gratitude and love this book is dedicated to my mother, Rachel (Wally) Tworkov, and to the most important of the subsequent mothers who nourished me with guidance, kindness, and wisdom: the teachers at Yeshe Nyingpo, Taizan Maezumi Roshi, and Yongey Mingyur Rinpoche.

Contents

PART ONE: ONE CUP OF TEA   1

A Buddhist Monk Sets Himself on Fire · East Twenty-Third
Street, New York City · The Mystery · Religion Versus the Tra-
dition of the New · Named After a Farmer · The High Priests ·
The Dalton School · Biala · *The Dharma Bums* · Back to Ohio ·
Psychedelics · Charles Mingus and Other City Forays

PART TWO: ASIAN TRAVELS   53

1965 · Japan · Mekong Adventures · India · Nepal ·
Between Kathmandu and New York

PART THREE: CAUSES AND CONDITIONS   103

Return to New York · 1968: Making the News · 1969: The
Moonwalk and Marriage · Montreal · Cape Breton,
Nova Scotia · Confounding Logic · The Arica School ·
My White Dog · New-Age Excursions

PART FOUR: ENCOUNTERING THE TIBETANS 135

Milarepa in an Oakland Gym · Dharma Diversity ·
Dudjom Rinpoche · Yeshe Nyingpo · A Bardo Retreat ·
Relax Your Mind

PART FIVE: CONVERGENCES AND FRACTURES 169

A Cabin in the Woods · Dharma at the White House ·
A House Blessing · Jasper, Meet Thinley Norbu · Lamas in
the Big Apple · Wind River Retreat · Family Problems ·
Falling Apart

PART SIX: WAVES AND WINDOWS 197

Zen in America · A Solo Retreat · Provincetown · A Peace
Offering · Ascending the Mountain · My Father's Death · The
View from the Kitchen Window · A New Morning · Maezumi
Roshi · A Winter in Cape Breton

PART SEVEN: THE *TRICYCLE* YEARS 243

When the Swans Almost Drowned in the Lake · *Tricycle: The
Buddhist Review* · Change Your Mind Day · One Death After
Another · 9/11 · Taking a Different Seat

PART EIGHT: WHERE IS YOUR MIND? 279

Return to Vajrayana · Mingyur Rinpoche · Change I Could
Believe In · Bodh Gaya, 2009 · Sherab Ling Monastery ·
Vietnam

PART NINE: THE BARDOS 301

The Bardo of This Life · In the Bardo of Old Age · America
in the Bardo of Dying

Acknowledgments 327

ONE CUP OF TEA

A Buddhist Monk
Sets Himself on Fire

Just before noon on June 11, 1963, a slow-moving baby-blue Austin sedan pulled up at a busy intersection in the heart of Saigon. Inside was the Vietnamese Buddhist monk and temple abbot Thich Quang Duc, along with two attendant monks. When the car stopped, the three immediately got out. One attendant placed a cushion on the ground, and Thich Quang Duc quickly sat down in formal meditation posture. The other attendant removed a five-gallon can of gasoline from the trunk and poured it over the seated monk. As three hundred monks and nuns from his temple stood by, Thich Quang Duc pulled a pack of matches from his pocket and ignited his gasoline-soaked robes.

The monk was protesting the government's crackdown on Buddhist clergy, an assault that most of the world knew nothing about, and it was not until the following morning, June 12, that the shocking image of Thich Quang Duc's self-immolation reached the United States. That's when I first saw Malcolm Browne's black-and-white photograph of an unimaginable sight: an elderly monk seated upright and straight as a statue as flames consumed his body. Browne's photograph later won a Pulitzer Prize, and no one who saw it ever forgot it. Within an inferno of his own making, Thich Quang Duc sat so still that the whole world stopped. When it moved again, to me it never looked quite the same.

I was twenty years old and had never seen a Buddhist monk before. I had no clear idea of where Vietnam was either. But I had been studying anthropology at Hunter College in New York City, and had been looking at photographs of strange behavior. Restless within the conventions of my own society, I had turned to anthropology as an avenue for exploring alternatives. Photographs of scarified faces, noses pierced by bone, and penises sheathed in dried gourds were part of my coursework; and I was drawn to anything that challenged prevailing authority: civil rights, women's rights, psychedelics, the Beats. Nothing prepared me for Quang Duc. He was certainly challenging authority—in his case, the powerful ruling regime of South Vietnam—but his method upended every idea I had assumed about human behavior. In order to make a political statement he reset the very parameters of human potential. It was impossible to imagine sitting in the midst of flames without flinching. Impossible. And no degree of political passion or moral righteousness could explain it.

Journalists had been alerted to a newsworthy event, but demonstrations in Saigon had become so common and without consequence that only a few had shown up. Those who did reported their visceral alarm at watching living flesh turn to ash, but no eyewitness in the English-language press attempted to describe Quang Duc's composure. His equanimity remained outside the media narrative, leaving it to hang in the air like a hologram: true but not real. It would have felt natural to project excruciating pain and anguish onto the monk. After all, he sat burning to death. Yet as much as I looked for signs of torment, the photograph does not show a man in the throes of physical or mental suffering. There was nothing to relate to, to identify with—and I kept wondering how this could be.

Thich Quang Duc (*thich* is the Vietnamese pronunciation of Sakya, the Buddha's clan name), then sixty-six, had made it his mission to draw international attention to the persecution of Buddhist clergy in South Vietnam by President Ngo Dinh Diem, a fundamentalist Roman Catholic. He fulfilled his mission so successfully that in the process of focusing worldwide attention on the plight of South Vietnam's Buddhists, he spotlighted Diem's regime in all its corruption, as well as its alliance with the United States military and the covert buildup of American troops. Though Quang Duc was not protesting American intervention, the image of his self-immolation became forever merged with the war itself.

Diem's cronies attributed his dramatic achievement to anesthetic drugs. Others might have categorized it as a one-off magic trick of sensational street theater. Or perhaps the Buddhist robes and formal meditation posture told a story of training and discipline, of a mind that could not be harmed by the flames that destroyed his body. This possibility was especially difficult to consider in the West, where the meditative disciplines of his tradition were still largely unknown. It was, however, the version I wanted to believe, and I wondered if it made sense to Buddhists, even while stumping the rest of us. After all, he was a monk within a celebrated religious tradition, a revered abbot, not a faithless misfit; nor was it just the lone warrior against the establishment that made me cheer Quang Duc. The inexplicable version of this event stirred up questions from my childhood that I had not considered for many years.

By the time I was five, I played private games of make-believe—becoming other people, living with other families, exploring ways to disappear in plain sight. Later in life, psychotherapists would try to help me figure out my need not to be where I was. Nonetheless I became familiar with hidden aspects of the mind—the ones that no one ever talked to me about and were not taught in school—and I learned something of how secret and invisible worlds could run interference with unwanted circumstances and emotions. I was an unhappy little girl, so my curiosity about how reality could be manipulated was not whimsical. There was a precarious safety in conjuring my own hiding places and knowing that stories that came from inside my head could make life less scary—at least for a little while. When my father was unreasonably and irascibly critical of something my mother served for dinner, and my mother sat withering at the table, I wanted to protect her, which I could not do, but I didn't have to stick around to witness something so troubling. I could remove myself to the safety of pastoral harmony, sunshine, and leafy trees. When the look on his face suggested an imminent explosion, or when his angry disapproval was leveled directly at me—for my table manners, my rude interruptions, dirty fingernails, swear words (which I had learned from him), or my insistence on trying to discreetly carve my name into the edge of the wooden table—then I would resort to the most reliable and recurrent escapes. In one favorite daydream, I was a ballerina in a yellow leotard with a matching tutu and a golden cardboard crown; in another I was Tarzan's Jane, swinging from jungle vines.

When I saw the photograph of Quang Duc, I had to wonder if he had used his mind to create a field of protection; or had told himself a story that had separated his mind from his body. As his body burned, where was his mind?

Through the therapeutic lens, my flights of fancy had been reduced to escapism. In some prototypical psychological portrait, daydreaming was always in a negative classification; no therapist ever suggested that it might have been a healthy search away from sadness. Anthropology was viewed as another dive down the rabbit hole; yet comparing different cultures had also revealed how the mind processed or distorted or restructured sensory and emotional matter. This version of mind made it a blank screen that reflected distinct values through varying interpretations of sensory input; and this could account for why some societies relished eating dogs, while others found this culinary delight repulsive yet chowed down on pigs and cows. Or maybe this so-called blank screen had sentient qualities of its own. Maybe it had the capacity to make choices and not be automatically subject to conventional dictates, or to sensory response such as, for example, extreme heat. Quang Duc raised the question.

Following his death, I began revisiting my little-girl strategies for coping with anxiety and fear. When I think back to 1963, I can't remember one basic feature of my life that didn't bewilder me: my mind, Quang Duc's mind, school, sex, drugs. But the encounter with Quang Duc inspired questions that felt more alive than my routine preoccupations with boyfriends, with how I looked and what I wore, and with what I wanted to be when I grew up. Within this muddle, Quang Duc roused my search for meaning, although it would take a few years before either Buddhism or the war in Vietnam began to shape the rest of my life.

East Twenty-Third Street, New York City

I've often been asked how I became a Buddhist. I've answered this question in different ways, sometimes including Thich Quang Duc, sometimes not. To my ears, all my answers have sounded hollow. Yet I've asked myself the same question, and have been as perplexed by my journey as others have been, for nothing about my family or education or childhood in New York City pointed to ancient India or to a 2,600-year-old spiritual tradition. When I consider the disjointed pieces of my own path, I am reminded of a teaching tale told by my Tibetan Buddhist teacher, Yongey Mingyur Rinpoche: A man is on a pilgrimage from Eastern Tibet to Lhasa, walking across snow fields. One day he stops for tea. He puts down his pack, digs out the flint he uses to light fires, and sets off in search of three small rocks. He returns and places the rocks in a circle. Then he sets off to find twigs. When he returns he places the twigs inside the circle, but he can't ignite the twigs with his flint. So he sets off again to look for dry grass in the crevices of nearby boulders. He returns and places the grass on top of the twigs, and this time the fire ignites. He fills his small pot with snow and sets it over the fire to make tea. When the tea is ready he leans back against a rock to enjoy his hot drink. Suddenly he becomes alarmed at the sight of dozens of footprints in the snow, coming and going in every direction. Once he recognizes that all the footprints are his own, he contemplates the many interrelated actions required to make one pot of tea. That's the end of the story, and it doesn't even include the history of the tea, the pot, the flint, the snow, or the man himself.

When I try to understand how I made my way from the cultural capital of the United States to sacred Buddhist sites in Asia, I feel like that man, perplexed by so many footprints coming and going in different directions without obvious purpose. The steps are distinct but when taken together, they reveal how thoughts and movements intersect to lead to one pot of tea—or, in my case, to a willy-nilly path of waking up.

Before my make-believe games came the impulse to invent them. Before that came the dynamics of my nuclear family, and before that, what little I know of the dysfunction of my parents' families. As the story of the man making a pot of tea reveals, nailing the beginning of anything requires an arbitrary choice. To begin my story about how Buddhism slowly reshaped my experience of myself and the world, I want to return to my childhood games.

One stands out because its lessons are still true today. I lived with my parents and my sister, Hermine, three and a half years older than me, in a railroad flat in downtown Manhattan on East Twenty-Third Street. Over the years we rearranged the apartment, and at different times I slept in different rooms. The game I remember most clearly started when I was about five and had a small room to myself at the front of the apartment. The privacy most likely factored into my investigations, for I never shared my games with anyone. At night, after I was put to bed, I would lie in the dark under the covers and run the fingers of one hand over the other hand. It felt soothing, a slight tickle. Then I would imagine what would happen if I turned on the light and discovered that the source of pleasure was a cockroach crawling on my skin. I would recoil, maybe scream. Once I got the gist of it, I played this game day and night, imagining touching different objects and confirming that the mind could transform what felt good one moment into something horrifying the next moment, even when the sensation itself remained the same. Intriguing, but just a game. It would take immersion in meditation decades later before I fully explored the power of preconception. Yet the game also emboldened other, less success-ful experiments, while providing a blueprint for a critical aspect of how the conceptual mind dictates experience, how it filters direct sensory input and turns it into something agreeable or not. Cockroaches regularly infested our apartment, and no one would think to allow one to crawl across their hand. How weird that experiences of *pleasant* or *unpleasant* were domi-nated by ideas and associations, not by direct experience.

This conclusion did not stop me from attributing my unhappy moods to my mother, father, and sister. Still, I would tell myself that if I could look at a flower and only a flower and think of nothing but that flower, I would be fine. If disturbing thoughts could not be willfully pushed out through the bones of my skull, I would smother them with imported nicer ones. I chose a sunflower by Van Gogh, as I had already spent many Sunday afternoons at the Metropolitan Museum of Art. It was a family deal: first art and then roller skating in Central Park. In my most distressed moments, I tried walking around with a sunflower inside my head, imagining that all the unjust hurt, the insults, taunts, and teases, had transformed into yellow petals.

I was often asked, even by strangers, why I was so unhappy. I had not been looking in a mirror and saying, *Gee, you look so unhappy, little girl,* so the question had the benign stupidity of asking a fish in water how it feels to be wet. I do remember wanting a different family: a mother who was not so melancholy, and a father who was not so volatile, and an older sister who didn't make fun of me and wasn't my father's favorite daughter. I fan-tasized that I had been adopted and was stuck living in the wrong family. Still, I wasn't beaten or abandoned or sent to bed cold or hungry. I had a home and knew where it was, and I had parents who loved me and tried hard to be good parents, although that role did not come naturally to ei-ther one. We had photographs of relatives who had been killed in the death camps. When I saw those photos, or images of starving or homeless chil-dren, I could acknowledge my own good fortune—but life as I dreamed it would be so much better. In a flash, I could swap urban grit for a bucolic idyll with the proverbial prince and white horse. When anger threatened to overwhelm me, especially in response to my father's harsh criticisms, I could disappear into the theater of my mind, dark and alone.

Dizziness was another game that explored how the world worked when I played spinning with the kids on my block. Twenty-Third Street was a main thoroughfare. This made for a lot of foot traffic, which did not prevent four or five of us from spreading across the sidewalk and spinning as fast as possible, then suddenly stopping and either remaining upright or falling to the ground. In my calculations, dizziness created an alignment with the rotation of the earth. If the earth was round and in constant motion, as I had been taught to accept as an indisputable scientific fact, then walking erect on a flat surface was an illusion, a big lie built into our most fundamental behavior. Everyone was in on the deception but no one discussed it, and everywhere people walked erect on a curved surface. This proved that nothing was as it appeared to be, and made me wonder if anything in the world could be trusted.

My father, Jack Tworkov, was an artist, a distinguished founder of what came to be called the New York School of Abstract Expressionists. This placed our family of four in a rarefied domain where the ranked conventions of class and money were displaced by the high value placed on making art. Today, making art has become so synonymous with making money that I encounter worldly people who register surprise on learning that in the years following World War II, making art was not a lucrative business. My father taught art, and my mother worked as a secretary. Our apartment, on the third floor of a four-story walk-up, was half a block east of the Bowery, and occasionally a boarder paid ten dollars a month to help cover the rent. To this particular apartment and to this crummy neighborhood, from time to time certain dinner guests arrived by taxi or a chauffeur-driven limo from Upper East Side townhouses or Park Avenue apartments.

I grew up among painters, writers, composers, and poets who were almost exclusively white men. Artists were not respected by our working-class Catholic neighbors, but in my childhood observations their preeminent status was defined by how they were treated by men of wealth and power who did not use public transportation when they came to visit. For these lawyers, bankers, and real estate developers, artists were the high priests.

From a very young age, I listened in on discussions of form and color, foreground and background, the use of perspective in Giotto's floors, Cézanne's mountains, making forms from emptiness, using emptiness to create form—ideas that applied to objects called *paintings,* to something called *art.* But such considerations of form and emptiness were never applied to the body or the mind. There was no opportunity to ask, *Did Cezanne's mountains exist outside his head? Are the images in a painting any more or less real than what we see in everyday life?*

These discussions about art never included anything I could understand, but they occurred with such confident ease as to make my teachers at Public School 40 on East Nineteenth Street sound simpleminded. Then again, I was not a good student, and with budding arrogance I attributed my poor grades to a worthless system. I was frequently caught talking in class or chewing gum, or staring out the window or doodling instead of practicing penmanship. I regularly got my knuckles rapped with a ruler or was ordered to sit in the corner with a wad of gum on my nose. These punishments did not correct my delinquencies and only affirmed that school was stupid. My poor grades were consistently explained by my uncooperative personality. It was not until I was past fifty years old that I was diagnosed with spatial dyslexia. This had not made it impossible to string letters into words or words into sentences, but reading was slow and frustrating and I gave up easily. To compensate, I experimented saying words that I couldn't read or spell; sometimes, I didn't even know what they meant. As for my uncooperative personality, it's possible that it was aggravated by dyslexia; yet I might have been just as uncooperative without any learning difficulties.

The conversations among artists often included names of European capitals and foreign museums and men of letters pronounced with foreign accents, and they sounded weightier and more informed than the conversations of other grown-ups I listened in on. They were more erudite than the conversations of not only my parents' wealthy friends and my schoolteachers but also the two grandparents I knew as a child. My father's mother spoke only Yiddish, and my mother's father hardly spoke at all. The language difference between my parents and their parents was one of many indications that we barely coexisted in the same country at the same time. My grandparents came from the Old World, and my parents were not just creating lives in the New World from scratch like our Irish and Polish neighbors. Experimental artists like my father had a different vision of accomplishment, and the New World—not just the shiny new world of materialism but also the new postwar world of possibilities—invited a leap into an unchartered future not captive to the past or present. This made the gap between us and my grandparents a divide of centuries.

All four of my grandparents were part of the great migration of Eastern European Jews to America in the early part of the twentieth century. Their shtetl confines in Poland, Russia, Ukraine, and Romania shared an immersion in undisputed orthodoxy. Once settled in New York City, my mother's family veered toward progressive politics, while my father's parents maintained traditional customs as best they could in their cramped quarters on Broome Street on Manhattan's Lower East Side. After leaving home, my father could not sustain the old traditions and never replaced them with secularized concessions. By the time I knew him, he was enjoying bacon for Sunday breakfasts and irritably refusing invitations from distant relatives to attend the bat mitzvahs of their American daughters.

How to move between the monotheistic morality of the Old Testament and the secular imperatives of the New World preoccupied my father until the day he died. For a time during the 1930s, his longing for a righteous doctrine was absorbed by communism, and even though that experiment didn't last, it's how he met my mother. In 1932, under the tutelage of her communist aunts, my mother signed up for an evening Russian language class, where she met my father. She was a sixteen-year-old virgin; he was thirty-two and twice divorced. Neither of them learned Russian.

My mother wore her long chestnut hair swept back in a bun, and her beauty was frequently noted. On outings with her daughters, she was often mistaken for the oldest sister. I know she had a quizzical intelligence, which I can almost bring to mind—though not quite. During social gatherings at our apartment she remained mostly quiet, as did other wives. I also remember a coquettish smile, but she was embarrassed by her rotten teeth, made more discolored by chain-smoking unfiltered cigarettes, and she smiled with her lips closed. She had friends who remember her as a *spitfire*—a jolting contradiction to the images I carry. What dominates my memory are her sullen withdrawals, those weeks when she spoke little, did not smile, and dutifully fed us and got us off to school. Had the smoke rings that she sometimes blew into the air formed a sign, it might have read, *Do not disturb.*

My mother was born on Elizabeth Street in Lower Manhattan, then raised by two of her father's sisters, spinsters who shared an apartment in Co-op City, a housing development in the Bronx known for its population of Yiddish-speaking, leftist garment workers, communists, socialists, and unionists, and was a prominent breeding ground for *red-diaper babies*—children of parents who were engaged with communism. Every few Sundays, my mother's father took the subway from his apartment in the Bronx to visit us. Max Waladarsky was lumbering, worn-down, dressed in a Sunday suit—brown with a matching felt hat—respectable, but looking as if life had collapsed in on him. He worked for the Department of Sanitation and spent his days pushing a gray canvas trash bin on a trolley with one hand while using the other to impale garbage with a metal spike on the end of a wooden pole. He always arrived at our apartment with a crumpled brown paper bag filled with gutter trinkets: single earrings, bracelets with broken clasps, eyeglass frames, beads, and busted fountain pens. With each visit, he brought the same kind of layer cake—all chocolate inside and out, with a maraschino cherry on top—from Entenmann's Bakery on Fourteenth Street, and he always gave Hermine and me a dollar each. Then he and my mother sat in the kitchen.

The long, narrow kitchen was in the back of the apartment and faced a courtyard. Lines of wash were strung between our side of the building and the apartments across the courtyard, which faced an open skyline, and the kitchen caught the sunlight. Yet I remember my grandfather's visits as always taking place on gray days. He and my mother sat at the kitchen table speaking Yiddish, and just as with toast left unattended, the atmosphere turned murky and ominous, making me wonder if their conversation involved the mystery of my mother's mother.

The Mystery

When I was four or five I started asking my mother questions about her mother.

Where is she?

She died, my mother said.

What was her name?

Anna.

How did she die?

She just died.

How old was she when she died?

I don't remember.

How old were you when she died?

I don't remember.

No matter how often I pestered her, I could not force the story out of her. Perhaps my mother and her father used their secret language to discuss my grandmother, for it turned out that she wasn't dead. For more than two decades she had been locked away in Manhattan State Hospital, an asylum for the insane on Wards Island, a speck of land in the East River between northern Manhattan and the Bronx. I later learned that my grandmother had come to New York from Romania when she was sixteen, penniless and alone. She landed a job at a garment factory on lower Broadway, where she worked beside Jenny Waladarsky, who introduced her to her brother Max, my grand-father. I don't know whether mental fragility drove my grandmother away from her family in Romania or gained its grip in the immigrant margins of the New World. At the time that she was first admitted to Manhattan State, in 1922 when my mother was six years old, it held the dubious distinction of being the largest psychiatric hospital in the world. That's when my mother and her younger sister went to live with their aunts in the Bronx.

My mother's ill-disguised lies did not just construct a secret, they im-bued it with disgrace. I took her discomfort to mean that my grandmother must have done something unspeakable, maybe criminal. Prostitution. Murder. Theft. I never guessed that she was alive while my sister and I were growing up. She died when I was sixteen, and I didn't know any-thing about this for another ten years. At that time, I also learned that the intention behind this secrecy was my mother's fear that her children might inherit this illness that had no name. Prior to having children, she had consulted doctors who had assured her that whatever had beset her mother was not genetic and could not be inherited. Still, she concluded that Hermine and I had a better chance of mental stability if we did not know this part of our ancestry. My sister, outwardly delightful and coop-erative, appeared to affirm my mother's reasoning. Looking back, I see Hermine burdened by the pressures of her self-appointed role of trying to ease tensions through smiling cheer. Taken at face value, this accentuated our differences: merry, gloomy; happy, sad. In my mother's perception, my despondency suggested an inherited dysfunction that ran straight through her own body and mind. We kept a close watch on each other, me looking for clues about what she was hiding, and she looking for clues about where I was heading.

My grandmother hadn't just been alive while I was growing up. My mother had visited her regularly. We had lived with an invisible presence, a phantom who moved among us, who communicated with the grown-ups, affecting the air quality. No wonder that appearances never seemed to be the whole truth of things.

I don't recall my mother as a schemer, yet arranging for her clandes-tine visits to Wards Island required a calculating finesse that involved both grandmothers. On many Saturdays, my father took my sister and me to visit his mother in Coney Island, an outing made enjoyable in the summer when we could swim in the ocean. This grandmother occupied a single room on the second floor of a boardinghouse one block from the beach. A kitchen on the first floor was shared by the residents, all elderly Jews from Eastern Europe. Even though the kitchen had an icebox, my grandmother stored used tea bags and honey cake on the sill outside the one window in her room. Entering the building, I was struck by a smell of chicken, garlic, and onions so pungent it was as if a soup had been boiled down to a paste that was used to plaster the hallway. Puke-pink in color, the hallway led to nowhere I wanted to go. My grandmother lived in America for forty-some years and never learned English.

My father, sister, and I would emerge from the subway in time to meet her at the synagogue as she came out from Sabbath services. She was small and hesitant and wore a babushka. Like both the synagogue and her boardinghouse, she appeared lacking in cheer, and our visits showed no signs of disrupting her glum bearing. From the synagogue, we walked slowly to her room and, depending on the weather, went upstairs or to the boardwalk or the beach. Either to relieve my father's anxieties about his mother's deprivations or to make the outing more appealing to his daughters, we never headed back to the subway without stopping for hot dogs from Nathan's and either a round of bumper cars or a few games of Skee-Ball, as those games were indoors and open all year. My favorite ride, the carousel, opened only for the summer season.

These outings to Coney Island allowed my mother to visit her mother. Saturday after Saturday she said goodbye as we left for Brooklyn and greeted us at the door when we came home. The grandmother who was supposed to be dead turned out to be alive, and the two grandparents I knew to be alive seemed somewhat dead. Neither of them took delight in us, even though Hermine and I, the grandchildren, represented the triumph of their sorrows. We were there to say: *You survived the pogroms, you outlived rejection and scorn, you saved your children from the Holocaust. We prove that you did. Look at us and smile.* But the weight of defeat was too heavy. They carried the Old World in their language and their food, in their melancholy and discomfort. I didn't ever want to kiss either of them.

I never associated our outings to Coney Island with my mother's secret. But she used to tell a story that suggests I never knew what to believe. Ostensibly, the story was about how difficult it could be for a mother to get five minutes to herself. She had left Hermine and me alone in the apartment one afternoon to shop at the local market. She returned carrying two brown paper bags. I asked where she had been. She said she had just gone to buy groceries. I said, *No, you went somewhere else.* I pointed to her name written on the brown bags, indicating that she had left the bags at the store after they were packed and paid for. I had gone grocery shopping with her often enough to know how this worked. She said she had just taken a walk around the block and seemed annoyed that I had been so accusatory.

Suspicion came so naturally to me that becoming a detective struck me as a professional option. On countless occasions when I was six, seven, eight, I got out of bed at night to investigate the darkened street. Anyone out walking became *a person of interest,* probably up to no good. I would then become the star witness in a trial: *Yes, Your Honor, he was wearing a raincoat and carrying a briefcase, and he appeared to enter the Steinway showroom*—which in fact was on the corner of our block—*with a key. No, sir, he was not wearing glasses, but he was wearing gloves. And by the way, Your Honor, would you happen to know anything about my grandmother?*

This was the era of listening to *Dragnet* on the radio, the detective show starring Joe Friday. *Just the facts, ma'am, just the facts.* In fantasy courtroom dramas, I would seek to unravel mysteries, as I had been trying to do with the mysteries of my grandmother and walking erect on a curved surface; and most pressing in ways too elusive to recognize, the mystery of my own mother. Behind her smoke rings and shield of protective darkness, I could not find her. My father was more knowable—not more approachable or more transparent, but he more fully inhabited his difficult personality. Despite his domineering role, he was the more playful of the parents, amusing us with hand puppets, teaching us to play checkers, and setting us up with pastels and sketch pads. Even his anger helped me know him—when to draw near or to stay away. Nothing about my mother was ever that obvious, and my efforts to wait and watch for opportunities to know her never paid off.

As it turned out, I did become a detective—of sorts. In my search for what was true and what existed beneath the appearance of things, I became a Buddhist and embarked on a journey of discovery without a beginning—like the man who made a pot of tea. I don't see footprints leading directly from my mother's heartbreaking deceptions to Himalayan monasteries, but seeking the truth—about my family or the power of the mind to manipulate direct experience—was not disconnected from investigations that took shape later.

Religion Versus the
Tradition of the New

We were secular Jews in a working-class Catholic neighborhood and when I was a child, religion represented bygone eras, taking the form of Jewish men who wore hats when they ate and Catholic housewives who cooked fish on Fridays. As far as I could tell religion was not modern and not democratic. It did not belong to the tradition of the new and could only be a backwater impediment to the ascendant vision of skyscrapers, airplanes, smokestacks, water towers, and elevators. Everything good and modern that inclined toward progress reached upward, trespassing on heaven as if to mock God's absence.

I don't remember when I first learned that Christmas celebrated the birth of Jesus Christ. The kids on my block dressed in their best clothes for church on Christmas morning, even when it was not Sunday, because they were Catholic; but we decorated trees and ate turkey because we were all Americans. We trimmed the tree with colored lights and glass ornaments and added strings of cranberries and popcorn, and turning on the lights was pure magic—even though we stuffed the tree, with ornaments still hanging, into a closet on those occasions when my grandmother visited during the holidays.

There was no context for discussing what religion was about, or why our neighbors went to church, or why we didn't, or why a decorated tree at Christmas would offend my grandmother. Consequently, objects rooted in religious meaning were taken out of context. From what I remember of conversations about art, this even applied to the overtly religious themes of painters such as Fra Angelico or Michelangelo. This also applied to a precious gift from my father. One Valentine's Day, when I was about seven years old, he came home with extravagant presents. This was most unusual and must have been occasioned by the sale of an artwork. He gave my mother a white silk scarf laced with golden threads that came wrapped in a lavender bag from Bendel's, the fancy ladies' store on Fifty-Seventh Street. Hermine's gift was a small white radio to keep by the side of her bed. Mine was three miniature clay camels, not more than an inch high, with a glossy finish the color of caramel. Each camel carried a bearded rider wearing a colorful robe and turban and holding minuscule reins made of wire, and tied to each saddle were cloth satchels. Generally, my response to gifts my sister and I received automatically concluded that hers were better than mine. Not this time. The camels came from a junk store on the Bowery that my father liked to frequent, and they made such an inventive and sin-gular gift that I understood them to have been chosen especially for me— small treasures to behold, not playthings. I kept them for many years, long enough to recognize that they were the three wise men following the star of Bethlehem to the newborn Jesus, and carrying offerings of gold, frank-incense, and myrrh. As a Valentine's gift, the baby Jesus played no part.

The disparities between us and our neighbors could be just as wide within my parents' own social sphere. The most outlandish juxtaposition stretched from the eccentric Bowery bum Joe Gould, aka Professor Seagull, to the Park Avenue real estate tycoon Alexander Bing. Joe Gould became a legend among the literati after his claims of genius were explored by the writer Joseph Mitchell. I will always remember him, but certainly not for his liter-ary reputation. His infrequent visits to our apartment were horrifying. This was in the late forties, and his days of drinking in Greenwich Village with other promising literary figures had deteriorated to living on the street and in Bowery flophouses. A small, balding man, he arrived disheveled and reeking of urine. Most disturbing, his visits were announced to the entire building by our downstairs neighbor, Mrs. Dunn, screaming at the top of her lungs, *Mrs. Tworkov, Mrs. Tworkov, there's a rummy in the hallway lookin' fuh you!*

Gould never left without getting a meal and a few bucks. I watched from another room, intrigued by my parents' kindness to this wreck of a man who—as they explained to me and Hermine—had fallen on hard times. But I was scared of getting too close, as if disgustingness was a contagious disease. Maybe disease was a real concern, for Gould always asked to use the bathroom, and the minute he left the apartment my mother would be in there with rubber gloves to scrub down every surface, especially the toilet.

Then there was Alexander Bing, the richest person we knew, who lived in a penthouse duplex as close to heaven as one could pay for. With his brother, Leo, Al Bing had developed the august Bing & Bing buildings along Park Avenue. The embarrassment of Joe Gould's visits was countered by the semi-annual ritual of Al Bing's chauffer pulling up to our building in a black limousine in order to drive our family uptown to his apartment for dinner. The chauffeur, Hadley, wore a charcoal-gray uniform and a matching cap. He stood by the limo with his hand on the opened door and waited for us to pile in. The kids on the block gathered around in astonishment, and I felt like a princess. I enjoyed the envy and admiration associated with limousines, but Mr. Bing was merely wealthy. Joe Gould was an artist.

That my family could be a connecting link between a Bowery bum and a real estate tycoon testified to our inclusion in the most progressive spheres of modern America. Unlike our neighbors, we were not restricted by the conventions of class and religious affiliation; we did not belong to a flock or a parish or a congregation. At the time, I did not know that this degree of social fluidity was more or less limited to the New York art scene; and despite my parents' apparent ease with such disparities, the divergent worlds that crowded our apartment had me taking comfort in the more consistent dynamic of the street, where I played with kids from my block after school, and became more familiar with their brand of Catholicism than with anything related to Judaism. Shabby, tinted posters of the dying Christ hung on the walls of their apartments and in the shoe repair shop, and in the store on the corner where men speaking Spanish rolled and cut tobacco for cigars, where my mother bought single cigarettes for a penny apiece. Christ looked out, eyes gazing upward, near naked, wounded, with blood dripping. I knew nothing about the teachings of Jesus but found it confusing that he didn't wear clothes, and that agony aroused awe and worship.

When the nuns and priests of the Church of the Epiphany, one block away, walked down our street, I would draw back while the other kids, all of whom attended both the church and its school, ran over to kneel and kiss their rings. My parents did not openly criticize our neighbors, but their own disregard leaked out, and I came to view kissing these rings or making the sign of the cross at the sight of a church as rites of superstition. Occasionally, my parents would refer to an acquaintance who attended church services or who, like the poet Robert Lowell, had converted to Catholicism, and their astonishment suggested that the local religion was not of merit. I concluded that our progressive bona fides extended far beyond abstract art; we were part of a post-religious world, scientific and democratic. We believed in human agency and the power of reason; organized religion was not creative, and not inspired. I did not know that a modernist dismissal of institutional religion revealed nothing of the private pursuit of religious meaning. Religion to me was delineated by material evidence—churches and synagogues, dress codes, rosaries, rites, and rituals. As far as I knew, those external forms had no connection to needs that were invisible and intangible. I didn't know that these needs, unnamed and undiscussed, could take many forms. I didn't know that making art offered a way to push beyond the boundaries of appearance and might even create furtive channels to God, or to merge a search for integrity with spiritual solace and satisfy a longing for transcendence.

I certainly knew nothing about the Jewish mystic Simone Weil, and I never learned why her books were stacked by my mother's side of the bed. Yet despite Weil's conversion to Catholicism and her scorching critique of Judaism, as well as my father's outspoken disdain for its reform versions, my mother concluded that her daughters would benefit from some type of religious education. One autumn afternoon she took Hermine and me, then about nine and six, to a reform synagogue, some ten blocks north of our apartment, in order to investigate its after-school program. It was during the Sukkot holiday, the weeklong fall festival that celebrates the harvest, and the synagogue had an outdoor display of colorful foods embedded in straw bales: pumpkins, apples, squashes, pomegranates, and grapes. Against traffic and concrete, this attractive fragment of rural life made a promising entryway.

The rabbi invited us into his office where, after a few questions, he scolded my mother for not lighting candles on Friday evenings. She ushered us out quickly, and the possibility of Jewish education was never revisited. As we walked home south on Second Avenue, I remember looking up at my mother with glowing pride in her unexpected flash of disobedience. My beautiful mother, with her private catalogue of punishing memories, knew better than a rabbi.

Named After a Farmer

Helen Boyd didn't make art and she didn't make money. She was a farmer in Ohio whom I was named after. We didn't meet until I was eight years old, and growing up in downtown Manhattan with only the occasional excursion to the countryside made being named after a farmer one of the more puzzling pieces of my collaged life. Helen had been married to a minister. Around 1918, not yet thirty and impelled by the suffragettes' fight for the women's vote, she abandoned her husband and their three small children and fled Ohio for New York City. In Greenwich Village, she threw in her lot with political radicals and left-leaning artists and writers. That's when she became lifelong friends with my father and his sister, Janice Biala, who also became a painter. My father and aunt were born in Biala (for which she named herself), a town that fluctuated between Russia and Poland, and they grew up speaking Yiddish. They learned English after coming to the United States in 1913, when my father was thirteen years old and Biala was ten. And despite Helen's Protestant breed of American legitimacy and farmland whiteness, they shared with her an untutored passion for literature and recommended books to each other until the end of their days.

Helen spent some fifteen years in New York City. Then her father passed away and surprisingly left his farm not to his only son, with whom he had quarreled, but to his scandalous daughter. Her decision to return to Ohio

and run Boyd Farm confounded her friends in New York, as it had confounded an earlier set of friends when she left Ohio. In the summer of
1951, my mother took Hermine and me on a Greyhound bus to visit
Helen: short, buxom, rimless glasses, no makeup, nothing frilly either in
looks or language, mousy hair in tight curls. We stayed with her in a stately
three-story Victorian house, formerly occupied by her father, on an elm-
lined street in the small Ohio town. I remember the wood, the smooth,
polished dark wood of the stairs and the banisters, the floors, the tables,
and chests. It darkened the rooms and made them cheerless. Compared
to our apartment, the house felt grand and intimidating, and eerily quiet.

Each morning during that visit, leaving my mother and sister behind,
I accompanied Helen as she drove her car from town to the farm, which
was sustained primarily by corn, hogs, and cattle. On arrival, she met with
her two resident farmhands. Notwithstanding her unassuming stature, she
was very much in charge, and although I had never before been in such
unfamiliar circumstances, I interpreted my special connection to the boss
as meaning that I had an inviolable right to be there, even though the
farmhands' kids made sure that I understood how ignorant I was about
every aspect of farm life.

I knew that Helen Boyd was a Protestant, which meant that she was not
a Jew or a Catholic. She had no evident church affiliation but didn't seem to
need one, as if being a white farmer in Ohio did not require the credibility
of attending church services. Even before I met her, I could not distinguish
between a religion called *Protestantism* and a country called *America*: both
were white, a perception not dispelled by living in a neighborhood with a
growing Hispanic population, and five miles south of Negro Harlem.

In my first years at Public School 40, I was taught that Protestants were
the first Americans. Indians were here first, but they didn't count because
they were not civilized, did not believe in God, and did not speak English.
We learned that Pilgrims deigned to celebrate Thanksgiving with their new
neighbors, the dark-skinned savages. Then these men became civic leaders,
statesmen, and preachers, and they signed the historic papers that made us
the greatest nation on earth and established elite universities for white men
who became the captains of industry: banking, shipping, copper, oil—they

owned it all. They held all the political and financial power and nothing much had changed in three hundred years: just look at Franklin Delano Roosevelt, my parents' hero. He had been the president of a very big club called *America*. This did not seem to be a religious club, but more like an English gentlemen's club, with paneled wood and genuine leather, cigars, and free newspapers—off-limits to women and Jews.

The High Priests

From reform to orthodox, my parents rejected any type of Judaism; and the nuns and priests of the Church of the Epiphany were distinguished from their parishioners by their long black robes, leaving my world devoid of any heroes more exalted than artists. The kids on my block made fun of the abstract art on our walls, confirming that art was special—misunderstood by the working class, the uneducated, and the unenlightened churchgoers. And that made me special too—misunderstood and apart but with coveted membership in this elitist club. When I reached adolescence, this template started to disintegrate as I came to recognize that adult behavior was not significantly different from children's behavior; and that making art did not make good people. It was a shocking acknowledgment that left the hierarchies in shambles.

My parents did not have the kind of earsplitting fights that came from other apartments. If my father was home when the screams got too loud, he would yank off a shoe and bang it on the radiator. But his temper could be scorching without the noise. And he was certainly not the only artist among his peers to voice bitter complaints about other artists and the art marketers. Their conversations could be competitive, judgmental, self-righteous, grandiose. Some of them drank too much; others cheated on their wives. One knocked up his mistress but would not leave the wife whose salary supported him; another was having an affair with his teenage stepdaughter. For a certain period, Bill de Kooning and Franz Kline were going out with twins and for some inexplicable reason, my parents found this hilarious, even when they stopped by for visits, uninvited, and all four smashed.

The other kids in the building might not have been privy to these kinds of antics and escapades in their parents' circle, yet their families were hardly paragons of good behavior. Two of the fathers in my building, both cops, regularly staggered home late into the night to be met with operatic rebukes from their wives. I understood no more about what went on in artists' studios than the other kids did, but I saw that artists shared with everyone else short tempers, impatience, competitiveness, agitation, something never being quite right. I listened in on complaints about who was stubbing out cigarette butts too close to turpentine-soaked rags, which sounded both legitimate and petty. Museum directors were mocked along with the artists who sucked up to them. I heard sly boasts of meager sales, eye-rolling disparagement, jealous dismissals of others' achievements. Pride, anger, lust, jealousy: normal human behavior that dramatized the cardinal sins in utterly ordinary ways. I wondered why these men, with their messy moral lapses and childish complaints were elevated to a special status, why their very ordinary behavior did not bring their preeminent rank into question. Grown-ups were supposed to be better than children, and artists were supposed to be better than other grown-ups; otherwise why would rich and powerful men venerate them? But venerate them they did, which made the rich and powerful collaborators in moral disorder. And so I entered adolescence with the same frightening conclusion reached by so many kids: The grown-ups are in charge and they do not know what they are doing. My father was preoccupied with making art. Even that configured into his ideals of goodness, and he most definitely wanted to be a good person. He was an Old Testament patriarch whose standards of goodness were biblical in their stature. Yet this didn't provide him with the means to control his fearsome temper, and we were too small a domestic unit to accommodate his outbursts. The circuitry between the four of us often malfunctioned like electric wiring not fit to handle the high voltage, causing the fuses to blow and leaving us in the dark.

The Dalton School

When I was thirteen, perhaps with the intervention of Al Bing, I received a scholarship to The Dalton School, a prestigious private school which, at that time, was all girls, on the Upper East Side. My sister would be a senior when I entered as a freshman. Despite Hermine's initial difficulties with the monumental inequality of wealth between us and the families of her classmates, she had proven to be an engaged and worthy student. My own tenure would not follow suit. In addition to my combative history with school, I entered with a specific grudge: I had to be tutored the summer before my first term because I could not pass the reading and writing entry exams. Once again, this was attributed to being uncooperative, not dumb. But in my eyes, accepting me made the school dumb. The city was filled with underprivileged children deserving of a scholarship. It was my father the artist who enhanced Dalton's diversity program—the rare, not-a-businessman father, not a real estate mogul or trustee, or Wall Street financier. I was not the one the staff respected, and in turn I refused to respect them.

I had made a seamless transition from disobedient child to sulky teenager. I was good at math, as numbers were easier than letters for me to read, but in my first year at Dalton the math teacher told me that since I had pierced ears—a rarity for white girls in 1956—I belonged in the art room.

In my second year, my disappearing acts in plain sight caused such alarm that I was hauled into the principal's office and asked, in the presence of my parents, if I was using drugs. Drugs? I had no idea what they were talking about. I had just been daydreaming, staring out the window, imagining better friends, clothes, parents. I don't remember teenage versions of the baby ballerina or Tarzan's Jane, but my guess is that they conjured country living, finding eggs in a hay loft, and riding horses. In animals, nature, and farm life, I identified a sanity that I could not otherwise locate.

There was an English teacher whom I found oppressively pretentious. I can still recall sitting through her classes, arms folded across my chest, making my disdain as obvious as I knew how. One day I challenged the use of the verb *to be*—the word *is,* I claimed, suggested the equivalency of two entities, as in *winter is cold; this teapot is small.* The usage fixed partial, restrictive identities, for *small* was one of a hundred words that could describe a teapot, while this grammatically conventional figure of speech conflated *small* with *teapot.* The teacher took my enquiry to be rude and disrespectful. I concluded that since she did not know how to answer, it meant that I was right. In her next class, I fell asleep. Then the school threatened to kick me out unless my parents arranged for me to see a psychiatrist. The doctor was an old-fashioned, on-the couch Freudian, and I was much too young and unwilling to talk into space with a cold, unseen presence behind me—no face of sympathy or affection. To be coaxed out of hiding, I needed more kindness.

My conscientious parents had tried to do the right thing. It had kept me in school but had wasted their hard-earned money, even though money was not as tight as it had been. My father's paintings had begun to sell, and after renting shacks on Cape Cod for several summers, in 1958 with the help of Al Bing, my parents bought a house in Provincetown's West End. A few years earlier, after years of going to night school at Hunter College, my mother completed her degree in early childhood education, and had taken a job teaching kindergarten at the Lighthouse for the Blind, providing the family with one steady income. At the same time, their newfound financial ease was hindered by my extremely expensive psychiatry sessions, and I felt bad about that.

In my junior year of high school, a most unusual encounter with my father took place in our apartment. He handed me a book, P. D. Ouspensky's *In Search of the Miraculous*. The book recounts the author's search for wisdom in the East, his meeting with the Western mystic G. I. Gurdjieff, and his subsequent immersion in Gurdjieff's system of self-realization. My father explained that a friend had given him the book, and although he wasn't much interested in these matters, he thought that I might be. I have returned to this exchange many times, baffled by my father's suggestion, for I cannot summon a memory of myself or of him that explains it. Could my smart father have confused a mind that was spaced-out and distracted and always elsewhere with some longing for transcendence? Or perhaps it was only me who could not intuit what might exist beyond the fog.

I was disobedient and, especially in his presence, surly. He also knew that I was having sex with my first boyfriend. We had met on the Cape the year before, and after a few terms at an art school in Boston, he had moved to New York City, and I had been caught sneaking out of school to spend time at the apartment he shared with other young art friends on the Upper West Side. I was relieved that my father had not commented on the disclosure about sex. The boyfriend was another story. My father did not like him and did not like his tipsy, café-society, art-dabbling, parents. He also knew that psychiatry was not making me more compliant at home or at school. To hand me this book, he must have seen something besides my disappearing acts and a *fuck you* scowl. I remember feeling utterly surprised—confused and flattered that he would pass along a book suggested by a peer as if, against all odds, I had made it into adulthood.

By this time, I had had two distinct experiences that actually had some resonance with Gurdjieff's work, but I would not realize their significance for many years. I never told anyone about them and still have no sense that they manifested in any way that could account for why my father gave me this book. The first happened when I was eleven years old. My father had arranged for us to spend a month on the Cape. He had lived in Provincetown full-time for several years when he was in his twenties but had not been able to afford to return. In 1954, he arranged to rent one of the Lemon Pie shacks, six wooden shanties that overlooked Wellfleet Harbor. He himself had to teach all month at Indiana University Bloomington in order to pay for us to have this vacation, but he had rented a car to drive us there. The final preparations during the morning of our departure had all four of us on edge with my parents snapping instructions to each other about suitcases, lists checked for swimming suits, shorts, sandals, cash, sandwiches, maps, driver's license, directions. The living room was in the middle of the long apartment, which meant it got no sunlight. In the midst of frantic activity, I found myself sitting on the couch in the shadowed room with tears streaming down my face. Very quietly. No sobs. That so much well-intended effort should succumb to such fraught anxiety felt completely normal—and unbearably sad. There had been no violence, no threats, no shouting, but something about the subtle, accepted, persistent ways in which people make themselves and each other unhappy came to the surface. Yet the *I* who was so used to feeling unhappy was not there. I knew what it felt like for Helen to be unhappy. This was different. I was not crying for myself or for my family in particular. None of the things that usually made me cry had happened. I had not been scolded, humiliated, or criticized. These tears were not independent of circumstances, but they came from a different place inside of me than other tears. My mother asked what was wrong. I didn't know and didn't answer.

The second experience occurred when I was fifteen, on a brilliant summer day on the Cape. I was walking with four friends along the dunes on the bay side of Truro. Suddenly, *I* disappeared. The environment became startlingly bright and vivid. I recognized where I was—the sand, the water, the friends—but *Helen* had fallen out the back of my head. Nothing that I perceived seemed connected to *me*. Just minutes before, everything I saw, whether a foot away or a hundred feet away, had seemed to be connected to my eyes by an invisible line that unspooled like a measuring tape. Suddenly, that line did not exist. Some version of me had exited through an invisible doorway. The sound of the surf and awareness of the beach and friends were there, but they existed independent of *me*. Everything was the same—and different. This lasted for three or four minutes. Then *I* returned to my body, and my senses resumed their usual function of funneling information to the switchboard of my brain.

I didn't tell my friends what had happened. I had no words, no language for it. The incessant mental chatter had been cut as precisely as scissors might snip a strip of film. Nothing disappeared—except *me*. I still didn't know about the grandmother who, at the time, was living in an asylum, but the incident had me wondering if I was crazy. The few minutes that *I* had spent without *me* were in no way unpleasant, though I had no idea *who* had had this experience. As with my childhood games, I had no reference for these incidents. No one I knew had ever talked about anything like them, and I did not want to be made fun of or have others consider me more lost and spaced-out than I considered myself. I had no reason to think that my parents would respond with anything but alarm about my psychological state; and I knew nothing of how a sudden break in the habitual loops of mental chattering could provide a glimpse into nonconceptual and authentic levels of reality.

Reading was still difficult, but my father's gift struck me as so exceptional that I determined to make my way through Ouspensky's journey. I struggled with the language, with new words and ideas that I had never before encountered, and I understood nothing—save for one story: Gurdjieff describes a philosopher king who exemplifies humankind at its most laudable. But when this great man, upon rising from his bed, cannot locate his bedroom slippers, he becomes flustered, even angry. Gurdjieff makes clear that this reaction reveals a man who knows nothing. His erudition, moral rectitude, and talent for discourse have left him pissing in the wind. The great man has a baby fit because he cannot find his bedroom slippers. I can't vouch for how much of this retelling synchs up with the book. Regardless, I took away precious information: the poet-artist knows nothing about how to live. Just as I had suspected—even though it deepened the question of why my father had given me this book, as he had shown no interest in teaching me this particular lesson.

In Search of the Miraculous also revealed that beings worthier of veneration than philosopher kings lived in these modern times. The only wisdom masters I had ever heard about—Jesus, Confucius, Buddha, Moses—were long dead. This meant that I was no longer stuck in a universe where the peak of human possibility was compromised by untamed and irrational behavior. Gurdjieff used the term *seekers after truth,* with its implication of *a path,* of *going forth,* of a journey and momentum. When I first encountered Gurdjieff, *truth* was still bound to a pedantic legal parsing of right and wrong. I still believed that it depended on facts and that facts existed beyond the limits of personal subjectivity. Truth meant certainty, and the intrinsic union of certainty and truth set the essential coordinates of a moral universe. This was not the truth to which Gurdjieff pointed. His truth existed on another plane altogether, cut loose from certainty, from conventional morality and fixed perspectives. It seemed that his truth rested with meaning, not facts, but I could go no further.

Biala

While Joe Gould and Al Bing represented the outer limits of visitors to our apartment, extremes closer to home existed with my parents' siblings. My mother's younger sister, Minnie, waitressed all her life and raised her out-of-wedlock daughter in a series of rat-infested apartments on the Lower East Side. My father's sister, Biala, had been the common-law wife of the writer Ford Madox Ford, and she had played a critical role in enshrining art as the apex of human endeavor in my world.

Biala was the only relative who, through blood ties and sensibilities, expanded some version of family beyond the four of us, and her outsized personality made her presence feel like an entire brigade even when she was not in the room or even in the country, for she lived in Paris most of her life and was an outspoken Francophile. Compared to civilized French children, Hermine and I were the barbarians, especially me—too loud, too messy, insufficiently courteous and demure; and she took every opportunity to score her points, often leveling criticisms that could be as harsh as my father's. My attire always provoked disapproval, although I couldn't be blamed for that; all our clothes came from thrift shops. Still, Biala told me I looked like an orphan, lending credibility to my suspicion that I was living in a family not my own—except for the curious contradiction that I shared personality traits with Biala herself.

Biala arrived at Ellis Island with her mother and my father. My grandfather, a tailor, had arrived a few years earlier. They lived on the Lower East Side in a tenement on Broome Street, and never forgot the lost pleasures of the modest home they left behind. This included a dog, a carriage, and a horse, and fruit trees in the front yard. None of them spoke English. Only the boy's education was encouraged. My father finished Stuyvesant High School and spent a few years at Columbia University. Biala left high school to work in a factory and devoured books from the public library. They both ended up studying art, and both became artists and made art all their lives. Biala was the name she used as an artist. I don't know where the name *Janice* came from. After she died, I came across a postcard that she had sent to her mother from Europe. It was signed *Ida*.

The Dharma Bums

Even without the dictatorial opinions of my high-minded aunt, my orientation toward Europe as a first travel destination was supposed to have been programmed by my private high school education. If the dreams of my pretentious English teacher had come true, I would have been enthralled by Henry James before graduation and planning to follow Isabel Archer across the Atlantic. Instead, in my last year of Dalton, I was caught out in school assembly reading *The Dharma Bums*.

Despite the title of Jack Kerouac's book and its page-by-page references to the Buddha and bodhisattvas, nothing in memory suggests that this book introduced me to Buddhism. I only remember reading it because once again I had been caught breaking the rules. The reprimand is what stands out—the phone call to my parents, the repeat of disappointment and frustration all the way around. In this particular case, my father's beleaguered attempts to explain the benefits of conforming to school regulations were compromised by disclosing that he had recently been to a party where the guests had included Allen Ginsberg and Jack Kerouac.

I read *The Dharma Bums* three or four years before seeing the photograph of Quang Duc. Some aspect of Buddhist dharma must have made an impression, but my memory of reading Kerouac for the first time relates to the Bums, not to their religious pursuits. These divine renegades could have sung the praises of Hinduism, Marxism, or Stoicism. Unshackled from formal religious or middle-class conventions, they represented a new brand of freedom, modern and subversive, and as wide open as the American West. What mattered most was their rejection of uptight Judeo-Christian morality and capitalist political hegemony—and their undoubted rejection of the elitist snobbery of The Dalton School. What compelled my admiration was their rebel spirit—their wildness and the tribal antics of loner subversives.

By the time I finished high school, *The Dharma Bums* was the text most likely to be stuffed into the knapsacks of a whole new breed of seeker. Young beatniks—guys alone or accompanied by girlfriends—were crisscrossing the country, hitchhiking and riding rails. Women did not travel alone like that yet, and I was not about to test those waters. I felt too fragile to cut loose; I needed to stay tethered to familiar posts. And so I plodded forth from high school to college, a sleepwalker bumping against the world with the disembodied presence of a ghost.

Back to Ohio

My grades did not allow me to join my Dalton classmates at Ivy League schools, and in the fall of 1960 I entered the University of Cincinnati, in part because of its proximity to Helen Boyd. Visiting her when I was eight years old had felt like a short excursion into real life. During that visit, the sensory richness of the farm became more interesting than fabricated stories of elsewhere: the odor of chicken coops, riding pinto ponies, tasting fresh corn. Fantasies of Tarzan's Jane had only drawn on visual imagination, not the smell and taste and touch of things. Compared to the skyscrapers and human hustle that enveloped New York, the sunlit, open-air operations of the farm pushed artists in their dusty studios into the shadows. This had led to questioning—in the confused logic of an eight-year-old—the primacy of the intellectual life of the mind. The superior place that the artist occupied in New York society had come into focus just enough to infuse this fumbling rearrangement of the social order with transgressive undertones. Ten years later, Helen Boyd, and by extension all of Ohio, held the promise of another escape into more compatible circumstances. I would leave behind the prized talents of the art world, the affectations of Dalton, and the bright-light entertainments of New York City, and strike out for the heartland, where real people lived and worked. A university in Ohio was as far as my rebel spirit would take me. I discarded my black turtleneck sweaters and arrived on campus with tailored blouses and a gray wool skirt. I still didn't fit in and cried myself to sleep for two years. After that, I transferred to Hunter College and moved back to my parents' apartment on East Twenty-Third Street, and then to a sixth-floor walk-up on Fourteenth Street between Avenues B and C.

By the time I returned to New York, adherents of Kerouac's rucksack revolution had been turning up on Zen master Shunryu Suzuki Roshi's doorstep in California. He had come from Japan to San Francisco in 1959, sent by Soto Zen headquarters to administer to the Japanese-American congregation. Soon he attracted barefoot Buddhist wannabes who arrived with Kerouac as their heroic guide, and in 1963, they participated in a memorial service that Suzuki Roshi held for Thich Quang Duc.

Psychedelics

In 1963, a Buddhist monk abiding in meditative stillness while burning to death was not the sole disruptive display of unknown realities. Psychedelic drugs were also beginning to fracture basic assumptions. Like Quang Duc, psychedelics burst into public awareness with headline news. On May 27, 1963, two weeks before the monk's death, Harvard University fired Timothy Leary and Richard Alpert (later known as Ram Dass) for violating the terms of their research for the Psilocybin Project. Today we know that LSD evolved through decades of controlled experiments, yet with the media exposé of the Harvard professors, psychedelics might have sprouted straight from the head of Zeus, so Olympian were the claims for their exalted benefits and so charismatic were their leading messengers. Furthermore, the dramatic debut of psychedelics in America's premiere educational institution made the drug seem as exclusive as the university itself. For further affirmation of its non-threatening properties, the LSD procured by the Harvard professors came from the Sandoz Laboratory in Switzerland. With its edelweiss and alpine air, Switzerland assured a pristine purity that stretched from the lab directly to the hallucinogenic promise.

The winter before Leary's and Alpert's dismissals from Harvard, a friend had introduced me to the professors. My experiences with LSD were mostly limited to the Sandoz variety and came through the professors when they were at Harvard, and later when they reestablished themselves in a grand, sixty-four-room mansion in the countryside near Millbrook, in the Hudson Valley, two hours north of New York City.

First LSD and then Thich Quang Duc: two very different encounters with indescribable states of mind. The media story about Quang Duc focused on politics. The story of psychedelics used the liturgical language of transcendence. According to their messianic envoys, psychedelics transported you upward, to lofty realms of boundless, formless, oceanic oneness, far removed from decaying urban 'hoods with broken vials and discarded needles, far from streets inhabited by despair and poverty, by Black men and jazz musicians. A clean, safe drug for clean, white people who paraded the same enviable wealth, class, and beauty that embellished the pages of fashion magazines, LSD was the harbinger of designer drugs that soon became fashionable.

Several years ago, I was talking with my friend Carole Tonkinson about the convergence of psychedelics and Buddhism in the West. We worked together in the early years of *Tricycle: The Buddhist Review,* the magazine I founded in 1991. Subsequently, Carole moved to London, but our conversations about Buddhism continued. On this occasion, I was on my way to Vietnam and had been speaking about Thich Quang Duc. We were sitting in her sunny yellow kitchen in Surrey, and she asked if LSD had influenced my curiosity about Quang Duc's mind. The question startled me, for I had never thought about those two distinct experiences in such consequential terms. The photograph of Quang Duc had seemed to appear out of nowhere, with no references and no context. Yet I have long assumed that the photograph lives in present history because it captures stillness and silence amidst circumstances that defy stillness and silence to exist. It frames reality upside down, no less astonishing than a wheel that rolls uphill. Any consideration that Quang Duc's behavior might actually indicate an authentic and awakened mind seems likely to have been influenced by my experiences with psychedelics, as they upended the accepted rules for everything.

The most fundamental assumption challenged by mind-expansion drugs was that an *I,* a *me,* a person called Helen, existed as a discrete entity, separate from everyone and everything around me; and furthermore, that this *me* habitually reaffirmed its identity by filtering, evaluating, accepting, and rejecting sense experiences based on rigid, preconceived versions that I had come to identify as my very distinct Helen identity.

With LSD, the mind that was normally filled with conceptual identifications floated away, allowing for a very different experience of reality. This state might be induced by a pill and last for several hours, but it shared similarities with that day on the dunes five years earlier when it seemed that for a few minutes I had lost *my* mind—at least the mind that I was familiar with, the one we call *normal*. The objects of sense perception— hand, shoe, tea—were there, but they were independent of any identification with *me*.

My excursions into psychedelic realities were entertaining, but despite the weighty implications, they remained superficial. They were fun, not transformative, and not sacred. Without a context that might explain the benefits of transcending the conceptual mind, they remained devoid of impact. Experience without meaning. The LSD gurus certainly had notched up many more trips than I could fathom, and they proved to be magnetic Pied Pipers, but I never viewed them as reliable guides. The weekends at Millbrook were whirlwinds of activity with Tim Leary at the center, always at the center, a mesmerizing magician, playing both king of the castle and court jester; a chameleon shifting forms between a baby prankster, an adolescent party boy, and a venerable elder. But neither the gurus nor the experiences themselves suggested how to be less confused, less depressed, or more curious about growing up. They did not tell me whether or not to stay in school, marry, have children, imitate my mother's role as a devoted wife, or be independent like Helen Boyd who abandoned her children, or like Biala who didn't have any. These pulls bedeviled me, and the temporary flights into realms of infinity and no-self and oceanic transcendence did not help resolve them. I also never forgot the liberating delight of being in the world without the cumbersome baggage of *me*.

By now, my childhood games about the malleability of mind had been mostly subsumed into patterns of disappearing. Over time I had concentrated on knowing my escape routes rather than on trying to know the many layered dimensions of mind. I could change the story, and in this way, knew something of how mutable the mind was; but was not yet ready to work with mind's fabrications as sources of suffering—of stimulating desires, hopes, fears that could take different shapes, but did not explore states of reality that dropped beneath the self-cherishing constructions.

Unlike the LSD avatars and their devout followers, I had no inclination to automatically identify a mind emptied of self-reference with mysticism. Labeling LSD trips as *mystical, religious,* or *spiritual* sounded disingenuous and self-aggrandizing. Some stubborn insistence on finding my own way saved me from a wholesale buy-in to the psychedelic movement. This resistance included a healthy measure of self-preservation, but also came from fear. I was far from ready to accept that the conventional, predictable sense of my identity was not real. Despite my games and my experience on the dunes, the dissolution of my mind and the dissolution of Helen felt the same. I *was* my mind, my fucked-up, neurotic, spinning, egocentric, self-centered, muttering mind. I was not up for an existential assault on the so-called normal self, especially as I could not discern any lasting benefits of dislodging the primacy of the ego.

I remember a spring night in 1963. I had brought tabs of LSD back from a weekend at Newton to share with my boyfriend, Bob Ross, an art student at Cooper Union (not the TV personality and artist of the same name). We dropped the acid in his apartment on East Tenth Street, and while exploring the beguiling movements of our hands and the intricacies of shoelaces and luminous, shifting colors, we decided to walk down six flights of stairs to buy ice cream. What lasts in memory is an ecstatic, wordless knowing that I was not *in* the world—that there was no world *out there,* no separation between the world and some personal, restrictive, solid, dense, concept-driven *me.* Something that I would still call *me* could see everything, hear everything, but through a different sensibility than the eyes and ears in my head. Though I could not apply this experience to my daily life, it introduced a lasting puzzle: knowing did not seem to depend on thinking. The mind, emptied of the constructed self, nonetheless experiences and perceives. *It* knows; whatever it is. Is *it* God, consciousness, awareness? How could the mind, unbound from the constructed self, know anything? How could it even function in this confused world? I came from a background that valorized the life of the mind—the smart, conceptually astute, witty, IQ mind; the educated, literary, historically nuanced mind. Yet when all those attributes dissolve, still we *know*.

What I also remember from that trip is the relatively seamless transition back to the self that identifies body and mind as having inherent, permanent, fixed qualities, the self that tells us each day, *This is who you are*. Even though fixity is manifestly untrue—otherwise we would still be in our baby bodies—our smart-IQ minds never quite disabuse us of this irrational belief in permanence. After the LSD wore off, I realigned with the typical markers of meaning: the daughter of, sister of, citizen of, girlfriend of. Under the influence of LSD, I might have become a cloud and seen mountains walking, but afterward I easily reinhabited the person named on the birth certificate and weighed in the doctor's office. I was pretty, funny, opinionated, insecure, arrogant, smart, quick to anger, and easily hurt. That was me. Any challenge to this sense of self might be amusing but was not to be taken too seriously. Tarzan's Jane was not real, and the baby ballerina in a yellow tutu was not real, but the blood-and-flesh Helen, with fixed traits trapped in a body like bees in a closed jar—she was real.

Charles Mingus and
Other City Forays

At the time of my first visit to the Leary-Alpert household, what stands out—more than the professors—was meeting Charles Mingus, the jazz virtuoso. We were sitting together at the kitchen table in the house in New-ton, both feeling out of place. I had hoped that pretending to be content in all situations would disguise feeling small, worthless, and concerned with whether I was liked or not, even though no one paid me any attention. I don't remember Charlie speaking about his unease, but his eyes darted about with guarded mistrust. We traveled back to the city together from Boston. I was staying at my parents' apartment while they were at their house in Provincetown, and Charlie was living in a loft a few blocks north on the Bowery. I was not immune to his celebrity, but my most indelible memory had nothing to do with jazz or his stature but rather that he intro-duced me to a restaurant on my own block that I had passed ten thousand times without ever going inside. More than just stepping through another new doorway, going to this restaurant combined physical proximity and social distance in ways that reflected a larger merging of opposites—or perhaps of my own slow-growing ease with disparities.

Connelly's Bar and Grill was on the southeast corner of Twenty-Third Street and Third Avenue in the shadow of the Third Avenue El, when

Twenty-Third Street was the unofficial northern end of the Bowery. Peri-odically the police would send paddy wagons to pick up bums from the areas north of Twenty-Third Street, then drop them off at our corner and tell them to head south. Right in front of where the paddy wagons stopped was the Irish bar and restaurant, its name prominently displayed on the glass windows in gold lettering. Despite its location in the creepy, dank shadows of the El, it featured starched white tablecloths and cloth napkins and lace curtains. Hermine remembers that in the spring of 1954 before we, or anyone we knew in our neighborhood, had a television, a black-and-white screen appeared in the window of the street side of Connolly's, and people gathered outside to follow the McCarthy hearings, and she went to the corner to watch with my father. But Connelly's did not enter my world until the summer of 1963 when Mingus invited me to share several Sunday lunches there with him and his son, Charles Junior.

Mingus was an outsized African-Chinese-White-American world-famous jazz genius. I was a white, Jewish, post-Beat lost child of the 1950s New York art world, closer in age to Charles the younger than to his father. Yet this notoriously prickly band leader and breathtaking bass player seemed to find solace in these outings to the Irish restaurant. Its prim formality and the classic dishes of an American after-church Sunday dinner appealed to his singular and complex sense of order. All the differences between us and with the other diners were leveled out in the great democratic mash-up of roast turkey with canned cranberry sauce, Del Monte fruit cups, and Parker House rolls. On several occasions Mingus willed us into his version of an American family. We sat in a booth by a window, with Charlie Senior facing me and his beautiful skinny son—dad and the kids on their Sunday outing.

These lunches registered as urban field trips, another excursion into new territory, like weekends in Newton or dinners at Park Avenue du-plexes, or the single visit to an apartment in the Bronx where my moth-er's father lived with his second wife, and a crystal bowl of silver-wrapped chocolate kisses sat on a low coffee table before an upholstered sofa. All were curiosities of varying degrees of interest, none of which asked any-thing of me. I could observe each from a safe distance, as content as when sitting in darkened classrooms at Hunter College, and watching documentaries about the lost tribes of the Amazon or New Guinea, or the Eskimos in *Nanook of the North*.

That summer Hermine turned twenty-four. For her birthday, Charlie took a group of friends including me, and Hermine and her husband, Bob Moskowitz, to the Five Spot to hear Thelonious Monk. It was the club's relatively new location on the corner of Third Avenue and Eighth Street, and it was packed. I already knew the club's owners, Joe and Iggy Termini. My father's studio was on the Bowery across from the original Five Spot, a few blocks south of Saint Mark's Place, and he was one of many artists who frequented the club. A few weeks after Hermine's birthday, I returned to the Five Spot to ask for a job. I had been waitressing at a coffee house on MacDougal Street. I had heard Bob Dylan sing "Blowin' in the Wind" at Gerdes Folk City and felt the wind picking up among beatniks who were hanging out at espresso cafés, but the Five Spot had more edge. I was too young to legally work where liquor was served, but Joe and Iggy decided that I could work the hat check. Given what went on at the club, this attention to legal detail now strikes me as both funny and touching.

The Five Spot was an exciting place to work, but also scary. I was adventuresome enough to get to the edge of an abyss but then faulted myself for not going further and jumping off the cliff into whatever—drugs, sex, music, anthropology—for the sake of fully inhabiting myself, of closing the distance between me and me. I had tasted this possibility with psychedelics but did not know how to bring it into daily life and continued to live with an uneasy sense of something missing, that my life lacked some crucial ingredient. But unlike Thich Quang Duc, or island aborigines, the otherness of Black jazz edged up close, the music invasive, and my attractions filtered through hesitation. Losing myself to a Black male world in a white female body threatened my own identity more than drug-induced non-dual perception in which culture, race, and gender disappeared altogether. The hat check was at the entryway to the club, but if I came around the wall of coats, I could stand at the doorway to the side of the low stage and watch the cigarette smoke curling through the darkened room and people moving in shadows, and listen to the piercing, untamed sex of solo horns. I hovered at the threshold.

LSD introduced the idea that all the culturally conditioned labels that I had used to identify myself were transitory, impermanent, and pliable. But without transformative momentum I returned to the strong habits of perceiving myself and the world around me as fixed, solid, and unchanging. However, the takeaway had a more immediate effect on my studies: LSD allowed me to recognize that my attraction to tribal societies was more than just neurotic escapism; anthropology did suggest journeys that led away from myself and the worlds that I knew, but it simultaneously invited a search inside myself. I came to recognize that embedded in my curiosity about tribal living was a yearning to reach outside or beyond the confines of selfhood, to be pulled into a universe or tribe or club where the solitary, separate self would welcome the dissolution of its boundaries. Psychedelics convinced me that the wish to transcend individual personhood did not simply express self-loathing and a desperate need to avoid this mind, this body, and this moment. Quite the opposite: that the longing for liberation into a greater, universal, welcoming love was normal, the ordinary yearning for union with the unconditioned universe. And that this longing, far from being compulsive or disturbed, arises from elemental sanity. Readjusting the value of my studies however did not mean enough to keep me in school, and I finally hit upon a viable plan for quitting. I would travel and see the world, an honored tradition for young women—with a twist. I had no intention of following the standard itinerary through European capitals and art museums. Experiences that had eluded meaning could still shape a search and suggest a direction, and between Thich Quang Duc and psychedelics, that direction pointed east.

PART TWO

ASIAN TRAVELS

1965

1965. The year before, I had left my job at the Five Spot for a more lucrative waitressing job at the Ninth Circle, a high-tipping steakhouse in the West Village. I had saved $2,000—enough, I figured, for a round-the-world plane ticket and expenses for five months. Perhaps it was a lack of courage or imagination that necessitated a return plan and not just to leave and say, *Goodbye—and see you whenever.* Maybe never. I was twenty-two years old.

I arranged to travel to Japan with an acquaintance my age whose family had emigrated to California from Japan. She had never visited Japan but her relatives in Osaka agreed to host us on arrival. For my first international journey, my mother gifted me with writing paper and envelopes, and demonstrating her idiosyncratic grasp of everyday minutiae, she included a roll of United States postage stamps.

Shortly before leaving New York, I had dinner with my friend Jo Eno, who said something that I tucked into my suitcase. Jo had grown up on a farm in Puget Sound, although she had the high forehead and strong jaw suggestive of a more jagged and remote coastline. She also displayed an enviable elegance that showed no alignment with any fashion style but synched up with an interior sensibility that was just as singular. She had known Bob Ross from their days in Portland, Oregon, and had come to

New York City from the West Coast in 1962 with Rudy Wurlitzer. They had been living together in California. Rudy's jukebox ancestry cast an aura of glamor, which his moneyed Upper East Side childhood and his tall, blond looks did nothing to dispel. He was not yet a published writer but could already be identified as a wordsmith, while Jo did not have an easy way with words and used them sparingly. Jo and I were having dinner by ourselves at an Italian restaurant near Tompkins Square. I had been talking about anthropology when she cut in: *You don't want to be an anthropologist, Helen; you want to be a Polynesian.*

For now, Japan would do. The most significant part of the itinerary was not my port of arrival but what I was leaving. I carried out the arrangements for quitting school, quitting my job, and giving up my apartment with the precision and excitement of planning a jailbreak, escaping from my family, my language, my society; from my confusion about how to be an adult and what shape that might take. Girlfriends were getting married, some already had babies, others were constructing brilliant careers. I assumed that one day I too would join the ranks of responsible adulthood. But not yet.

Japan

Traveling with my Japanese-American companion allowed for an easy entry. Then I went to Tokyo on my own, where I had arranged to meet up with Yoshiaki Shimizu, a Japanese painter I had known during my last years of high school. In America, Yoshi had lived a ragtag life, first in Boston and then Manhattan, but he had returned to the straightened modes of his home country and at the time of my visit was residing unhappily in Kyoto with his Japanese wife. Straddling the world of his upbringing and the *gaijin*—outsider—community, he had a circle of foreign friends, many of them writers and poets influenced in their choice of Kyoto either by Gary Snyder or by Japhy Ryder, Jack Kerouac's portrait of Snyder in *The Dharma Bums*.

Yoshi came from Kyoto to meet me in Tokyo with his friend Brian Shekeloff. The three of us climbed a hill above the city. It was a brilliant clear day, and we sat on the ground looking out over a wide urban expanse. Out of the blue Brian began quoting Ford Madox Ford. The name landed like a sucker punch. I had come to the far side of the world only to discover I couldn't escape my family or the route mapped out by my European art heritage. I asked Yoshi if he had known that my aunt Biala had lived with Ford, and he had not. I had anticipated a straight line away from New York, and while Yoshi felt like an accomplice to that end, Brian's reference to Ford felt intrusive and introduced me to how zigzag my life could be—would always be. At that time, I only knew that I could push away parts of life, forget them, deny them, pretend to be more confident and cheerful than I usually felt. I had not yet learned that everything that I wished to change or leave behind would haunt me until I turned to face it. Despite the invasive interlude, we continued to have a grand day. They both seemed to revel in the role of being my guides, and by late afternoon it was agreed that I would return to Kyoto with them.

Japan was utterly new and unknown, but more surprising to me was how quickly I became new and unknown to myself. With stubborn pride, I forced myself to learn the currency, to buy bus tickets, and to identify my designated stop. Hot in the face with embarrassment, I sat in restaurants alone, trying to manipulate chopsticks for more subtle maneuvers than shoveling food into my mouth. Squat toilets? No problem.

After my mother died in 1991, I discovered that she had kept my letters from Asia. In one, I describe a tea house that I rented shortly after arriving in Kyoto. It had just been vacated by American friends of Yoshi's who themselves had relocated to larger quarters that had become available when the poet Philip Whalen returned to San Francisco. I wrote:

My house is 15,000 yen a month ($41.67—4 cents less than I paid in N.Y.—rents are high!). The rooms are measured by the number of mats. I have a 3 mat room (about 9'x6') and a six mat room (9'x12') plus a large closet and a small kitchen. The house is part of a large house owned by quite a wealthy family. You enter through a sliding wooden door, which looks like a wall from the street, and enter a garden full of tall bamboo & flowers. There is about a 4' wide garden along 2 sides of my house, and one side has a little platform of sorts where I eat breakfast in the morning sun.

The houses in this neighborhood are almost all big with a real sense of classic Japanese beauty. To one side there is a temple close enough to hear the monks chanting in the evening. To the other side is the Kyoto zoo & in the morning I can hear the lions roaring. The Museum of Art is just down the block, as is Kyoto's famous Heian Temple—a big

gaudy red thing. And it's a ten-minute walk to the center of town.
Ideally located is what you would call it.

Just as foreigners took over each other's residences, they did the same
with jobs teaching English. Within a month, I was earning a living by
following a mimeographed manual for teaching English as a second language to middle-aged, middle-management businessmen in chemical and
technology companies on the outskirts of the city. A few evenings a week,
dressed primly in a skirt with my long hair pulled back, I arrived by com-
muter train at large, dreary, concrete industrial buildings filled with men
in suits. I was bemused by the irony of my position, given my own trials
with learning English, even though it was hard to go wrong if I followed
the printed instructions. If my students had any reason to question my
proficiency, they were too polite to show it.

Within a month of landing outside my own country for the first time, I
was living in a tea house and teaching English and studying spoken Japanese from a paperback primer that had been designed for American ser-
vicemen. I soon abandoned my initial plan to return home in five months.

The previous spring, I had met Gary Snyder in New York City when he
gave a reading at Saint Mark's Church on East Tenth Street. We were introduced by my then boyfriend, Bob Ross. The two of them shared an abiding
admiration for Lloyd Reynolds, an esteemed professor of calligraphy who
had taught them both at Reed College in Portland, albeit a decade apart.
Not long after my arrival, Snyder returned to his house near Daitoku-ji,
the Zen temple complex in the northern section of Kyoto. He spoke fluent
Japanese and rode a motorcycle. Somewhat sententious, especially in the
company of young women, he was also a lot of fun and generous with advice on making one's way through this lacquered land. In New York I had
chafed at social propriety. In Japan, I wanted to get it right. I approached
the hole-in-the-wall convenience store at the corner near my tea house
with itsy-bitsy steps as if my knees were tied together, and upped my voice
two octaves to ask for cigarettes, then bowed too low, smiled too broadly,
and teetered back to take shelter and smoke Winstons. When students in

my English-language classes invited me to visit their homes on holidays, it felt crucial to arrive with the appropriate bean-cake sweets. I fretted over whether to wear pants so that I could sit *seiza*—on my knees—or to wear a staid, knee-length, herringbone suit that I had uncharacteristically purchased before leaving New York and ask for a chair. Whatever I wore, I was always too imprecise, too casual, too American. I was trim and not tall, but in Kyoto I felt like an unwieldy affront to Japanese delicacy. At some point Gary explained that no matter what I did it would be wrong. *Gaijins* could not get it right, he said, *so just relax.* He told me that after years of living in Kyoto, his former wife, the poet Joanne Kyger, never left their house alone without carrying a stack of magazines pressed to her chest. I understood this to mean that she needed the physical weight to tamp down a fluttering anxiety. When I moved about the city on my own, I too felt the need for a shield to protect against feelings of vulnerability and displacement. Visiting Zen temples intensified this need, for the monks were austere, unfriendly, and relentlessly masculine—career monks strutting with their wash buckets, barefoot in winter, their stride full of virile bluster.

It took dutiful visits to every historic Zen temple to conclude that I made a terrible tourist. Surveying the world from the margins of my own culture had offered a choice perch, but being an outsider in a foreign land was less compelling, especially when I felt a diplomatic duty to display curiosity and appreciation for temple art and rock gardens and flower arrangements. But give me a cup of coffee at a café anywhere in the world, and I can sit and watch for hours.

What did I want to be in Japan? Not a Polynesian, not a tourist or a Japanese person or a Zen Buddhist. Perhaps I was too far from home—or not far enough. I tried reading the prolific and influential Zen philosopher D. T. Suzuki but came up against a torrent of words as impenetrable as the walls that surrounded the Zen monasteries and lined the streets of my aristocratic Kyoto neighborhood. I had already heard something about Suzuki from his tenure in New York City. Under the sponsorship of the toilet magnate Cornelius Crane, he had lectured at Columbia University in 1950 and attracted a number of artists, some of whom were friends of my parents'. Yet I did not know when I left for Japan that, thanks in large part to Suzuki's influence on the Beat writers, especially Jack Kerouac, Zen was already taking root in America.

A quick look through Suzuki's writings revealed the intricate density of his language, tempting me to not even try. But I was in Japan, Suzuki's home territory, and I was living in a tea house in Kyoto, the divine abode of more than a thousand temples. I felt obliged to learn something about Zen though I wished that it could be through experience, not language. Suzuki pointed to a reality beyond words, but made the point with an abundance of words. His tireless efforts to introduce Zen to Westerners relied heavily on philosophy and disquisition. It was an exhaustive approach to what I later learned was a tradition that claimed *a special transmission outside the sutras*—outside the written canon. While Suzuki's work extolled the penetrating pith of haiku, none of it sounded like the splash of Basho's frog jumping into an old pond—the most iconic of all haiku imagery. And then, while sitting in my tea house, I stumbled on a simple statement that Suzuki had made about death, something along the lines of, *Well, that's the way it works, folks: we are all going to die.* It was astonishing—not to learn that we are going to die but to encounter someone stating flat out, *We are all dying,* without camouflage, distaste, or apology.

Shortly before leaving for Japan, I had read Jessica Mitford's *The American Way of Death,* a groundbreaking best seller that summoned the nation to confront the corporatizing of the death industry. Mitford's exposé targeted the mercenary tactics of the funeral trade, skewering the sales reps who preyed on vulnerable families, exploiting their grief to sell expensive arrangements. The book offered none of the Buddhist incentive to recognize our fleeting time in these temporary bodies as the key to a meaningful life. However, Mitford's account made clear that the heartless professional care for the dead could only become a lucrative industry in a society where spiritual values were subverted by greed.

On the heels of Mitford, Suzuki's words on dying cut through a thick layer of cultural conditioning. Throughout my childhood the subject of death, like cancer and polio, was banned from polite conversation. I couldn't remember attending a funeral, not even that of my father's mother, who died when I was thirteen. Death loomed as the enemy of life, and it seemed only a matter of time before America, recent liberator of the death camps and conqueror of polio with the Salk vaccine, would once again use its brilliant might to defeat the ultimate foe.

In talking about death, Suzuki did not invoke a Shakespearean rant against an unjust universe or rely on histrionic displays of love and loss, of anger or derangement. I concluded that Buddhists told the truth about things that Americans lied about. First a Vietnamese monk burning to death while sitting in meditation, embodying a truth too profound to comprehend; and then a Zen master speaking of death without embarrassment or despair.

I made friends among Yoshi's group of foreigners and was soon touring the hills and rural roads outside of Kyoto on the back of Gary's motorcycle and bathing in the local communal bathhouse, where I learned to contend with unabashed interest in my light skin. Naked women, friendly and giggling, would come near in the pools or the dressing room and run their hands over my arms or through my hair.

Soon after settling into the tea house and keeping Suzuki's books at the side of my futon, I twisted my legs into full-lotus meditation posture—my ambitious bid to be Japanese or at least to participate, alone and out of sight, in an essential aspect of this peculiar country. I cannot remember if I ever outgrew the pain of this arduous position, but its accomplishment helped piece together a story of my life in Kyoto: meditating in full lotus and living in a Japanese tea house with a bonsai garden and red Japanese maples.

Once the congratulatory thrill of attaining full lotus wore off, I didn't know what to do. On my black meditation cushion, set on a tatami mat in my perfect tea house, the past was replayed, the future invented. I could have been in New York City, on the Twenty-Third Street crosstown bus or alone at a diner eating a tuna salad sandwich. I assumed that meditation meant not thinking and that elimination of thoughts was the goal. And yet, the thoughts came, and came relentlessly. Consequently, every thought—dozens and dozens each minute—represented failure and frustration. Thoughts had a life of their own, dominant and dictatorial. Suzuki spoke of the essential emptiness of all phenomena. If this were true, then thoughts must be empty too, I reasoned. But they felt dense as bullets.

I had courted thoughts all my life, had relied on them to construct fantasies that had made life bearable. I had used my conceptual abilities to say things that attracted attention, things that were witty or funny or smart. I had used thoughts to fake knowing more than I did or to hide behind when I was too uncomfortable to keep my mouth shut. I could name a hundred good, useful, rewarding, worthwhile attributes of thoughts, so I wondered if maybe I didn't want to let them go. But really, I didn't have a choice. I couldn't have stopped my thoughts even if I'd wholeheartedly wanted to.

To my astonishment, I discovered I wasn't the only one in the world plagued by uncontrollable thoughts. I was shocked to learn that everyone talks to themselves. I had assumed that the incessant internal dialogue of the muttering mind was endemic to my personal dysfunction. There was no way to know otherwise. No friend had ever asked, *Do you ever talk to yourself when you're walking down the street, sitting on the bus, in the bathtub, falling asleep?* No one had ever asked the more pressing questions: *Do you ever stop talking to yourself? Does the mind ever come to rest? Does* your *mind ever come to rest?* From the photograph of Thich Quang Duc, it appeared that as his body burned, his mind had come to rest.

My attempts to manipulate the thoughts that ran through my head in fantasy and projection—maintaining a double life as a ballerina or a jungle acrobat—had not been successful strategies for well-being, and sitting on a black cushion was not easing my mind either. I had anticipated that with the traditional accoutrements—cushion, tatami, incense, posture—I would attain elevated, uplifted states of calm, maybe even states of bliss, of ecstasy. I would disappear—not be who I was, where I was. And yet, in my projection of what meditation was supposed to accomplish, the self that dissolved during meditation would afterward reassemble in a recognizable form. Sort of like my experiences of LSD, although I assumed that the authentic state arrived at through mental discipline rather than drugs would mean that the reassembled me would be transformed and improved. I would be nicer than I was by predisposition, less congenitally depressed, more empathetic and patient. I would enjoy ease in my own skin and in the world and would smile more. I felt certain that transcending the mind that talks to itself through traditional spiritual practice would cultivate qualities of goodness. As my experiments with meditation dragged on, however, indulging in fantasies of spiritual attainment while maintaining an uptight Zen posture did not shift a thing. I felt defeated by my inability to stop thoughts, and the time on the cushion became interminably long, disappointing, and very boring. Still . . . it was a start.

Being in Japan and reading snippets of D. T. Suzuki also provided the first real challenge to my long-standing yearning for a static and certain truth. In the otherness of Japan, I began to view the quest for certainty as both immature and unattainable. My assumption that *truth* and *fact* were interchangeable—first challenged by reading the book on Gurdjieff—was falling apart. Even though I had studied other societies in the classroom, this was my first actual taste of another way of life, another language, dress code, aesthetics, food. And even then, I had assumed that these distinct cultural variations manifested essential human qualities that were universal and that laid a grid for a kind of absolute truth.

So much of Kyoto was literally walled off and out of public sight. Even when my English-language students invited me to their homes, I never got past a reception area near the entryway. At the same time, what did appear in public offered an abundance of otherness. All the elderly ladies wore the traditional kimono, and in Kyoto at that time, so did the younger women, and to my eyes, each one looked as dramatically posed as a high-class geisha, without the whiteface—quite a contrast to bare-breasted Polynesian women in their short grass shirts.

That everyday Japanese dress could display so much care and elegance was a cause of constant wonder, even as I acknowledged that I could never get underneath the external layer. For any clue to the mundane emotional lives of the people that I passed on the streets or in the grocery or the baths, I had to read novels. This reversed my childhood relation to books. My parents always encouraged me and Hermine to read, but while my sister spent her after-school hours with a book, I was always on the street. It had made no sense to read about other lives when I could be living my own.

Junichiro Tanazaki became my guide to Japanese people, their precise social rituals, and their philosophical, otherworldly aesthetics. I especially loved *The Makioka Sisters,* and reading about Japanese customs in Japan was my first experience of befriending literary characters, of caring about what happened to them, about their loves and losses. For the first time I loved reading, even as the process continued to be slow, but this did not change my newfound understanding that there was no firm ground anywhere from which to measure, judge, compare. No universal yardstick. I began seeing that the efforts that went into small gestures like exquisitely wrapped packages or bigger enterprises like monastic architecture, rock gardens, and temple murals were all activities conditioned by time and place, changeable and changing, neither true nor not true. So many aspects of Japan—a bonsai tree, a haiku—felt grounded in exactitude while expressing ethereal realities at the same time, as if experiencing the entire universe through one atom.

However opaque I found Suzuki's writings, he had pointed to the truth of ineffable states of mind, states in which the very concepts of fact and certainty and even truth itself dissolved into sky-like spaciousness, far removed from words and ideas and consensus reality. According to how I understood Suzuki, they were all just concepts. That did not make them meaningless or insignificant. It was just that concepts were not intrinsically tied to anything unchanging and substantial. It was beginning to occur to me that instead of weaving a comforting tale about what was right and wrong, true and false, *reality* was more like a floating stage with no anchor.

Being outside the United States for the first time also brought into question issues of national identity. These surfaced with my English-language students. In the US, I was more at ease with the identity of being a New Yorker than with being an American. I wasn't quite sure what it meant to be a *real* American—i.e., not a New York Jew. I wasn't quite sure that Jews qualified as real Americans. But in Japan it seemed natural to identify myself as an American, even if my father made abstract art and Hermine and I were not Girl Scouts. In Japan, the distinctions between New York and Nevada, painting houses and painting pictures, lost relevance. The question of nationality was intensified in the many times I tried to explain to the middle-management men in my English-language classes the apparent disparity between my surname and my nationality.

Yes, I would say encouragingly, *that is correct. Tworkov is a Russian name.*

You are Russian?

No, I am American. My father was born in Poland, but his name is Russian: Tworkovsky.

So you are Polish?

No, I am American. I was born in America.

Was your father Russian or Polish?

Neither, really.

But your name is Russian.

But I am not Russian.

If your father is Russian, then you are Russian.

I was born in America. I am an American.

People of Korean descent who had lived in Japan for hundreds of years are still called *zinichi,* meaning *staying in Japan,* implying itinerant or stateless status. I could not explain to myself, let alone to businessmen trying to practice their English, what it meant to be Jewish, or what it meant to be Jewish in Russia or Poland in 1900, or what it meant to be American.

The more familiar I became with the Japanese refusal to accept my American nationality, the more I appreciated America for providing me with any nationality at all. Being a foreigner bid me to explore what it meant to identify with a nation, to acknowledge nationality as a gift, not take it for granted, and to consider what it had meant for my relatives to have left countries where they were not wanted, and even if they remained dislocated in the New World, to give their children a shot at living where they might belong. My aunt Biala could rail against America, but before ever visiting her in Paris, I knew that she was not French. She would never be French. The French would not tolerate it.

Listen to me, Mr. Japanese person: I am an American. Listen to the ease with which I recall my country's short history, how we started with a confederation of colonies and became a nation in 1776, and yes, you are quite right, our first president was George Washington. No, Thomas Jefferson was our third president. Our *president. Thomas Jefferson was* my *president. And we built the railroads, and we invented refrigerators and airplanes, and I am a* northern American. *We fought against slavery in the Civil War.*

My people fought against slavery in the American Civil War? Into what depths might I carry this convenient, continually revisionist version of my American heritage. In a letter to my parents from Kyoto I wrote:

> *The five or six people that I have met here tease me about staying for years as they have done. But that would surprise me. A lot of the problem, I think, is identifying Americans living abroad with negative, ex-pat attitudes, like Biala's. Intellectually, I know that this isn't necessary. I also know that I don't have it in me to stay away for these negative reasons, that I will not live, could not live comfortably out of the States for a long time until I successfully disassociated it from anti-Americanism—or other forms of escapism. Besides a real identification and genuine feeling for the US, I find that recent political activity reveals America's fears, problems, and sincerities more than ever before. I think a lot about America, often with tremendous pride—but a kind of pride that previously I would have associated only with the sentimentality of the Salvation Army and the Daughters of the American Revolution combined.*

This cozy tryout of patriotic pride proved to be short-lived. The war in Vietnam continued to divide the United States, and I knew which side I was on.

Mekong Adventures

I stayed in Japan for six months, until the extensions on my tourist visa ran out. From Japan, I flew to Taiwan and then continued on to Hong Kong and the casinos in Macau, willing to be seduced into staying anywhere. Not finding a foothold, I stayed on a westerly homeward track and bought an airline ticket to Phnom Penh, Cambodia. After taking off, the pilot announced an unscheduled stop. It was now 1966. The Saigon airfield had been turned into a military base with commercial flights banned. Apparently, we had a VIP on board who needed to be dropped off. Soon the elongated Vietnamese landscape came into view, slithering snakelike between the sea and the mountains. Below us was the man-made gash with the pitiless name: *17th parallel,* the military demarcation separating North and South.

On landing, a young white man, blond, reddened by sun, wearing a seersucker suit, white shirt, and tie, stepped onto a movable flight of stairs. A greeting committee of Vietnamese military stood at attention. They presented their visitor with a bouquet and escorted him to a waiting car. Vying for a better look, hundreds of GIs pushed forward. The dapper guest turned out to be Winston Churchill's grandson, a VIP of no consequence to the American soldiers. Without explanation, the pilot then announced that we would remain in Saigon for a few hours and were free to disembark. Under a hot midday sun, my appearance at the top of the movable stairs caused considerably more commotion than the grandson's: hoots, shouts, and wolf whistles, just like when Marlene, Rita, or Marilyn entertained the troops. My thick brown hair flowed loose below my shoulders, and I was wearing a matching indigo cotton blouse and skirt that had been custom-tailored in Hong Kong. Over the noise I finally made out the one question screaming from every direction: *Where are you from?* When I said *New York,* the congested crowd of army fatigues opened to allow the home boys to come forward and escort me to the canteen.

The serendipity of being in Saigon felt momentous, auspicious—even if I could not calculate why. Was there some reason I had landed in a war zone? Was I supposed to make something of this unexpected stop in Quang Duc's country—rally the troops to mutiny, preach Gandhian pacifism? I sat in the canteen with the GIs from New York and drank Coca-Cola. Mostly what I recall is how young these boys were. I had celebrated my twenty-third birthday in Kyoto, and most of them were younger—Cheerio-fed baby warriors, pleased with the surprising chance to flirt with an American girl. The war was theirs to win with Mekong adventures and a hero's homecoming parade. If fear of death tormented their dreams they did not show it, although unlike Thich Quang Duc's, their deaths would be anything but serene. While this surprise stop was uneventful, it still felt full of significance.

A few days later, on the rickety front porch of a run-down guesthouse in Siem Reap, Cambodia, it became evident that there were many ways to fight this war. Siem Reap sits just north of the temples of Angkor Wat. I was waiting for dinner in the moist, mosquito twilight with the one other guest, also American: white, with black hair, a beer belly, and something of the pirate in his affected bravado. We may have been close in years, though he seemed aged by disenchantment, and he had been drinking. He said he had been in Siem Reap for several weeks and identified himself as a Harvard graduate. In this outpost, you could invent any story and there'd be no reason for it not to stick. I could have been a Harvard graduate myself. He told me, *Might head to Laos; might cross the Mekong north of the seventeenth, check out what ole Ho's up to.*

The noodle soup hadn't arrived before I endured a torrent against the masters of war: *Fuck Johnson, fuck McNamara, fuck Curtis LeMay, fuck Joseph Alsop, fuck Westmoreland. Make no mistake about it, this is Kennedy's war—fucking shanty lace mackerel snapper.*

Oooh. Maybe he *had* gone to Harvard.

Angkor Wat had always been described with such hushed awe that this vitriolic harangue violated the mystique. I felt uneasy with so much hyped-up rage, and since foreigners in Siem Reap came for the temples, it seemed appropriate to steer the conversation in that direction.

Excuse me, Mr. Erudite Harvard man, can you tell me about the transition of the temples from the Hindus to the Buddhists in the latter half of the fourteenth century?

Excuse me, little miss white American girl, slumming through hell, masquerading as the non-imperialist memsahib, high off meeting real GIs in real Saigon who will really get their balls blown off: Did you tell Winston Churchill's grandson to fuck off?

The next morning, I set off on my rented bike for the temples, glad for the company of a skinny little Brit, still in university. We had met in Phnom Penh, and he was staying at a nearby hostel. By then I was familiar with the loose confederation of world travelers on the move with little money and less purpose. We traded information about cheap hotels, student hostels, bus lines, and the best cafés and noodle joints in the capitals and temple towns east of the Bosporus. English functioned as the common language though we came from everywhere.

We biked along overgrown pathways that wended through hundreds of stone structures. The damp interiors of the temples and the abandonment of the complex hundreds of years ago had turned Angkor into a reptilian utopia. Particularly threatening were cobras from below, and from above the green pit vipers, camouflaged by the foliage, that attacked the necks and faces of hapless wanderers.

In steaming humidity, we rode for miles without seeing another person. The absence of human sound or motion amidst such massive displays of human invention created an eerie atmosphere. Angkor had been known to the West since the mid-nineteenth century, yet none of the reconstruction that has since elevated it to Pyramids-of-Giza tourist status had begun. The temples stood in glorious, jungle-choked decay. Every evidence of civilization was decomposing, with assertive roots and tentacles pulling rocks back into the ground. What made this damp fungal site particularly menacing was the possibility that not everything that once lived here was completely dead. The temple walls featured extensive bas-relief carvings that described the history of various saints, deities, and Khmer kings. In the years before international efforts renovated the structures, these stones were encrusted with moss and lichen, and the imagery could not be read in sequence. Then, from behind soft feathery vegetation, a human face or limb or part of an animal appeared with a suddenness more alive than dead.

When I returned to the guesthouse the American lay reading on a hammock at one end of the porch. He immediately placed his book on its back, but not before I caught the title. How strange that he would want to hide *The Quiet American*. Every traveler through Indochina reads it. At dinner, together again at the single table, he was less contentious, perhaps less drunk. I did not mention the book, but Graham Greene's vision of bullying American naïveté made me wonder why he had edged up so close to a war that he claimed to despise. Perhaps his trail was closer to that of the riverboat captain Marlow in Joseph Conrad's *Heart of Darkness* than to Greene's Alden Pyle, presaging the superimposition of the Congo onto Vietnam in the movie *Apocalypse Now*. Perhaps this tormented American boy-man was scouting the Mekong for a hidden valley where he could experiment in private with the forces of barbarism and civilization that vied for his soul. He seemed just angry, young, and cocky enough to picture himself as Lord Jim or Kurtz.

I speculated that he was drawn to the tragedy of Vietnam, that he felt compelled to stick his nose close enough to taste its blood, to die from it or be redeemed by it. He had to be there, to get snug with what he most dreaded. I further projected that his need to be intimate with the destruction had nothing to do with whether he was for or against the war. He wasn't—in my imagination—driven by moral imperatives but by a hidden need to make himself whole. The war that he identified with was over there, and for whatever reason, he was over here, and that divide became intolerable. Politics aside, he might have been trying to mend a tear in his heart.

Or perhaps I mixed him up with my own need for mending. I would not be subject to the draft and was so protected by gender that even my right to question the war felt compromised. But as the war continued, I edged closer to Buddhism, safely removed from danger and closer to the primary religion of the people who were being obliterated.

India

I reached Delhi by plane from Bangkok. By the time the cycle rickshaw pulled up to a YWCA not far from Connaught Circle, I was near tears with fright and the effort of fending off a swarm of young men outside the airport. They wanted to carry my bag, know my name, country, address, be my guide, my boyfriend, my husband, my translator. They wanted to know why I said no. They wanted to know why I was so unfriendly, they wanted to know if *no* meant I did not like them, and did not trust them. All the time they pressed in as close as possible, and I did not like them and I did not trust them. The YWCA was run by Episcopal Indian nuns in long blue habits with large gold crosses around their necks. Whatever biases I held toward organized Christian establishments, I nonetheless identified the religious habit as a symbol of safety.

For my first day in Delhi I dressed primly in a long-sleeved blouse and knee-length skirt with the intention of walking the few blocks to a tea shop near Connaught Circle. I was quickly besieged by men on bikes, in cars, on the crowded streets. Across one of the wide avenues, I saw a row of outdoor bookstalls. I made my way to stacks of used, cheap English paperbacks, bought half a dozen, then hailed an expensive car-taxi for the short ride back to the nuns.

For several days, I did not leave their premises, moving between an interior courtyard and my room, where I lay in bed and read Western novels including E. M. Forster's *A Passage to India,* which seemed like an obvious choice. Big mistake. Even under the protection of the nuns I became terrified for Adela Quested, that silly prig of an Englishwoman who is—or is not—molested in the Marabar Caves. When I first read *A Passage to India* the ambiguity surrounding the Marabar incident seemed to amplify India's tumultuous political, racial, and religious tensions. After being in India for two days, Adela's quandary about whether or not she was molested took on a new integrity and perspective. I wanted to leave India. I was also growing weary of the hippie trail—a few nights here and there, hours figuring out routes and transport schedules, and the sundry rewards of itinerant friends. But I could not leave Asia before visiting Kathmandu.

Nepal

I first learned of this Himalayan capital shortly before leaving the United States from a man whose name I can't remember but whose insistence I can still hear: *If there's one place in all of Asia that you must visit it is Kathmandu.* He had a beard, and, in my memory, he stood in front of an easel with a map propped in place and held a pointer, lending a professorial authority to his assertion. Yet the setting had been a gracious mill house in upstate New York owned by Rudy Wurlitzer's mother, and I do not recall any schoolroom paraphernalia on subsequent visits. In her absence, Rudy and Jo Eno had invited a few friends for a summer weekend. It had been a glorious day. We had taken peyote in the morning, waited for the nausea to wear off, and spent the following hours exploring manicured lawns and playing in the stream. Toward dusk we drifted back into the house, ready to eat dinner on the screened-in porch and listen to Asian adventure stories. That's when the bearded man said, *If there's one place . . .*

The small propeller plane flew north to Nepal from the Indian town of Patna. Soon we were flying parallel to the highest peaks of the Himalayas. Below, the city of Kathmandu emerged from the valley floor like an ant hill, a diminutive brown bump. From the plane window, I could see a few structural clusters among low buildings, a winding river, narrow dirt roads, and moving dots that suggested the occasional car. A dirt town surrounded by green fields, and the sacred mountains not yet obscured by pollution from a million vehicles.

From a letter home:

> *Guess what? I am not going to Greece or Europe right now. I came to Kathmandu last week and met a guy who was just about to leave on a two-month camping trip and offered me his house and his English teaching jobs in his absence. It's a little tiny house with windows over-looking the Himalayas! (really only the foothills) but it is so beautiful. I will be teaching at a US-English school for Nepalese—the woman who hired me is Mrs. Unsoeld, wife of the first American to climb Everest.*

Never before had I known such immense power of place. The mountain peaks showered indiscriminate luminescent blessings on the ragged capital, and my muttering preoccupations evaporated, at least momentarily. The mountains evoked intense happiness, accompanied by a physical sensation of expansion, as if breathing out could last long enough to make room for the clarity of Himalayan light to enter.

The tiny thatched-roof house—actually a hut—sat to the side of the courtyard of a three-story brick house, on a street that sloped toward the river away from Durbar Square—a complex of temple structures that made up the heart of the small capital. The house sat about forty feet back from the street behind a mud wall, and each floor consisted of one large room. My landlord, Mr. Ratna, and his young wife occupied the first two floors, and a European man lived above. A large garden that extended from the house to the mud wall was planted with roses and dahlias and a border of fragrant gardenias—a little oasis in a city over-whelmed by punishing poverty. Mr. Ratna spent hours each day tending his flowers.

The streets that led off Durbar Square were narrow and densely resi-dential. The small dilapidated houses featured latticed wood shutters and carved wooden balconies groaning with age. On the dirt streets, vendors squatted over vegetables laid out on cloths. Cows and mangy dogs wandered between rickshaws and bicycles, and men and women bent by heavy loads of wood or grain on their backs walked barefoot.

In Kathmandu rats ruled the gutters. Men, women, and children peed and defecated everywhere. Nepal had its share of beggars, which, as in India, included teen mothers with babies, cripples, and blind boys. But Nepal lacked the teeming density of India, at least from what I had observed in Delhi and on the train ride from Delhi to Patna, where I had boarded the flight to Kathmandu. People were polite and friendly, with none of the invasive harassment of their southern neighbors. And Nepal had the mountains.

Mr. Ratna was proud of having Western friends and enjoyed the chance to practice English. He was a short man and self-conscious about his badly pocked face. As if to thank you for being forced to look at his condition, he offered an endearing, tender sweetness. The previous occupant of the thatched hut had left behind a bedroll and minimal kitchen equipment. The bathroom was on the ground floor of the main house, a stone's throw away, and featured a hole in the floor, a tap that ran cold water, and a large stone bathtub used for rinsing dishes before they were carried to the river to wash. The hut was cheap, convenient, and charming in its fashion, yet daytime viewing showed no evidence that by night the rats that lived in the thatching scurried down looking for food.

From a letter to my family, spring 1966:

> *Kathmandu is a town out of the Middle Ages. Right now I am sitting in a restaurant for early morning coffee. In front, I watch people pass, barefoot in the muddy street—grey, dirty people taking vegetables to the market, children 10 years old carrying 100 lb. bundles of wood on their backs with rope pulled across their foreheads. Dirty saris and loincloths.*
>
> *Kathmandu often reminds me of etchings of Medieval London. Too many people tired and dirty; crowded, overworked (human labor is the cheapest commodity) with too much sickness, disease, too many rats.*

There was no point in complaining about the rats or the ubiquitous piles of shit, or the flies that blackened the meat stalls, or the loose feces splattered onto market vegetables by sacred cows. By American standards, the place was a cesspool, take it or leave it. I was happy to take it. Every moment in the presence of the mountains felt like a benediction. The peaks themselves could split the mind and shatter the chattering that went around and around—incessant, unbidden, unwelcome, inconsequential. Their soaring, sentient magnificence bestowed an intoxicating, thrilling moment of newness that more than compensated for the filth below.

But I could not stay awake any more nights fending off rats with my inadequate artillery of books, shoes, pots, and cans. I pleaded with Mr. Ratna to move me to the top of the waiting list for the soon-to-be vacated room on the top floor, from which two windows looked west to the Bagmati River. The river supplied water for washing bodies, clothes, and kitchen utensils—all at the same time. Then more fields stretched out to the great Swayambhu temple complex with the spherical form of its central stupa just visible. Once installed on the top floor I discovered that rats climb walls. By then I had made the acquaintance of an official in the USAID office. With welcome American efficiency, he disembarked from his jeep one afternoon gallantly carrying sheets of screening, a ladder, nails, and a hammer, and set about securing the windows.

It took a few minutes to walk from Mr. Ratna's house to the Tibetan Blue, a popular restaurant that specialized in *thukpa,* a thick-cut noodle soup with slivers of onions, green peppers, cabbage, cauliflower, and sometimes buffalo. The restaurant attracted the incipient tourist trade, creating more than usual foot traffic for a side street, and this made the corner a suitable spot for Tenzin, a Tibetan trader. He had a resigned smile, and the ends of his two long black braids were tied together at his back with red thread. In hot weather or cold, rainy or dry, he wore a ratty black woolen *chuba*—the traditional Tibetan outer garment—often with the top part off and the long floppy sleeves tied at the waist. Over many layers of shirts and sweaters a variety of neckwear covered his chest. The rosary-type beads called *malas* hung in separate strands of ivory, turquoise, bodhi seed, coral, and human bone—or so he explained in scarce English and extravagant gestures. He also wore around his neck, hanging from leather cords, several sizes of pendant-style engraved silver boxes. These portable shrines, called *gau,* held protective images and amulets. Tenzin's seat was a wooden crate turned upside down. He sat with his knees toward his chin and watched over a cloth on the ground where more treasures were set out for sale, including conch shells, skull cups, butter lamps, wooden bowls, and thigh-bone trumpets. These ritual objects, used to transform worldly ways into a sacred outlook, were the warm remains of a culture newly slaughtered, still leaching the smells of incense and rancid butter. Now, pale foreigners in pressed khakis and hippies wearing Mexican *huaraches*—all at the fever pitch of tourist greed for native trinkets—jostled over Tenzin's wares. They stuffed holy artifacts into their bags and backpacks, souvenirs from Shangri-La. At dusk, Tenzin returned to makeshift refugee tents at the edge of the city that were clogged with smoky fires and crying babies. He dispersed scant sums to those whose religious possessions he had sold, kept his cut, and went off to buy beer. I passed Tenzin several times a day, going to and from the Tibetan Blue.

The owner of the Tibetan Blue, Kelsang, offered to exchange meals for English lessons—fried eggs and toast in the morning, and *thukpa* for dinner. This arrangement suited me fine. I liked hanging out with him and his helper, Pasang, toothpick-skinny and mournful, who cooked and served and begged me to take him to America. The dining area off the street had blue walls and half a dozen Formica tables. The lessons were held upstairs in a room that combined living quarters with storage. Amid sleeping rolls and boxes and under burlap bags of rice and flour hanging from the rafters, we sat on the floor, drank milk tea, and said words out loud in English. Whenever I became flustered by nearby rats, my earnest pupils laughed at me.

I did not linger at Tenzin's, but I learned about him at the restaurant and about his escape from Chinese-occupied Tibet. It took him ten months to cross the Himalayas, moving only at night, sleeping in caves, at times gnawing on his leather belt to blunt his hunger. He had started off with a party of a dozen other men, but some were shot by Chinese soldiers, others died of starvation or illness, and less than half crossed into Nepal. He had made his way to Kathmandu to seek work and try to get his family out.

Then, with the first news of home, he learned that once his escape had been discovered by the Chinese, his wife, son, and baby had been shot in front of their house. After that Tenzin got drunk every night.

One morning I went out early, and Tenzin was just setting up. There were no shoppers yet, no static between us. He yelled out: *Where from? America?*

Yes, America.

America good?

Yeah . . . America's good. Land of the free.

You like Buddha?

I like Buddha.

You husband?

No husband.

You marry me?

Ha, ha.

Time for breakfast. On leaving the Tibetan Blue, I passed a group of young Germans, disheveled and blond, moving away from Tenzin's corner. Their boisterous manner felt out of step with the early hour of the day, and Tenzin's gaze followed them with unfiltered bafflement. No judgment, no interpretation. Then he noticed me watching, and he saw that I found his bewilderment heartbreaking.

The next day I flew west to Pokhara, in the foothills of the Annapurna mountain range. A cow pasture doubled as a landing strip for the small planes that made up the fledgling fleet of the Royal Nepal Airlines. There wasn't much of a town, but with the opening of the airfield less than ten years earlier, Pokhara was just evolving into a starting point for trekkers heading farther west. On returning to Kathmandu the following week, I immediately went to the Tibetan Blue. When Tenzin saw me, his face lit up. *Lotus Girl!* he cried out.

I laughed. *Yeah, that's me. Lotus Girl.*

By then he knew from Pasang that I made regular trips to volunteer at a Swiss-run Tibetan refugee camp a day's trek from the Pokhara airstrip. He beckoned me over. He seemed excited to see me. He was finishing up a transaction with an older European couple. Once they moved on, he knelt on the ground and fumbled around under the box that he had been sitting on. Standing up, he handed me an ivory mala that had a few beads of turquoise and coral. I shook my head no. He held the mala toward me: *No sell. No money.*

I cannot accept this from you.

Lotus Girl, for you. You take Buddha beads to America.

He placed them over my head and waved me away. I brought my palms together and bowed in gratitude. When I emerged from the Tibetan Blue he was gone. I stayed in Kathmandu for another six months, but I never saw Tenzin again.

Shortly after arriving in Kathmandu, I had three jobs teaching English: at the Tibetan Blue restaurant in exchange for meals; at the USAID school, which paid enough to cover my living expenses; and at the Royal Nepal Airlines in exchange for free passage. At that time, the Royal Nepal Airlines operated less than half a dozen routes, including Delhi, Calcutta, and Annapurna.

I took advantage of free plane tickets to fly to Delhi. My time in Kathmandu had made me feel better able to handle India on my own. From Delhi, I traveled south by rail to Benares, the spiritual heart of Hindu India. More commonly known today as Varanasi, this is home to the legendary ghats—riverfront steps to the banks of the holy Ganges, where the dead are burned and the devout come to bathe. Walking along the promenade above the river, I stared at naked, ash-smeared Shaivite mendicants with their painted faces, dreadlocks, and jangling staffs, and pretended not to see their flaccid cocks, while below, women washed dirty linens and clothes at the river's edge, and bathers dunked their bodies into the ash water, which was strewn with yellow and orange marigolds that had been offered to the dead.

I anticipated that stopping to sit down would mean being encircled by aggressive monkeys, and beggars with outstretched hands, young girls holding infants, men too deformed to stand who pushed themselves forward, dragging their legs, and the blind and the destitute. For several days in a row

I returned to the ghats in the early morning and walked slowly back and forth, avowedly modest in dress, shoulder bag snug at my side, as I weaved in between chai *wallahs* holding the wooden handles of large metal pots and carrying small clay cups, snake charmers who carried their livelihood in round baskets that looked like a grandma's sewing kit, and men practicing arduous yoga poses. I walked up and around the burning pyres and looked down on stacks of wood and families who had gathered around their loved ones. Wrapped from head to feet in white shrouds and covered in fresh marigolds, the dead waited their turn, while cows and goats munched on the floral discards from previous funerals. If the family could afford it, musicians played drums and flutes, and invocations to Ram filled the smoke-choked air.

Allen Ginsberg, always quick to take off his clothes in public, had jumped right into the Ganges when he and Peter Orlovsky, Gary Snyder, and Joanne Kyger had visited Benares a few years earlier. Maybe Ginsberg had been transported by spiritual ecstasy or maybe he was just showing off, but part of me had wished that I too could jump into the Ganges and swim, without inhibition or fear, in waters alive with death. Everywhere in India neat, clinical distinctions between living and dying melted and liquefied and came together again, but Benares amplified this perpetual transformation into a throbbing rhapsody. Of course I would not jump into the Ganges. I was a girl, alone without friends, and already self-conscious and uptight and conspicuous. I envied the freedom that those guys had, but India was not where I wished to challenge the limitations of my gender—at least not any more than I was already doing.

From Benares, I went to nearby Sarnath, where the historical Buddha gave his first teaching, and southwest to Bodh Gaya, home to the Mahabodhi Temple, where the Buddha fully awakened under the Bodhi Tree. At that time, both Bodh Gaya and Sarnath were mudholes, barely towns, not yet tourist attractions and only occasionally visited by even Asian pilgrims. As he was dying, the Buddha extolled the benefits of making a pilgrimage to four sites in northern India: his birthplace, Lumbini, in what is now Nepal; Bodh Gaya, where he had his great awakening; Sarnath, where he first turned the wheel of dharma; and Kushinara, where he died. That doesn't quite explain what compelled me to visit these places. I still found Buddhist texts and commentaries impenetrable; I couldn't meditate. I was young and uneducated, but it's hard to imagine that I could have been so ignorant as to think that sitting down under the same tree as Shakyamuni when he had his great awakening would magically shake off my own habitual inclinations to daydream and sleepwalk; or that in sitting on the grounds of the Buddha's first teaching, the truth of suffering might penetrate my bones. I didn't even know what it meant to be a pilgrim. I was there to *get* something, to take and to hold, to check off another experience on my to-do list. I did not travel with the mental posture of a pilgrim. My mind was open to new opportunities, but I was too preoccupied with protecting my body to travel with an open heart. What I recall is a young woman meandering, picking her way through rubble, wary of rabid, mangy dogs and starving pigs, uncomfortable with the attention paid to a young foreign woman alone. Nonetheless, those footsteps reappear today in memory as having pressed seeds of possibility into my mind-field. Footprints with more obvious consequences came from free plane tickets to Pokhara, a one-hour flight east of Kathmandu, and to the Swiss-run Tibetan refugee camp situated a day's trek from the airstrip.

On my first visit to the refugee camp, I was accompanied by an American woman, Alexis, several years younger than me, who had known about the camp and suggested the visit. Alexis had the sturdy look of a Roman stoic: white, solidly built, with short brown hair, blunt-cut at the top of a square forehead. Her looks proved misleading. She was neither sturdy nor stoic and took the lead in trouble. On the flight to Pokhara she divided a sticky ball of hashish and handed me half. As the plane descended, women in colorful saris cleared a field of cows. We put on our backpacks but didn't get far before collapsing by the side of the road. By the time we could walk we had lost too much time to reach the camp before nightfall and ended up in a one-street village where we were given curried potatoes and tea for dinner and invited to sleep on the dirt floor.

We reached the camp the next afternoon and settled into an area assigned to guests: a raised platform with piles of bedrolls at one end of a large rectangular wooden building, which functioned as a community center. Opposite, some forty feet away, were vats of noodle soup on top of propane burners and tin kettles of tea for anyone who could pay or barter. A table between the kitchen and the platform was occupied all day, children ran everywhere, and at night groups of men sat on the floor drinking *chang,* a barley beer, and loudly gambling with dice.

The camp encompassed about three dozen tents placed some fifteen feet apart in no particular pattern, made of varied fabrics—hide, canvas, nylon—in all different colors. Some had lines stretched between them holding laundry, airing clothes, or flying prayer flags. No tent was more than eight feet square at the base; each housed a family of five, six, or seven people. About three hundred feet from the tents was a long bank of freshly piled dirt, and behind it a trench used for the common lavatory. Young girls walked there together, arms looped around each other's waists.

There were people in the camp so old and bent that their escape from Tibet over the Himalayas could not be fathomed. Dressed in traditional robes and high felt boots, they walked everywhere with prayer wheels in one hand and malas in the other, their lips never taking a break from mantra repetition.

The camp was administered by a young Swiss couple. Before the visit ended, I arranged with them to return regularly and provide English lessons for the children. If not for my teaching responsibilities in Kathmandu, I might not have left at all. Amidst all the heartbreak, the isolated cluster of tents sat beneath the sweeping white mountains like a secret enchanted garden, in the world but not of the world.

During that first visit Alexis and I walked away from the camp, following a narrow footpath used to carry firewood down from the woods above. Quite quickly we found ourselves lost in piney thickets. Our efforts to retrace our steps did not lead to the path but to a circular clearing, maybe twenty feet in diameter. The abrupt change in the forest floor and the symmetry left by the removal of trees indicated that this was not a natural opening, yet no signs of stumps existed. We moved around the circumference warily, afraid to disturb anything or anyone, wondering in whispers if it was used for ritual or worship. The space seemed fashioned for prayer or propitiation, designed to protect something, maybe the sacredness of silence.

We had been gone for several hours and were growing fearful. Finally, we sat down within the circle, and only then did a figure appear half-hidden behind a tree, allowing us to notice it, and we understood that it had been watching us for a while. Torn and filthy maroon robes, shaved head, mala. We were given a few minutes to get acquainted at this distance, just mutual staring and sniffing like dogs. Only when the figure moved into the circle could we see its female form. An *ani*—Tibetan nun—face brown and wrinkled, bare feet scratched and cracked. No facial or hand movements attempted an introduction, not a bow, not a smile. She walked over slowly, squatted, and displayed an affectless curiosity about our hair, clothes, and backpacks, running her hands over the fabrics and across our cheeks. She said nothing. After a few minutes we tried to pantomime our predicament: the camp, below, down, lost, looking for path, do you know, can you help? No recognition crossed her face. No sound. Finally, she stood and beckoned for us to follow. She passed through interlocking branches like wind. We had a hard time keeping pace though she looked twice our age. After a while we picked up the trail but she stayed ahead of us, leading us down the side of the hill until we could see the tents and prayer flags. When we got to within about five hundred feet of the outer tents, she pushed us forward to go ahead on our own. As she began walking back up the trail, a group of men came rushing in our direction with rocks in their raised hands and began hurling them at her. She ran. They chased her until they reached the edge of the opening.

At the guest area, eating noodle soup and drinking tea, we were told that she was a bad person, an evil character who endangered the welfare of the camp. She was accused of coming around at night and stealing food. I knew that Tibet had a tradition of yogis who chose independent and harsh lives without the protection of monastic affiliation. Later I learned of another type of yogi who pushed the boundaries of extreme circumstances by deliberately courting rejection and ostracism as part of their spiritual evolution. Some descriptions sounded just like this woman, and I have wondered if our protectress was such a *yogini*, a supremely accomplished practitioner committed to adding wood to the flames of her awareness so that her ego-self could burn more completely and her hidden wisdom flourish. Or perhaps she was just crazy.

In Kathmandu in the mid-sixties, it became difficult to distinguish between what looked crazy, what really was crazy, and how much of what looked crazy made some sort of sense. Alexis presented this kind of predicament. She left Nepal a couple of months after our visit to the refugee camp, but before leaving she had been running around Kathmandu wearing the maroon robes of Tibetan monastics, bonkers on drugs, and her crowd was growing every day. When she returned to the United States, her parents committed her to a psychiatric hospital. From the few letters that she sent back, it was far from clear which induced more trauma: too many drugs or returning to the United States when the madness of Vietnam made the lunatic fringe look sane.

From the time I arrived in Kathmandu in the spring of 1966 to the time I left at the end of that year, Kathmandu transformed from a low-wattage town in an obscure hidden valley into a theater of the super hip and strung out. At first, on any one day, there were no more Westerners than a few dozen well-heeled tourists, as many hippies, and a couple of dozen Peace Corp volunteers, along with a few dozen Western residents who had moved out of guesthouses and into more lasting accommodations. Some had lived in the city for years and had become legendary for their eccentricities, like the diminutive dark woman of indeterminate origin who only employed Nepali eunuchs for staff. Her duplex featured funky traces of Raj decadence such as moth-eaten tiger skins draped over frayed silk couches.

From a letter to my parents, June 1966:

Today I organized my teaching schedule—6 hours a week for US Info Service Eng. School and 10 a week for Aid for International Development. The latter should be very interesting as the kids have been selected to study in the States next year. Working for USIS and AID and watching the official Americans who run it—and listening to their introductory speeches—I feel like the newest member of

*the walkie-talkie, wind-up, American, anti-Communist doll club. In
fact, I am technically an employee of the Gov't!*

*Every evening there are groups of people playing music everywhere.
Generally I go to one temple to watch a group of old men singing with
all their hearts, playing drums, a harmonium, a flute, and a triangle.*

*Yesterday I went to a Tibetan monastery and watched the monks
chant while people streamed into the temple to pray. Many elements
of Eastern religion (Buddhism) are much more easily comprehensible
to me than Western. . . .*

*The monsoons have not broken yet. The city continues to get dustier
and dirtier. I envy you in Provincetown, swimming in the cool ocean.
I hope you are well.*

Much love, Helen

I wrote that letter more than half a century ago. Visits to Kathmandu
in recent years affirm that the dust, in addition to the congestion of vehicle
exhaust, still makes the stretch just before the monsoons the most trying.
So I can see that a swim in the Provincetown Bay might have seemed
enviable. Yet this line does not ring true, and all these years later, I am
left to question why I lied and what I meant. Both my parents remained
enmeshed in unresolved personal matters, but the breaks from their own
histories in terms of religion, language, aesthetics, values, and the ways that
those ruptures allowed for vibrant, creative, large lives, retold the quintes-
sential American story of starting over. But I believe that breaking from
their past fulfilled only half their dreams. The other half was creating a
legacy in their own image. So far, I had not shown any inclination to com-
ply with this, not with studies or travel destinations or immersion in art.
Hermine had already become an artist and had married an artist. Perhaps I
could be a little less disappointing by pretending to love swimming in the
Provincetown Bay. What I had really hoped for was that I had the courage
to swim as far from them as they had from their own families, but I did
not have my father's taut resolve and feared that, like my mother, I would
always—for the most part—be towed along.

Meanwhile, a shadow had been encroaching on my happy months in this Himalayan outpost. Suddenly hundreds of Westerners were crowding into Kathmandu. Something was happening here, some kind of tipping point phenomenon spurred by an accretion of ear-whispered recommendations, gossip, tall tales, letters, and returnees who said, *If there is one place in all of Asia . . .* By Christmas the road to Kathmandu was thrust into the limelight as the trail to paradise. This tiny idyll became the trendiest destination for every seeker, hipster, lost child, deranged aspirant, and soulless entrepreneur of religious goods. Overnight the place was overrun with wannabe Himalayan mystics, madmen, and Westerners wearing Buddhist robes, yogi robes, bathrobes, kimonos, or no clothes at all. They wore their hair twisted into topknots, in dreadlocks, cut like Japanese samurai, or swaddled like swamis, their bodies laden with sacred beads and amulets. Explorations of new fashion were fueled by marijuana, hashish, opium, heroin, or by LSD licked off the backs of stamps on letters posted from friends back home—which is how Alexis had secured her steady supply. Intermittently, through static-hissing radios, came the Beatles and the Rolling Stones, the Mamas & the Papas, Barry McGuire singing "Eve of Destruction," Phil Ochs's "I Ain't Marching Any More," and Bob Dylan's "Ballad of a Thin Man": *"Something's happening here, and you don't know what it is, do you, Mr. Jones?"* As much as I wished to identify with Bob Dylan, my insecurities brought me closer in character to Mr. Jones, still carrying a pencil, still trying to make sense.

From a letter home:

Last Saturday evening I sneaked into the American movie at the Embassy—supposedly only for the Embassy people—but the Nepalese doorman of course would not stop a young, white memsahib. The movie was Bridge on the River Kwai—*which was great—but it was very upsetting to hear the American kids, sitting with their parents, applaud when the Japanese train and bridge were blown up—especially because I'm not sure that these 8 to 10 year olds distinguish between the Japanese and, say, the Nepalese . . . or the Vietnamese.*

I did not see the war in Vietnam as the logical step in a brutal history of aggression and greed that started with the slaughter of native peoples by white imperialists. I understood that my public-school education about Jamestown and Plymouth had been patriotic propaganda. But that didn't make the mythology of America easy to give up. It still isn't, for I was born Jewish during the Holocaust. The mythology of America accounts for my grandparents coming to America, and their stories—my story—are no less consequential because the mythologies that powered the migrations remain wanting in historical accuracy. The streets were not paved in gold and money did not grow on trees and opportunities for all were not equal. Still, public schools and free libraries and museums provided my parents with options they would never have had in Eastern Europe, even without the Holocaust. Art. Literature. Vast and wondrous worlds became available even to immigrant kids speaking Yiddish and living in tenement slums. Even today, that strikes me as remarkable. And the Americans defeated the Nazis and liberated the death camps, so it seemed that, on balance, I owed my life to America—even if being an American was not always an easy fit, and some shade of disorientation had hovered close since my days of playing on the street with the sons of Catholic policemen.

In Kathmandu, my chronic disorientation played out in maneuvers between the Peace Corps volunteers and the growing tribe of outliers, not fully in one camp or the other. The English Language Institute, where I had been hired to teach, was run by Jolene Unsoeld, whose husband, Willie Unsoeld, was a famous mountaineer and the head of the Peace Corps in Nepal at that time. On occasion, they gathered Peace Corps volunteers in their home for evenings of real hamburgers (cow, not buffalo) with stateside ketchup and ice cream, and they would add some young strays like myself. The house was suburban USA with couches, wing chairs, and family photos. I went for the food and because this family shared something with family friends from my childhood. These friends engaged in exotic outings called *family vacations*: Mom, Dad, and the kids. One Christmas when I was about eight, I learned that all four members of this family were skiing in Colorado. I asked my mother if we could ever do something like that, and she said no. But her answer implied that the reasons were not just financial. When I asked why not, she said, *We're not that kind of family.* She made no attempt to explain what kind of family we were, but when I met the Unsoelds, I understood that they belonged to the other kind. They shared hobbies and sports and ideas of what fun looked like. Their good cheer seemed not so dependent on self-consciously constructing things like art or dinner or parenthood.

May 7th

Dear Mummy and Daddy,

Sunday was so beautiful I decided to walk out to a Tibetan temple—about a two-hour walk from here, along the most beautiful road, one step out of the city and you're in the villages. I was about to start back when it clouded up and began to pour. This is becoming more frequent as the monsoons approach. To get out of the rain, I went back to the monastery where there seems always to be continual chanting and the monks and lamas are always very cordial about letting you listen—since I was already dripping wet they offered me some Tibetan tea—which was very nice of them—and which I could hardly refuse—and it was warm—but Tibetan tea is made with a lot of salt and rancid butter, which so turned my stomach that I had to spend all of Monday in bed.

Every few weeks I arrived at the refugee camp with a backpack stuffed with crayons and pads. The classes started whenever enough children gathered in the community center. We would all climb up on the platform used by overnight guests and start the baby drill: *What is your name? Where do you live? How old are you?* Ages varied from three to fifteen.

A few Tibetans spoke minimal English, but aided by gestures and patience, they told their stories. Many entailed horrific details of leaving behind beloved family members, or losing them to starvation or illness on the risky trek across the mountains or to capture or death by Chinese soldiers. Many cried as they remembered those left behind.

Every week new arrivals showed up at the camp hungry and tattered, their grief etched into their faces. They might bring good news to a family whose relatives were still alive, but that did little to diminish the big picture of continued slaughter and torture of monks and nuns, the destruction of hundreds of monasteries, and the desecration of temples. The drama of any single tale veered at right angles from the ordinary hardships of human living. Yet the exceptional degree of suffering did not inflate emotional reactivity. I never once perceived that sorrow had been embellished or over-stated for effect; or heard misery used as currency, or tales exaggerated for sympathy. This was a different relationship to misfortune than what I was used to. No attempts to glorify suffering or make it noble, or to use it as a bargaining chip. Sadness without the drama, without self-pity.

One time I arrived at the camp between monsoon downpours after days of canceled flights. I had proceeded to the camp on the slippery mountain path, taking shelter under trees until giving up on staying dry, and had arrived at dusk soaked. The more industrious families had trenched their tents to little avail. The ditch used for the latrine was overflowing with excrement, creating a consensus that the path leading toward it was just as good a place to squat. The next morning, I awoke to more rain and to people piling into the flimsy shack to dry out with hot tea and to sit around and tell stories. The old people never stopped fingering their beads and turning their handheld prayer wheels. Men sat on the floor in small groups, gambling and yelping loudly with each throw of the dice. The rafters were soon laden with wet clothes. When the steam from the cooking vats reached the soggy wool sweaters and *chubas,* the room filled with a soft loamy stench. I drank milk tea under the covers, deeply content with so much commotion at just the right distance: not too far and not too close.

At dusk the rains stopped. The evening sky cleared, revealing a full moon. Tibetans celebrate the thirteen moons of their calendar by communal dancing. After the evening bowl of soup, everyone streamed toward a flat area to one side of the tents. The singing began, and men and women danced in separate circles. Against snow peaks lit by the moon, they slowly raised one knee toward the chest as the body turned and the circle rotated.

As raised arms swayed back and forth, the elongated sleeves of their traditional dress waved like flags, and in the icy glare of the moon their faces radiated exultant joy.

I watched transfixed by their easy abandonment of suffering. Nothing in my background suggested that a people persecuted with the intention of extinction could express carefree exuberance. If Jews had known laughter and merriment at the worst of times, I had not been aware of it. I had never been to a Jewish wedding which, I have since learned, includes ecstatic dancing. My experience of secular Judaism suggested that suffering was the noble attribute of an examined life and that liberation—even on a political or social level—should never be an excuse to tamp down the ardor of sadness. Jews were chosen to bear witness to suffering, and those who survived owed the world our misery.

My mother believed in the value of suffering. Her motherless childhood provided her with much to grieve for. She never spoke about her past but referred to happiness as if it were a disease. She conjoined *happiness* with *fun,* a word she used with particular derision, as if planning for fun was a folly of utmost stupidity. Perhaps this explains her reference to the family who went skiing together. In her view, Anglo Californians displayed an intemperate appetite for the pursuit of fun, and she refused to accompany my father on his visits to their state.

In childhood, I did not make a distinction between personal loss and the suffering of an entire people. The ennobling of suffering did not appear confined to any individual situation, especially as I did not yet know about my mother's childhood. The people I knew to be Jews, especially my disconsolate grandparents, made it difficult to separate the Holocaust from endemic despair. True, my family gathered around the radio on Sunday evenings to listen to Jack Benny, who was almost as funny as watching my father weep with laughter. My father also loved the Marx Brothers, and for their first date, took my mother to a Marx Brothers movie, but I had no idea that these comedians were Jewish. That was not the case with Ethel and Julius Rosenberg. Their execution took place one evening in June when the light stayed late. I was ten years old and had been playing outside with the boys from my building. Their mothers sat on folding chairs on the sidewalk hunched around a small radio that was plugged into Mr. Barrett's street-level hat shop. When the ominous countdown began, the Catholic mothers gathered their children to their sides. I ran upstairs to find my parents sitting at the kitchen table. They too were listening to the radio, holding hands and both in tears. Innocent or guilty, more Jews had just been killed. To let go of suffering was to let go of the history and identity of Judaism.

In the Tibetan refugee camp, I began to learn that suffering had a size and shape independent of circumstances. What a shock to consider that past events, no matter how tragic, did not inherently condemn an entire life to wretchedness, that people had choices, that something inside of us could be, if we allowed for it, bigger and braver than our losses and hurt, our grief and torment. I assumed that the Tibetans' capacity to be joyful amid suffering related to Buddhism, although I had no understanding of how that might work.

Years later, I read a story about His Holiness the Dalai Lama that still reverberates and brings me back to the refugee camp. He was being interviewed by a French journalist and spoke of an elderly monk who had requested his permission to undertake a particular practice. His Holiness explained that the physical demands of this practice were best suited for younger fellows and suggested a less rigorous alternative. The old man listened respectfully and left. Soon after, His Holiness learned that the old man had taken his own life. Apparently, he aspired to be reborn as quickly as possible so that he could engage in the more demanding practice.

That's the first part of the story. What sticks is the following: the journalist then asked, *How did you get over this?*

Get over this? the Dalai Lama repeated incredulously. *You don't get over something like this.*

It sounded as if regret or sadness or whatever the Dalai Lama meant by *this* is not forgotten but does not tyrannize the heart and mind, as it had for my mother. It's there without defining you or imprisoning you, without screaming for attention or keeping you submerged. *This* takes an appropriate place among a lengthy directory of hardships, thereby losing its power to control or condition or define an entire life. For the Tibetans, the jubilant full-moon festivities did not deny or circumvent the ongoing destruction of their people and religion; rather their capacity for living expanded beyond the shape of sadness.

Mingyur Rinpoche once shared the journalist's assumption that an evolved spiritual being *got over* one's own difficult experiences. His father, Tulku Urgyen Rinpoche, was an eminent meditation master, and from listening in on dharma talks from his earliest days, Mingyur had concluded by about age seven that becoming enlightened would erase all negative emotions and experiences. To make sure he had gotten this right, one day he asked his father, *When I get enlightened, will I remember me? My old self?*

His father found this question hilarious. He then explained that enlightenment is not about forgetting the self that we know but uncovering inherent qualities of wisdom that already exist within us—dormant, yet ripe for awakening. Recognizing new dimensions of ourselves will transform how we relate to our familiar selves, but this change will not come from erasure or avoidance or denial. Even though my mother traveled very far from her origins, she could not dislodge the primacy of her motherless childhood. The Tibetan refugees introduced an entirely new possibility for how to relate to difficulties—even to extreme suffering. Yet to apply this lesson to my mother, I would have to stop perceiving her as victimized by forces outside of herself. I might have had to look at the ways that she had kept her sad story in place. At the time, I was far from ready to apply that version of accountability to my own life, let alone hers. I already experienced her as entrapped in an interior darkness, and to criticize her for not taking responsibility for her own despair would have meant asking more of her than I ever could. I wished that she could have turned her suffering into her salvation, that she could have used the agency of her own resolve to open to something vast, outside of herself, beyond fear and hope, to find her own asylum, an interior place apart just for her, a place to rest in the absence of her congenital dysphoria. I loved her so much, but that was not enough to pull her to the surface, and I had wished for that too.

Following one visit to the refugee camp, I left at dawn to return to the airstrip in Pokhara. The camp connected to a dirt road by a narrow footpath not more than a mile long. At the last turn on the descent, the road below came into view, and suddenly twelve to fifteen young men appeared in the process of saddling horses. Many wore their thick black hair parted at the center and loose to the waist and had thin, long moustaches. They wore high boots, some made from the traditional red felt, and they had wrapped colorful woven sashes around their waists. The horses were small and of all colors. The wood and metal saddles were covered by thick decorative carpets, the same material used for the saddle pads. It looked as if any minute a Hollywood crew might arrive to film young braves in a cinematic burlesque featuring the most dazzling knights in the kingdom. And didn't they know it, especially with an enthralled young foreign woman looking on.

The horses began pawing the ground, tossing their heads. Time to go. A few people from the camp had gathered: awestruck young kids and some old people fingering their malas and turning their prayer wheels. For their final maneuver, the buccaneers slung cumbersome muskets across their lean torsos and leapt onto their saddles. With hoots and cries they slapped their horses, kicked their flanks, and galloped straight across the fields, dirt spraying in all directions.

On my next visit, I learned from the Swiss directors that these striking young Khampas—men from Kham, the eastern part of Tibet—used the area as a base from which they made raids to the Nepal–Tibet border with the intention of killing Chinese soldiers. Neither their successes nor losses were known. They were banned from the camp, but their proximity nonetheless guaranteed food and supplies. Despite many attempts, I never saw them again, but once was enough to set about locating a horse to ride. From my earliest memories, horses had starred in a variety of dreams.

From my bedroom on East Twenty-Third Street, the clacking sound of the mounted police brought me rushing to the window. When I was little, on hot summer afternoons my father would occasionally walk me down to the police stables near the Canal Street tunnel, where the officers allowed us to stroll up and down the wide aisle with the stalls on either side. On visits to country places, I jumped at any chance to ride even though I did not know how, and only luck rescued me from stupidity. But the closest I ever came to a fatal mishap happened near the refugee camp.

I was on a gray mare and as usual set off without a plan, elated to be cantering through fields in sight of the mountains. I turned onto a road that I mistakenly thought led back to the stable. The road soon tapered and before I knew it there was no room to turn around. To the left was a wall of rock, and to the right a sheer drop hundreds of feet to a river below. The path was not more than thirty inches wide. The small, surefooted horse remained calm, and we proceeded at a steady walk. Then we happened upon a trickle coming down the wall of rock from above. The water crossed the path making a small puddle and continued over the ledge. The horse would not cross the puddle. She would not move. Neither side allowed room for me to dismount. For several hours, we remained at that spot. Intermittently, I whispered encouragement, to no avail.

Late in the day a Tibetan came walking toward us. He stopped and stared. There was no room for him to get around us. He shook his head in what must be a universal gesture of stunned disbelief combined with searing disgust. He walked up, lifted the reins over the mare's head, and walked forward. She followed. He led us for about half a mile, until the road opened up again, then handed me the reins and quickly turned back. That put an end to my riding adventures in the Himalayas, and I soon left Nepal to continue west.

Between Kathmandu and New York

My aunt Biala lived in Paris. All my life her exalted descriptions of the City of Light had infused her determination to convince me and Hermine of the unparalleled civilized superiority of her adopted home. To choose any destination other than France for my first experience of foreign travel had been interpreted by my aunt—and my father—as among my most transgressive rejections of their own values.

After so much time in Asia, the worn tropes and obvious differences between New York and Paris seemed less distinct. On arriving from Nepal, I looked warily at streets free of litter and garbage, and lined with tended trees; where groomed dogs were walked on leashes; where buildings appeared defined by size and heft; and everywhere, fast traffic and impersonal encounters. But what really made Paris feel so close to New York was Biala herself, and for the ways that she was so like my father. Yet her impudent social habits were so contrary to the self-effacing presence of my mother and most of the other women I knew of her generation that she also inspired my admiration. And while she grandly essentialized the supremacy of European art, and high-handedly criticized all things American, she could also hold her own with my father, which neither my mother nor my older sister nor I ever figured out how to do.

At the time of my first visit to Paris, I was twenty-four years old, the same age as Biala had been when, with one marriage behind her, she was taken to Paris by a wealthy doctor and his wife. Photographs suggest a sassy young lady who knew something of fashion, smartly dressed in clothes made by her father. Not long after arriving in Paris in 1927, she learned the address of Ezra Pound. One day she knocked on the poet's door and introduced herself as a fellow American artist. It was lunchtime, and Pound invited her to join him and his dining companion, Ford Madox Ford. Apparently, it was love at first sight, with Biala writing to my father that she was *head over heels* for this man who was twice her age and, in another letter, that she was *up to her neck* in love. In terms of age, education, and religion, it was an improbable match, but they shared a passionate immersion in art and literature until Ford's death in June 1939.

My sister, Hermine Ford, born three weeks after Ford died, was named for him. A few months later, Biala returned to live out the war in New York, but for the rest of her days and all through her next marriage, Ford represented the gold standard for every object and idea that held significance in the history of the world. This meant the world made manifest by creative effort, by art.

Her next marriage was to Daniel Brustlein, a painter from Alsace who was also known as Alain, the name he used for the cartoons that he had drawn for *The New Yorker*. In 1955, after crossing the Atlantic at regular intervals, they settled permanently in Paris, buying two chicken coops in the backyard of a handsome apartment building on the Left Bank; they renovated the coops and added two rooms on top for their studios, creating a modest, boxy, four-room house.

I arrived in Paris on an inhospitable gray November day. Compared to French women, I had never looked more like an orphan in my eyes or in my aunt's. But even if I had looked chic, French women could not have been counted on for a friendly smile. I missed the welcoming smiles of Nepalese and Tibetans. Amidst the stately nobility of French architecture, I missed the squalor of Kathmandu. I longed for the mountains and lacked the proper enthusiasm for the Louvre and Notre-Dame and the bridges of the Seine. Stories about Tibetans fell flat. Over the years, Biala and I had acknowledged a genuine affection for each other, but I was still the American barbarian, her embarrassing niece, uncivilized in my disregard for the preeminence of European culture.

The kitchen of her little house was the size of an airplane bathroom. A lauded cook, Biala prepared meals sitting on the worn, cat-scratched sofa in the living room. One afternoon we sat there together, each with a platter of raw green beans on our laps. We were snapping off the ends and tossing the separated parts into two bowls on the low table before us. She started criticizing my clothes, an easy target. She criticized my not speaking French, which she had always done. And my American manners, another favorite. Soon she reached her grand finale, screaming, *You are only interested in the stuff that fills graveyards!*

I continued snapping the ends of the green beans. Did she mean refugees? Nepali people? Polynesians? People who did not make *real* art? My dignified uncle emerged from his studio, unhurriedly descended the stairs, and calmly addressed his wife in French. Fortunately, the dinner guests were quite lively. For the next several days I went out alone to sightsee. I returned before dinner and regaled my approving aunt with animated descriptions of the nearby Rodin Museum, the Musée de l'Orangerie, and, oh my god, the water lilies. Lunch at Deux Magots and a skip over to the Abbey of Saint-Germain-des-Prés. All lies. Each morning I studied a guide book and spent the days at a nearby bistro playing pachinko machines with men who drank beer.

With sightseeing lies intact, the visit to Paris ended with a cheerful French-style kiss-kiss on both cheeks. I took a train to the Le Havre seaport, and returned to New York on an ocean liner. Transatlantic winter crossings were generally turbulent, and after five days of lurching down corridors, hanging onto rails, and seesawing through unappetizing meals, land could not appear soon enough. Once the skyline of Manhattan's southern tip came into view, I stepped outside, made my way to the bow, steadied myself with feet wide apart, and faced the Statue of Liberty. I did this in some kind of inchoate tribute to my immigrant heritage, for one of the few childhood memories relayed by my father and my aunt described a scene from their own Atlantic crossing in 1913: As their overcrowded, stinking, lice-and vermin-filled ship sailed into New York Harbor, my grandmother—whom I had only known as a glum vestige of the huddled masses—apparently shook her children awake in their bunks and hustled them to the deck in the dark and up against the railing so that they could see the Statue of Liberty in the dawn light just before the ship docked at nearby Ellis Island, the processing center for newly arrived immigrants. Recalling this story, I feel my grandmother's gesture of hope, of optimism for their new lives, maybe even of gladness, though I myself never saw any of that. What I saw suggested that the relative safety and political promises of the New World could not dispel the sorrows of displacement; or of the crushing blows of two children who between them married five gentiles, and who both pursued outlier careers and never achieved any recognition or financial stability during her lifetime.

My stance on the bow had the straight-ahead resolute fortitude of a figurehead, even though the motive remained too elusive to identify what I felt so resolute about. By inhabiting the memory what comes into focus is a sense of gratitude; of wanting to lean into that same gratitude that my grandmother must have felt when she ushered her children to the deck; and to say to her, fifty years later, *Hey, I know it didn't work out so well for you, that in this land of plenty you shuffled through days of loneliness and grief with your heavy cotton stockings slack around your ankles. But here I am, newly returned to a country that I call my home, holding an American passport that gives me the right to enter and to be here. Because you were a miserable refugee, I am a citizen. My gratitude to you is the only gift I have. Please accept it.*

This newfound appreciation had slowly made its way into my awareness through the English-language students in Japan who did not accept that I was an American because my name was Russian; and through the heartbreak of the Tibetan refugees; and through recognizing that Biala could have been an American but she could never be French. This gratitude felt true, even if somewhat repellent in its mushy sentimentality; and further compromised by not wholeheartedly wishing to be in New York. Hermine was expecting a baby, and I wanted to be home for that. But Paris had felt fancy and fabricated. Its art and symmetrical gardens and architecture, and haute this and that—all the touted refinements that had made Paris the crown jewel of the Western world for Biala, and for Ford Madox Ford and legions of other expatriates, had felt suffocating to me, too mannered and uptight. And so I continued west, while wishing I was heading east—not to Japan, which had felt as restrictive as Paris, but back to Nepal, to Kathmandu and the Tibetans.

When I was a kid, Biala and Alain's arrivals in New York City occasioned a celebration. My mother stayed home to cook while my father took Hermine and me to the long pier that jutted into the Hudson River to wait with other eager relatives. I remember the dark water, brackish and threatening, smacking up against the hulking ship as the passengers lined the decks waiting for the crew to land the gangway. A burst of excitement always erupted when we first spotted each other, waving wildly as if this reunion was a triumphant surprise, when in fact it was all we had talked about for weeks. Now I had traveled the world and come back. I was not a refugee, but I did not yet know the meaning of *home*.

PART THREE

CAUSES AND CONDITIONS

Return to New York

The same day that I returned to the United States after an absence of almost two years, I heard of a massive protest against the American war in Vietnam in New York City planned for the following day. What good timing. I immediately learned from my parents that everyone we knew had voiced their opposition to the war. My own had percolated in relative isolation and now the prospect of solidarity provided a welcome dimension to my homecoming. Gary Snyder, visiting from Japan, would be at the front of the march with other poets, and he invited me to come to Allen Ginsberg's apartment in the East Village afterward where he was staying.

For my first outing in New York City, the congestion of the protest turned out to be claustrophobic. I took heart in the energetic dedication to stopping the war, but I was by myself and I still felt wobbly from the ocean crossing, and the attraction to solidarity did not staunch my aversion to loud crowds pressing in. After an hour, I returned to my parents' apartment but left for Allen Ginsberg's later that evening.

At Allen's, a group of about ten people sat on the floor, including the Swedish former model Nena von Schlebrügge, whom I had known slightly in Millbrook when she had been married to Timothy Leary. That evening she was with her new boyfriend, Robert Thurman. In another fifteen years Bob would be a leading scholar of Tibetan Buddhism, and Free Tibet's

most passionate and vocal champion. Also in attendance was Alex Way-
man, an eminent scholar of Buddhist and Sanskrit studies at Columbia
University, and his wife. The conversation moved from poetry to the war
in Vietnam, from Zen in Japan to Vajrayana in Tibet.

I still had sea legs from the ocean crossing, but my mind was even shakier,
roiled by the bewildering convergence of poetry, politics, and Buddhism. I
had spent my first and, so far, only night in New York with my parents on
Twenty-Third Street. I had not begun to digest my travels or figure out how
experiences embedded in Asia would play out in New York. And then, much
to my astonishment, the vajra universe of the Himalayas and the emptiness
domains of Zen showed up in a cramped tenement living room—an intense head-spinning evening of somewhat familiar subjects woven into hori-
zons that stretched with unprecedented continuity across the world. Similar
scenes, with a few of the same characters, had informed *The Dharma Bums,*
but that night I could neither track the references nor figure out how all
these worlds had come together. The conversation left me exhilarated and
disoriented. I had returned from my journey thinking that what I had done,
where I had been, how long I had stayed away, were pretty special. None
of my friends had yet wandered through Asia. But the conversation among
these Western men whose experiences in Asia and whose knowledge of Buddhism were light-years ahead of my own put me in the back of the pack. I
felt robbed of something personal and singular before I had time to figure
out where I was, where I was headed, in what ways I had changed or not, or
what I had learned.

At the end of the evening, Bob and Nena hailed a taxi to go uptown
and offered to drop me at my parents' apartment, but I had already accepted a car ride. The next day I learned that their taxi had been in an
accident and that Nena was in the hospital with a broken collarbone. The
near miss compelled me to walk over to the hospital. Behind a curtained
cubicle, Nena was sound asleep with Bob sitting by her bed. He suggested
a cup of coffee in the basement cafeteria. In the elevator, he disclosed that
it was an especially hard day because on top of this accident, he was scheduled to see his young daughter for the first time in many years. An old

association clicked, and I blurted out: *You're Christophe's ex-husband!* We were both taken aback.

Christophe de Menil was an occasional guest of my parents. Her Texas-oil family were art patrons, as was she by then. Tall, slim, somewhat French, with breathless, parted lips, she had an ethereal elegance that looked decidedly out of place on East Twenty-Third Street. Most intriguing had been learning that her American ex-husband, who had lost an eye in an accident that involved changing a tire, had become a Buddhist monk in the Tibetan tradition and had been living in India—information that sounded as rarified as learning about life on Mars. At the time, Western Buddhist monastics were exceedingly sparse, and within the Tibetan tradition, Thurman was the first to ordain. I never expected to meet him and by the time I did, he had disrobed. I also never expected my parents' world and my Asian journey to overlap. This convergence wasn't quite the sucker punch I experienced when Yoshi's friend quoted Ford Madox Ford shortly after my arrival in Japan, but I wasn't pleased either. In some inarticulate way, I still identified my Asian journey as a route away from myself, and this extended to my family. Yet however startling, this meeting initiated a friendship, and when Dore Ashton, an art critic and family friend who was then head of the Humanities Department at the School of Visual Arts, asked if I knew anyone who could talk about Buddhism to her students, I arranged for Thurman to give a lecture. This was before he acquired a reputation as a brilliant and mesmerizing orator at Amherst and later Columbia University. Nonetheless, the amphitheater was packed, and a rapt audience listened to a logical, soundly reasoned lecture on why all cows had been one's own mother at one time or another. I marveled at Thurman's choice of subject. Rather than riff on a more accessible topic such as loving-kindness and compassion, he chose sacred cows, reincarnation, continuity of life, and continuity of mind. Everyone loved it.

In New York I felt more displaced than I had during my travels to exotic places. I was betwixt and between, a familiar and recurring feeling from the days of being a foul-mouthed street kid of intellectually elite parentage. Pulled in every direction, wishing to go nowhere, I feared being left behind. In the midst of this ambivalence I stepped onto the safest raft available by returning to school at the Graduate Center of the City College of New York. I identified Tibet as my area of interest, and for the first time in my life became an engaged and earnest student. Tibetan studies barely existed in the United States then, and I was assigned to work with a professor who specialized in Outer Mongolia. Close enough. Another professor in the East Asian Department was a short, plump, awkward man, unassuming, with a kindness that did not typify the professors I knew. He had lived in Nepal for several years, studying its many languages. I enjoyed stepping into his office, where we traded stories about Kathmandu. One day I told him, *I'd like to know how the Tibetans can be so happy in the midst of so much suffering.* With a sorrowful sincerity, he said, *I'd like to know too.* Then he said that what made people happy could not be learned. I said I thought that for the Tibetans it had to do with their Buddhist religion. He agreed, but added that an academic study of Buddhism or Tibet would not help much. Soon after, I quit school again.

By then, I had returned to my old waitressing job at the Ninth Circle and had rented an apartment in the tenement section of Yorkville, in the East Nineties, a few blocks away from where Hermine and Bob were living. Bob used a nearby apartment for his studio, while Hermine had interrupted her own work when their son was born. For several years, both Bob and my father were in the preeminent Leo Castelli Gallery at the same time. Like my parents, Hermine and Bob's friends were artists; their dinner conversations were about art and artists—dead and alive; their outings were to museums and to gallery openings. Hermine and I had finally outgrown the competitive contention of our earlier years, and I saw her frequently, yet my own interests continued to diverge from art, except for Tibetan art.

I enrolled in a night class on Tibetan art at the New School. It was the closest I could get to signing up for a class on Buddhism, though learning the Sanskrit and Tibetan terms for highly stylized, crazy-looking iconographic imagery and being told that these images supported meditation practice remained incomprehensible. One classmate, Jonathan Altman, took off his shoes and socks during lectures in order to listen better, which struck me as an odd rejection of the Western esteem for brainy learning, but we became friends anyway. Jonathan invited me to a party at his loft in Tribeca, which by night was still a desolate outpost of downtown Manhattan where artists lived illegally in warehouses that had been vacated by factories once used for printing or making products like shirts, shoes, and dolls. At the party was a tall man with a shiny shaved head, wearing the kind of black cotton jacket worn by Zen monks. Over the jacket was a *rakusu,* the patchwork bib that represents formal entry into the Zen tradition. Having visited Japan, I easily identified the *rakusu,* but it was a startling presence in the United States, especially on a white American. The man turned out to be Richard Baker, subsequently the abbot of the San Francisco Zen Center (SFZC). During my stay in Kathmandu, Buddhist robes worn by Westerners had mostly been acquired with black market cash, not by rituals of faith; and posturing in holy outfits had created the impression that converting to Buddhism was inherently handicapped by cultural dissonance, and would never be more authentic than putting on a costume. By the time I came back to America a different picture had emerged, and it was intriguing to learn that after years of attracting interest through philosophy, poetry, and literature, Zen had taken form in institutional stability, with Zen communities buying land and building centers and publishing newsletters.

As the American war in Vietnam intensified, so did a growing interest in Buddhism. More troops, more body bags, more meditation gatherings throughout the country. The quietude of a residential Zen center made for a peculiar pairing with the raucous and increasingly encompassing response to the war. Each news hour brought horrific footage of death and destruction. You didn't need to take sides politically to recoil from the brutality. But when the anchormen politely said *good night,* America changed channels. People who shook their heads in disbelief at hippie communes where children ran naked between teepees could not yet bring themselves to oppose military operations that wiped out entire villages, even as they watched dumbstruck as this unfolded on television. Psychedelics were criminalized while Agent Orange rained down from Air Force heaven like manna. *They* were doing incalculable harm in Vietnam while in Washington, DC, *they* armed themselves with reasons, anti-communist slogans, and lies. *They* made it so easy to say: *Don't tell us we're crazy*—even if we were. Zen lunatics, hot barefoot babes, space cadets in full lotus, dropping acid in the zendo, smoking dope against the rules, having sex, having fun, and dancing to music with lyrics besieging us to drop out, do drugs, and warning us not to get sucked into the socially respectable government-engineered avalanche of annihilation.

At houses of worship where the clergy sermonized in cahoots with the government, congregations grew restless. The Berrigan Bothers and Thomas Merton and eventually Sloane Coffin, and by 1970, other representatives of organized religion spoke out against the war. But in 1968 ethical objections from the clergy were the exceptions while the pervasive interdenominational support for the war provided the opposition with storehouses of moral ammunition. American clergy failed to provide a reliable ethical compass; they failed to offer an intelligent and compassionate counter to an unjust war. They could not bring to bear the teachings of Jesus Christ to reset the dial on the first commandment; rather they turned the pulpit over to the war machine, and the people turned away. The moral vacuum created by mainstream religions was more like a wind tunnel than a static void; and Buddhism, hovering in the wings, swept through, sucking into its energetic promise an angry resistance to received wisdom and a genuine wish to help create a less violent world.

1968: Making the News

If you don't like the news, go out and make some of your own. This tag line ended the weekly radio show on KSAN in San Francisco hosted by Wes Nisker, who subsequently became a Buddhist meditation teacher. No one took Nisker's invitation further than the Youth International Party, known as the Yippies. A lot of us wanted to stop the war and change the world. The Yippies wanted to make the news, and guided by the shrewd media savvy of Abbie Hoffman, they succeeded in a big way at the Democratic Convention in Chicago in 1968.

I had become acquainted with the Yippies the previous spring at Hofstra College in Hempstead, Long Island, where I had been teaching introductory courses in anthropology. I was living in a small loft on West Twenty-Third Street just east of Seventh Avenue and took the Long Island Rail Road to the campus several times a week. My students introduced me to the Yippie meetings, and I sat with them at the far end of student lounges and listened to Jerry Rubin and Abbie Hoffman make their pitch for resisting the war, burning draft cards, and joining the Yippies in Chicago to disrupt the Democratic Convention. Shaggy and charismatic, they made radical opposition more appealing than peace-and-love flower power, and promised more fun than the starchy recruiting officers from ROTC. Every week another young man hovered nearby my desk at the end of class to explain that he had been drafted or had enlisted and would not be returning to school. Supporters of the war and resisters were both a couple of years younger than me. Gestures of swag and bluster and faces of fear appeared on both sides. My heart went out to all of them, although the rate of survival would not be equal.

The Chicago convention started with another Hoffman spectacle: the nomination of Pigasus the Pig for president of the United States. The police quickly confiscated the 150-pound hog, but the Yippies scored their point peacefully and comically. On the evening news Pigasus successfully competed with Vice President Hubert Humphrey, the Democratic candidate.

The Chicago police acted more viciously than during the race riots that had erupted with the assassination of Martin Luther King, Jr., a few months earlier. Watching them crack the skulls of young white protesters with clubs turned people of all political persuasions against the cops. The media slammed them, handing the moral high road to the opposition. The opposition, with the Yippies at the forefront, had correctly calculated that TV coverage of police brutality would work to their advantage.

I knew which side I was supposed to support—but both were equally repellent. The middle-class white kids, like the Yippie followers at Hofstra, behaved with unchecked arrogance, calling the cops *pigs,* cajoling them, daring them, shouting at them with as much disgust as white supremacists had displayed for their victims. But they were not nonviolent southern Blacks or followers of Mahatma Gandhi facing Raj overlords. They could afford to act entitled and condescending, as if they had the power, because in terms of the media, they did.

In the big view of a calamitous year, this response to the Chicago convention registers as a blip, but it was complicated. My parents were still living on East Twenty-Third Street, and my mother had reported that half the boys I had grown up with had followed their fathers into the police force. The Yippies were supposed to be my people, my tribe—antiauthoritarian, antiestablishment war resisters. But for all their lofty proselytizing, their brilliant street-theater comedy, first-class education, and media support, the very best they could do was engage in class warfare.

Chicago didn't change my mind about Vietnam, but I was less certain about how to effect social change. The Chinese were still exterminating Tibetans, and the Dalai Lama had still not incited rage against the perpetrators. Neither Martin Luther King, Jr., nor Gandhi had called for violence. It took educated white kids to act out the most conventional sandbox strategies, pitting themselves against the Other, the enemy, the ignorant. They appeared no more thoughtful than the cookie-cutter Chinese soldiers in their crisp military uniforms, who were carrying out orders to annihilate an exceptional Himalayan culture. But the Chinese were friends of Ho's. Ho was against American intervention in Vietnam. We were against American intervention in Vietnam. That made us Ho's best friends. But what difference did that make? Nobody cared about Tibet anyway.

I had befriended the staff at the Office of Tibet, which shared its eastside neighborhood with permanent missions to the United Nations, although thanks to Nixon's China policy, a seat at the table was never an option for Tibet. A few months after the Chicago demonstrations, I received a phone call from this office asking if I might show a visiting Tibetan dignitary around New York City. Asia Society had organized an exhibit of Tibetan paintings that had traveled to New York on loan from Tibet House, New Delhi. The frail, highly revered monk Domo Geshe Rinpoche had been invited to the opening celebrations to represent the Dalai Lama, who at that time was persona non grata in the United States.

Wafer-thin and short, Domo Geshe still carried the effects of his incarceration in a Chinese prison camp. His light brown skin was yellowed from liver malfunction. Our outings included the Empire State Building, the Statue of Liberty, and the Metropolitan Museum of Art, where he lingered before Rembrandt's portraits of elderly men in black hats against black backdrops. I catered to what I imagined he might like, as he expressed no preferences. Yet nothing offered a more telling measure of negligible interest in Tibet in 1968 than for me to be escorting Domo Geshe Rinpoche. For all my humanitarian sympathies, I was not a student of Buddhism or of Tibet and had no proper understanding of who Domo Geshe was, his history, his predecessors, his status, or his wisdom. There was simply no one else available. Philip Glass was already Domo Geshe's student, having met him in India a few years earlier, but between composing music and earning money as a plumber, Philip was only free to see Domo Geshe in the evenings.

Rudy Wurlitzer had introduced me to Philip shortly after Philip and I had both returned from Asian journeys with an interest in Tibet. They had known each other from their days of hanging out at the legendary West End Bar near Columbia University, a 1960s hub for student activists and literary subversives. Rudy never shied away from the associations between his name and the wildly popular music machines, although his own father had run an instrument repair shop near Carnegie Hall that catered to orchestra musicians. I have no sense that music itself played a critical role in their long friendship, although Rudy had first described his friend Philip Glass to me as a musician who made glass instruments. This turned out not to be true, but Rudy was not a musician. He was a storyteller. By the time of Domo Geshe's visit, Rudy had moved into the rent-controlled apartment on East Twenty-Third Street that my parents had vacated when they bought a loft building in Chelsea in 1968. And Rudy had moved out to allow Domo Geshe to stay there, so my days of sightseeing with Domo Geshe started off in the apartment that I had lived in most of my life. Behind me, all of my childhood, and ahead of me, days of shepherding my fragile charge though the city, feeling at times like a tree guarding its last leaf, making sure he did not get blown off the ferry or slip through the observatory railings. At the end of the day, I left him in Philip's hands.

1969: The Moonwalk and Marriage

The summer after the violence of the Chicago Convention, the television highlight featured Neil Armstrong walking on the moon. Images of one world, borderless, unified, and beautiful were quite a change from divisive hostilities. Yet it was hard to work out the follow-up, to figure out how best to get past the Hallmark connotations of *one world*. In ways similar to LSD or the serendipitous stop in Saigon, the moon walk felt portentous and full of meaning, but with no clues as to how to make it meaningful. I watched the moon walk with a group of friends that included Jim Strahs, whom I married a few months later. Jim had been involved with experimental theater and puppetry. A handsome oddball, he was socially ill at ease, wired and intense, exceptionally bright and very funny. He had been a debate captain in his Jesuit college, and although I had made a good enough sparring partner to enliven our disagreements, I never won an argument. He was also wanted by the FBI for resisting the draft.

Jim worked at Max's Kansas City, the outré hip restaurant near Union Square whose back room would function as the inner sanctum for every downtown artist and drug-addled bad boy and was frequented by the likes of Andy Warhol, the Velvet Underground, et cetera. His job included remaining after closing to scrub down the bar. One dawn he came home looking like he had eaten rotten seafood. A party of eight had come into Max's for dinner. They lived in New Jersey, in the town where he had grown up, and were still friends with his older brother. They exchanged greetings. By then Jim's family had moved to Illinois, but he had feared that his brother would report him to the FBI if his location became known. He never returned to Max's. Since he had not been indicted, his passport was still valid. At the end of November 1969, we married, partly for love and partly out of legal considerations, for we understood that a wife had more standing with the authorities than a girlfriend. The next day we flew to Madrid, where we had been offered a place to stay.

We traveled aimlessly, and not happily, through beach towns on the Costa del Sol and villages in southern France, homeless, not refugees, not quite criminals, but on the lam from an arrest that could have been made in our own country; always wondering if this might be a good place to decamp and if we should spend money in a restaurant or purchase snacks. I had been hoping to return to Nepal, and after a few months on the move, Nepal began looking like a reasonable destination. In Istanbul, we holed up in a squalid guesthouse, drank strong sweet Turkish coffee in dainty glasses, and waited for what was called *the hippie bus* to arrive from London and take us through Afghanistan and the Khyber Pass to India. We checked the bulletin boards of several coffee houses each day for postings of when the bus might arrive. Except for the Blue Mosque, the city had the grainy ambience of a gravel pit, made drearier by gray skies and frequent rain.

The ancient bus, round at both ends, had the same shape as the boa constrictor in *The Little Prince* after it swallowed the elephant. It broke down often and died one day in the frigid Caucasus Mountains, forcing its twenty passengers to spend the night in a concrete box of a room in a gas station, sleeping on the stone-cold floor. A leaden dawn revealed a black bear chained to a stake in front of the building, gnawing on a frozen camel. I remember incidents like this because it became a story I repeated often with the punch line *And in the morning . . .*

The whole trip never left the waiting room. The familiar agitated distress of waiting shadowed me. We waited for the hippie bus, waited to be rescued from exile, waited for the war to end, waited for a place to live—we waited in anticipation of nothing in particular and with anguish about everything. Each destination, including Kathmandu, lengthened the list of where not to live.

Montreal

May 8, 1970: We arrived in Montreal—sixty miles north of the US border—with the intention of making Canada our home, but we steadied our gaze on American news. The Weathermen had just accidently blown up a townhouse in Greenwich Village; Laos had become the target of more US bombs than Vietnam; and just a few days earlier, four kids at Kent State had been shot dead by the Ohio National Guard. We were missing out. Missing the action, away from where we thought we should be and grateful not to be there. We shared remorse, relief, and shame in leaving the scene of a crime, pride in opposing the war, and a queasy discomfort with unearned safety.

After staying with a friend of Hermine's, also a draft resister, we moved into a railroad flat in a complex at the edge of the old Jewish quarter, which by then was mostly inhabited by Greek immigrants. The building was at the corner of Esplanade and avenue Du Mont-Royal, and faced the Parc du Mont-Royal, which allowed the front room to fill with light. We applied for residential visas, filling out forms that included military status. A few weeks later our first visitor rapped on the front door. Following Canadian protocol, a polite RCMP officer handed Jim his official indictment. He was now wanted by the US government, a formality of no consequence—as long as he stayed north of the border. Canada did not grant amnesty to draft resisters; the government only agreed not to hold an indictment for refusing military service against a request for permanent residence.

With our papers filed, we made an appointment for our official entry interview at the immigration office. We waited in a large room, with honey-colored wooden floors and high ceilings, and sat among anguished families speaking among themselves in Jamaican, Haitian, Spanish, African languages, Slavic languages, Hindi; mostly not white, none speaking English, all looking up with fearful, pleading faces whenever a freed-up officer came out from one of the interview cubicles to call for the next applicant. We did not wait long. Somehow, our names had been moved to the top of the list, but *why* we had been given preferential treatment was not wasted on anyone. At least we didn't take up much time, and passed back out through the waiting room with our heads down. As a young American couple with college degrees, and the potential parents of white Canadian citizens, our applications were accepted with few questions asked. As we walked down unfamiliar streets, I understood that while we would live in exile from the United States, to be a white American refugee in Canada was not exactly being a refugee at all. Not like being a Tibetan.

Jim lined up a teaching job in the English Department of a junior college, Dawson, for the coming fall. We painted the walls of our new apartment and rummaged through junk shops for furniture. After a year of miscellaneous jobs, I began teaching introductory courses in anthropology at a junior college. We became a young married couple who resembled other young married couples, a description not altogether attractive. Separately and together we breathed more easily as outliers. Even so, for a few years we were happy with each other.

Around the same time that we immigrated to Canada, I learned from an article in the newspaper about a small community of Tibetans that had been newly settled by the government in Longueuil, directly across from Montreal on the Saint Lawrence River. They were refugees: disoriented and somewhat shell-shocked, strangers to urban landscapes, to the languages, the food, the rituals, the clothing. Only the extreme cold of winter provided familiarity. Within a year, the Dalai Lama—head of the exiled government—sent Geshe Kundrup, a Buddhist monk, to administer to the community's spiritual welfare. Jim and I offered to help him with his English. He started coming to our apartment regularly, and we went to Longueuil for festivities and to eat *momos*—Tibetan dumplings. In the cramped apartments in Longueuil, we represented white mainstream Canada. I don't think our hosts had a clear understanding of our own immigrant status, and in their presence, neither did we.

Cape Breton, Nova Scotia

July 1970. Two months after arriving in Montreal we were invited to the west coast of Cape Breton. The summer before, Philip Glass and JoAnne Akalaitis had driven there from New York with their infant daughter to stay in a farmhouse owned by the late conceptual artist Geoffrey Hendricks. On arrival, they discovered that the decrepit dwelling had no running water or electricity and JoAnne said *no*. They ended up in another old house with an indoor pump which spared them the inconvenience of washing diapers in a stream.

The following winter, Philip returned to Cape Breton with Rudy and together they bought a camp ten miles north of the town of Inverness, which stretches for a mile parallel to the St. Lawrence Seaway. At that time, the land that sloped down from the main street to the long beach—about a hundred and sixty acres—was covered with irregular chunks of blackened rubble, the enduring evidence of a coal mine that had closed twenty years earlier. In 1970, no industry had yet replaced the mine, leaving the town struggling to stay alive.

The camp consisted of a large rectangular lodge on a bare bluff that faced Margaree Island and the seaway. Behind the lodge, a dozen A-frames were interspersed in the spruce woods, and for several summers these cabins housed friends who gathered at the big house for evening meals. In addition to Jim and me, among those who returned to Cape Breton and bought places of their own were the sculptor Richard Serra, the performance artist Joan Jonas, and the writer Steve Katz. JoAnne and Philip had been working with a theater group in New York City and during the first summer they invited other members to join them. They created a rehearsal space in an old boathouse and named themselves Mabou Mines, the name of another costal mining area south of Inverness. For a few summers, Jim and I stayed in an A-frame, and then bought a remote piece of mountain land where we set up a campsite accessible only by a footpath.

I came to love Cape Breton slowly. Initially, its feral dimensions frightened me: the rugged coastline with battered cliffs gouged by coal veins; hidden coves with precarious rocky slides; blackened sand; remnants of defunct slips on the beaches—a maritime topography totally the opposite of Cape Cod's cosseted and picturesque charms. Nothing within sensory reach offered protection from vast empty northern skies or dark woods. The environment can be loved, feared, venerated, but not caressed, and left me feeling vulnerable and unprotected. I felt like an animal that had been living in urban captivity and then released back into the wild, but still looking for a snug corner, a hollow in a tree trunk, or perhaps a secure little cave. Even while appreciating the political asylum that Canada offered, in Cape Breton I yearned for some physical sanctuary within this unforgiving ecosystem.

It wasn't just the stark untamed physicality of Cape Breton that made the first summers difficult. The social dynamics centered on the New York artists. This was particularly hard on Jim, as he had not made incisions into the type of career path that would catapult some of these same artists into superstars. It was easier for me because in general, despite the inclusion of innovative artists like Joan Jonas and JoAnne Akalaitis, the expectations for women were lower; and also because I already had experience hanging around artists who saw themselves as superior to those in more conventional professions. Jim and I were the only ones who were in Canada specifically for political reasons, but everyone was against the war, and that cut us some slack. Had it not been for exile, I might never have returned to Cape Breton, as I had been so uncomfortable in the landscape and in the town; and with that group of ambitious New Yorkers, although certain of them have remained among my closest friends. Still, throughout the 1970s, barred from the United States, this summer cohort offered a connection to what I could not quite leave behind.

As I became less afraid, the island's pristine, primordial beauty began to captivate me to the core, and I came to welcome its challenges. I made friends with local people and enjoyed learning about the history through their stories. The mining towns of Cape Breton had long been disparaged by the farming communities. The children had been darkened by dust and many fathers were lost to black lung disease. The men in the bars got into brawls and gave the towns a reputation for being tough and rowdy, and with a supply of ladies of the night for *the men of the deep*—a description of miners. Not that the farmers led abstinent lives, but Inverness was criticized for taking on the ways of townspeople. In Mabou, ten miles south of Inverness, villagers still complain that folks in Inverness talk too much. Many people had abandoned their farms for the steady work of the mines but when the mines closed they did not wish to return to farming. Abandoned houses sold, when they could, for very little and often to people *from away* who had no intention of enduring the brutal winters. It took several summers before I came to recognize that surviving this harsh environment had forged reserves of dignity and humor. Growing up off the Bowery had left both Hermine and me with an intense aversion to drunks, and it took time to learn that among these tough town guys, drunk or not, there was nothing to fear.

In 1973 Hermine, Bob, and their young son Erik came to Cape Breton to visit Jim and me. After several summers of camping on land they had bought, they purchased a Victorian house on the other side of Inverness, along the same coastline. With the house came a large, substantial barn that they converted into two studios, and they have been returning to Cape Breton ever since. It will never make sense that horrific, hellish events can have transcendent consequences, but that was our route to Cape Breton. Some days, I'll join my sister at the beach, and have been with her when she has come in from a swim, arranged her towel, flopped down, and exclaimed, *Thank God for the Vietnam war.*

Confounding Logic

The same confounding logic by which the tragedy of Vietnam led to a lifelong love affair with Cape Breton applied to losing the baby. In the spring of 1972, I miscarried during the sixth month, far enough along to have prepared the little room, the mobiles, arranged the baby clothes sent by Jim's sister, the blanket knit by his mother. The doctors offered no explanation. That such malignant forces could not be identified felt like an intolerable second blow.

During the time of the historical Buddha, a young woman came to him carrying her dead infant. She could not let go of this child and basically arrived before the great sage asking him to raise her baby from the dead. The Buddha told the woman to return to her village and collect a few mustard seeds from each family that had never known death. The woman set off to follow the Buddha's instructions. When she returned she carried no seeds, but no dead baby either. With the acceptance that everyone experiences loss and grief, she had let go.

I could not let go. Initially the loss strengthened a marital bond that had already been Saran-Wrapped in the romantic appeal of suffering together in the embattled domain of exile. But in the months that followed, Jim righted himself and was ready to move on, while my own depression solidified. In order to let go I needed to put down a lot more than a lifeless bundle. I needed to put down a bundle of badness, of being so bad that I was not even good enough to have a child, this most primitive, biological imperative. The baby was incomplete because I was incomplete, physically handicapped, genetically distorted, my deficiencies circulating through my body like poison. I resented my husband's return to cheerfulness, and he resented my resolute sorrow. Then we began to dislike each other. I accused him of being insensitive. He accused me of indulgent self-pity. I did feel very sorry for myself, closed-in and stuck. As for the marriage, it was the beginning of the end. One morning, I found an image cut out from a newspaper that Jim had left for me on the kitchen table. It was from the sports section, and displayed an engraved trophy with the heading: *Best Defensive Player of the Year.*

After a cold, dark Montreal winter of deepening depression, I began to consider some form of spiritual practice. I did not know what this might look like, yet my curiosity was disturbed by an uneasy sensation of *cheating.* I surmised that the quest for awakening should not be brought low by anything as mundane as sorrow, loss, or despair—as if my own personal predicament could discredit this noble path. I did not yet understand that ignorance is the only starting line, and that the Buddhist path is nothing but the path of confusion. Something called *enlightenment*—ineffable, unknowable, as shimmering and solid as Mount Everest—was far away, where I wanted to be. In my calculations, seeking solace through spiritual practice was a cop-out, a way of elevating my anxieties to a loftier plane than banal psychological issues best treated by therapy. Yet I had not forgotten the Tibetan refugee camp, where unfathomable suffering was fluid—not fixed and immutable. The possibility of becoming bigger than the pain held out more promise than therapeutic analysis. Something inside would have to shift and expand. Maybe that would look like acceptance or compassion or detachment. I didn't know—only that some internal ratio would invert and shrink the wound to the manageable size of a pearl. The Tibetan refugees suggested that my whole life did not have to be haunted by grief, and that I was not destined to inherit my mother's legacy of loss.

The Arica School

At this time, 1973, Rudy and his girlfriend, Roberta Neiman, had become avid proponents of the Arica School, one of several human-potential movements that emerged from the counterculture. Influenced by their enthusiasm, and finally finding my own depression intolerable, I quit my teaching job and left Jim in Montreal to attend a six-week Arica training in Los Angeles.

Oscar Ichazo, founder of the Arica School, was born in Bolivia in 1931. As a young man, he studied with a Gurdjieff-influenced group in Buenos Aires, eventually ending up in Arica, Chile. He took the name of his school from this high desert town where, in 1970, he conducted a ten-month training program. About fifty spiritual adventurers, mostly American, joined in response to praise for Oscar that was spread by several influential thought leaders of the Esalen Institute, the new-age mecca in Big Sur, California, and specifically, by Claudio Naranjo, the prominent Chilean psychiatrist who had met Oscar a few years earlier.

Ichazo borrowed from Gurdjieff the replacement of the traditional role of the guru with a group process, and advertised a wisdom tradition independent of an enlightened leader. The original group of students trained by Oscar ran the subsequent programs, and Oscar no longer accepted new students. Arica's promotional language turned the promise of wisdom into currency: sign up, pay money, get enlightened. It sounded embarrassingly corporate and trippy. Yet every encounter with traditional guru devotion had evoked the same antiauthoritarian attitude that I had brought to the war, to the government, to school teachers, and to my father, making the leaderless aspect of Arica particularly appealing. Roberta had been living in Los Angeles and had become an Arica instructor. I stayed in her comfortable Beverly Hills house and every morning drove with her to the program site, a large rectangular room in an industrial building on Wilshire Boulevard.

Despite the sloganeering, the school offered an exquisitely executed six-week program. I did not have any *aha* awakening moments, but the program affirmed that awakening could be primed through intention and discipline, which contradicted my jauntier, drug-influenced projections of mind-shattering thunderbolt openings. Every detail was calibrated and sequenced to maximize the effects of bringing body, speech, and mind into alignment. With each passing day, the restricted diet in tandem with aerobic and yoga exercises began to shake out some of the sadness that had clung to me like the sour smell of cigarettes. As the tight grip of depression began to lessen, my confidence in my own capacities began to increase, and I felt more open to the difficult work of unpacking psychological knots. Guided meditations designed to expand the mind beyond its normal habitual boundaries also helped to reconfigure the predominance of psychological identities.

Four weeks into the program all sixteen students gathered at the upscale hillside home of one of the participants. We settled into garden furniture in a shaded area by the pool. The assignment required recounting a story that held emotional charge. I picked the miscarriage. There was one rule: you could not use a personal pronoun. *I, me, mine* had to be replaced by *a* or *the*. Not *my* body, *my* baby, but *a/the* baby inside *a/the* body. Each person had to repeat their story as many times as it took for the heat to cool down.

Romantic heartbreak, loss, and betrayal were common themes. Participants relived incidents of sexual and emotional trauma, crying, and raging at perpetrators. The exercise came easily to no one, but I had the hardest time. *This was my body,* I protested. *There was no "other" out there. This was inside. Giving it up was not a choice that I got to make. This loss was more like blood type or eye color.* The two instructors listened to my resistance, then gently and firmly one said: *Please repeat the story.* As often as they said *the story,* I could not hear that it was a story—an invented narrative based on the habitual delusion of innate, immutable deficiency. I repeated my version, my protests, my deafness. Everyone sat silently, patiently, as they had for each of the previous participants. It took many retellings before I could begin to separate the frame-by-frame details from a story that I had woven into the fabric of my life, my neurosis, my self-deficiencies; a story that kept me fixed, that reaffirmed my sense of lack, a story that told me that this is who I am, who I always was and will always be. I could barely fathom that these patterns were habitual, self-imposed wounds and that holding them in place was ultimately a matter of choice. This understanding demanded that I see myself in a wholly new light. It was so hard to accept that the charged-up heat lived inside the story, not the event, not the miscarriage. The event remained neutral. No single aspect was inherently good or bad—not *my* life, not *my* body. The emotion resided in the story, my old story.

Once the heat died down, and I was able to repeat the sequence of events in a neutral tone, sentence by sentence, my turn came to an end. From start to finish, the exercise took me from a fixed, unchanging version of personhood to a self who could not be found—a self that did not exist. Every deliberate suppression of the customary use of *I* or *my* forced a step-by-step dis-identification with the assembled collage onto which I had affixed an immutable persona. Every moment of surrender had been a death blow to this small, defended ego-self, and the ego had fought back, fiercely, as it always does; but—for the time being—without quite the same crippling force.

I left Los Angeles feeling newly energized and ready to get on with my life. I hadn't known what form that would take, but it became obvious the minute I walked through the door of our home in Montreal. Jim had gone to excessive lengths to create a happy homecoming, filling the house with flowers, candles, incense, and gifts. Yet every gesture intended to affirm his affections felt like a rope tightening around my neck.

By the fall of 1975, we were living separately in New York City. I moved in with Pat Steir, a painter who had a loft on Mulberry Street, near Canal, when the neighborhood still showcased its Italian heritage. The man she had been living with, Jimmy Starrett, had recently relocated to Los Angeles. He and my brother-in-law had been best friends, and I was still in high school when I first met Pat.

I signed up for the advanced three-week Arica training in New York City. Early every morning I left Mulberry Street for the swank Arica headquarters on Fifty-Seventh Street between Fifth and Sixth Avenues. Nothing came close to the lasting effects of the first six-week training. Nonetheless, it reset my life in New York City, and at the end of that training, I got a job working in the Arica administration.

The elders of this group shared several apartments in a high-rise apartment building on the Upper East Side, nicknamed the Stacks. I began going to parties at the Stacks. The apartments occupied the upper floors, thirty to forty stories up. This was *the seventies*—a euphemism for promiscuous sex and lots of dope. At the Stacks, there was also a lot of talk about Oscar, which made it obvious that this school, which promoted a teacherless path, had a teacher—but only for the first group of students, not for subsequent members like me. Arica had provided my first taste of dismantling the ego-self through practice. I was willing to go further, but I was not inspired by the instructors. Arica's path without a guru had been the initial attraction, and after two years, it became a prime reason for leaving.

My White Dog

The summer after Jim and I split up, I planned to return to the remote campsite. Not exactly alone. I needed a dog and started to ask around. Meanwhile
I stayed with Joan Jonas who had not yet built her own house and was living
by herself at Richard Serra's. According to local lore, that house was haunted.
Richard did not believe this and neither did I. But Joan did. She heard footsteps in the night and refused to sleep in the house. A petite powerhouse,
she dragged a double mattress some eighty feet from the house into the large
barn, which had holes in the roof and was full of animal shit. But she had a
dog, a mostly white short-haired mix named Sappho—part cattle dog and
part white shepherd—with one blue eye and one brown, and Sappho slept
on Joan's mattress. Even though I claimed not to believe that ghosts lived in
the house, I didn't want to stay there by myself, so I also dragged a mattress
into the barn, although I was afraid of the bats.

One Sunday Joan and I went to the annual concert held on the grounds
of St. Margaret's Parish on the other side of the town—a grand celebration
featuring the Scottish traditions of Cape Breton including fiddling, step-
dancing, bagpipes, and Gaelic singing. It started midday and continued as
the sun dropped behind the stage and into the seaway. We were sitting on
folding chairs among a crowd of hundreds when this cute, freckled little
boy came up to us and said, pointing to Sappho, *My dad has a dog that looks*

just like that tied up in the barn. According to the boy, the dog in the barn had run a sheep off the cliff, and as soon as his father had filed the papers to get reimbursed for the value of the sheep, he planned to shoot the dog. He had to wait for the sheep to wash up on shore, then cut its ear off and drive it to the authorities. I told the boy, *Tell your father not to shoot the dog. I'll be there tomorrow.*

This is how I came to live with Inook, an ardently independent, gorgeous part husky, part Samoyed, with a thick coat white as snow. She often took off for hours at a time while I became her lady-in-waiting. If others were kept waiting on my account, I might put on a show of exasperation, but privately I adored her inconvenient wildness. She resembled Sappho mostly in size and color, but that was enough for me and Joan, on outings with the two dogs, to make an odd quartet. At the end of that summer, we drove between Nova Scotia and New York City together, as we would on many subsequent occasions, and it was not uncommon for the border guards to pull us over.

New-Age Excursions

New York City in the mid-seventies offered weekly opportunities to check out an Asian holy man or new-age avatar. I went to an event for the imperious Tibetan teacher Tarthang Tulku, sat in on séances in a darkened hotel room near Carnegie Hall led by a woman named Hilda, took the subway to Brooklyn to see a crazy lady named Joya—first sanctioned by Ram Dass and later repudiated by him—and went to an auditorium in midtown for the sixteenth Karmapa's special esoteric Black Crown Ceremony, and spent weekends at Swami Muktananda's ashram in Sullivan County and chanted *Ram, Ram, Ram* all night long. I hoped that I might learn what I was looking for.

Later that same year, I returned to Los Angeles for a few weeks. I had reconnected with Jerry Rubin through his interest in Arica. He was in LA at the same time and invited me to tag along with him and Phil Ochs for a visit with John Lilly, who himself was among the first Aricans to train in Chile with Oscar Ichazo. Phil Ochs, the iconic hero of brilliant and angry protest songs such as "I Ain't Marching Any More" and "The Draft Dodger Rag" sat in the passenger seat and spent the drive to Lilly's house speaking of his depression.

By the time of this visit, 1976, interest in Lilly lay with the sensory deprivation tanks that he had developed, and with ketamine—street name *vitamin K*—the newest, coolest aid to mind expansion, of which he had become the leading proponent. The tanks, which came to be marketed as float tanks, were billed as yet another path to expanding the mind—even into the no-mind realm of enlightenment itself. A tank sat on the floor of a garage attached to the main part of Lilly's house. It resembled a black coffin and was filled two-thirds with a saline solution. I took off my clothes and got locked in the tank. Absolutely nothing could be seen or heard and nothing extraordinary happened. No death and rebirth. No out-of-body revelations. A degree of trust was required to count on someone coming to open the tank, as it could not be opened from within, and placing my life in that trust might have been the single most salutary aspect of the afternoon.

Afterward, I joined Lilly, his wife, Toni, and others in the living room for tea. I was not in a good mood. All these experiments with tubs and tanks and drugs were beginning to add up to a big pile of nothing. I was sick of them. And felt stupid for chasing after easy promises, too lazy to do the hard work. Something was all wrong. I had never met Lilly before, and his background in medicine, physics, and neuroscience defined him as a polymath genius. Yet he shared with other Pied Pipers of priestly Aquarian status a frightening certainty in his view of what the world needed—coincidentally just what he had to offer. I benefited from his generation of mind pioneers, but I was beginning to identify them as ego ideologues more attached to what affirmed their own schemas than to staying open to the whole shebang. I was sick of listening to entitled white guys who knew everything and loved the sound of their own preachments and kept peddling their spiritual projects and utopian dreamscapes—sick of them because I had been such a sucker. I couldn't wait to get out of there, and as far as I can remember, the deprivation tank was my last flirtation with a new, hip, cool, flash-in-the-pan mood-bender and mind-changer. I can't remember whether Phil Ochs tried the tank or not. If he did, it didn't turn his life around, for soon after he hung himself in his sister's house, age thirty-five.

• • •

I have heard many teachers, especially among the Tibetans, reproach Americans for our supermarket approach to spiritual paths—tasting, testing, moving from aisle to aisle. With all due respect, I think: *You were born in Tibet, and you grew up in a monastery and never knew that any other path existed except the Tibetan Buddhist path, and now you are a Tibetan Buddhist. Well, well . . . bully for you.* Because we had so many choices, we had no choice but to taste and test. But maybe it was time to try something more traditional.

PART FOUR

. . . .

ENCOUNTERING THE TIBETANS

Milarepa in an Oakland Gym

A few days after sampling Lilly's tank, I came across a flyer tacked up on the notice board at the Bodhi Tree Bookstore on Melrose Avenue in LA that advertised a weekend workshop in Oakland with Chögyam Trungpa Rinpoche. A few years earlier, his book *Cutting Through Spiritual Material-ism* had been passed around among the friends in Nova Scotia. For the first time, I had heard an Asian Buddhist teacher talking to me, an American, a modern Westerner. Even being a woman did not seem to present an insur-mountable obstacle. His language, fresh and inventive, poked holes in the saccharine speech balloons already hovering over followers of Asian spiritual traditions. If you just acknowledged the most ordinary onslaught of daily dissatisfactions—of wanting what you didn't have, not wanting what you did have—then he was right there. This was the first book that made me seriously wonder if Buddhism really could expand beyond cultural containers, really could be for people outside of Asia, even women. I had also heard enough gossip to keep my distance. Students bowed to Trungpa Rinpoche as a sacred embodiment of the Buddha, kneeled before him, adored and revered him. Too cultish. Then, too, in the five years that he'd already lived in the United States, he'd earned a reputation for heavy drinking and having sex with many students, which factored into his crazy-wisdom mystique. Whether or not this behavior expressed genuine, enlightened commitment to waking people up through shock and contradiction, or expressed selfish indulgence or addiction, I had no idea. Truthfully, I didn't care. I was not attracted to his scene, but I remained too attached to counterculture hipness to judge substance use or the sexual behavior of anyone, including gurus.

The workshop was held in a large gym with high walls and small windows at the top, mats and cushions laid out on the floor. Trungpa Rinpoche wore a dark blue suit and sat in a straight-back chair, often resting his elbows on its arms. His bearing expressed gravitas and refinement, while his squeaky thin voice was a comical counterpoint. A group of manicured young men, also wearing suits, accompanied him to and from the hall. His subject was the songs of Milarepa, the beloved eleventh-century saint of Tibet. At the end of the Saturday session, one of his young handlers approached to ask if I would like to meet Rinpoche later that evening. I politely declined.

The weekend incited no particular interest in Trungpa Rinpoche. Yet between him and Milarepa—the most extraordinary exemplar in his own Tibetan Kagyu lineage—I came away with an unexpected appreciation for the potency of lineage. So far, none of my experiments included wisdom that had been digested and then passed down, or maybe predigested, like a mother bird that regurgitates nourishment for her young. I had been drawn to the made-in-America variety of teacher, self-made—like my own family and many of the Americans I knew—cut off from past traditions, especially those associated with religion. Thich Quang Duc had been authenticated in part by his stature, his Buddhist robes, and the support of his monastic community. His context suggested that he was the real deal, whereas by now, homegrown gurus were springing up like mushrooms, without roots, without responsibility to lineage families or to a past that nurtured humility and obeisance. A newfound feature of spiritual virtue emerged from connecting Trungpa—attired in a formal suit, the glass beside him rumored to be filled with sake—with his dharma ancestor Milarepa, an elusive mountain yogi who roamed naked in Himalayan winters, turned green from eating only nettles, and radiated brilliant attainment through poetic songs. That Milarepa's wisdom had been preserved and embodied through successive generations endowed it with a vitality that was not wholly dependent on its living messenger—but was not separate either. This creative flexibility between generations and through centuries exceeded individual personhood, and something called *lineage* took on a disembodied dimension of dharma that felt alive and, perhaps most important for me, felt trustworthy. I could relate to these lineage figures through their human bodies—their flesh and blood was the same as my flesh and blood—even though it was the invisible sky-like mind that lived on in successive generations. How wondrous and paradoxical that what was transmitted through the centuries were dimensions of mind that eluded ideas and preconceptions about mind—like the dimension of Thich Quang Duc that had remained so enigmatic.

A week after Trungpa's workshop, I found myself lost in a desolate section of San Francisco on a Sunday afternoon—a warehouse district, deserted, nonresidential with gated concrete lots, little traffic, and no passersby. Increasingly uncomfortable, I suddenly noticed, half a block ahead of me, a commotion: a small crowd had gathered at the top of steps that led to a community hall or maybe a church, and then I recognized Trungpa Rinpoche. He was with a woman and a baby, presumably his wife and their child, maybe ten months old. They came down the steps and into a waiting black limousine. Following them was a gigantic Tibetan, who I would come to know as Dilgo Khyentse Rinpoche. He followed them to the sidewalk, and once the family was seated inside the car, Trungpa Rinpoche rolled down the window and held up the baby while Khyentse Rinpoche bent down, so that their foreheads touched. The window closed and the car drove off.

Dilgo Khyentse Rinpoche moved like a mountain in motion. It was hard to take my eyes off him, and I thought to myself, *How amazing to have stumbled onto this scene.* How lucky . . . unless it was not a chance encounter but . . . but what? Back then, the word *karma* netted more points for usage by hipsters than as a reference to a cornerstone of Buddhist teachings. Either way, the encounter was decidedly curious and the first of two surprise meetings I had with both gurus. The next one occurred a few months later in New York City, when Vivian Kurz needed help hosting another Tibetan VIP.

Vivian grew up in Kew Gardens, Queens, the younger daughter of sophisticated Viennese Holocaust survivors, making her background worlds apart from the shtetl origins of my family. The refined appreciation for the arts enjoyed by Vienna's assimilated Jews characterized a sensibility that my own parents had cultivated from scratch. By the time Vivian and I met, her parents had made adjustments to the crass mediocrities of postwar USA, and somewhere in that slippery transit between the old and the new, Vivian and I, born in the same year, became fast friends. We had met briefly in our teens through the friendship of our eccentric boyfriends, and more than a half century later, those choices still make us laugh. By the time we reconnected, her life centered on incipient Tibetan activity in the United States.

With fluttering eyes set in a cherubic face surrounded by ringlets, Vivian conjured the baby sophisticate Betty Boop, a darling quality that belied her defiant willfulness. She started her Buddhist studies with Trungpa Rinpoche, but by the mid-seventies she was studying with Dilgo Khyentse Rinpoche. Various part-time jobs allowed her to assist Tibetan teachers with their early American tours. In the late spring of 1976, after returning from California, I had sublet an apartment on Cornelia Street in Greenwich Village which, at Vivian's request, I vacated for a Tibetan teacher named Dodrupchen Rinpoche. A Buddhist path had not come into focus, yet the weekend workshop with Chögyam Trungpa, followed by the serendipitous encounter with him and Dilgo Khyentse Rinpoche, had suggested the comforting possibility that the aggregate wisdom of generations—totally absent from Arica—could offer a ballast against the vagaries of any individual in it, and this softened my resistance to gurus.

Vivian thrived as the self-acclaimed director of Tibetan protocol, a role she trained for under Trungpa. Particular flowers were selected for specified vases and set on indicated surfaces. I was dispatched to Chinatown to buy an appropriately decorated tea cup with a matching lid. Water must be served in a glass with a cloth napkin covering the top and placed on a coaster. Vivian had to teach me the correct way to approach a *rinpoche,* how to serve his tea, how to remove used dishes. For the benefit of my education she lay down on the bed in projected imitation of the tiny Dodrupchen Rinpoche.

When she was a college student at Brandeis, Vivian had starred in a few of the artist and filmmaker Bruce Conner's early movies, and never again were her dramatic impulses more activated than role-playing for the lamas. I didn't know what the little guy might look like at rest, but Vivian managed to cross Mimi dying in *La Bohème* with Manet's *Olympia*. She directed me to enter the bedroom carrying a tray with the newly purchased tea cup, the pot, and a cloth napkin. Short of walking on my knees I could not make my head lower than Drodrupchen's—or his surrogate's—as required by Mandarin manners. We would have to settle for a back-breaking stoop. Then came the rehearsals for leaving the room by walking backward, head bowed to my shins, in order not to offend by turning my back on the living embodiment of the Buddha. My etiquette mentor was not immune to the comical aspects of training, but proved to be a demanding taskmaster nonetheless.

Dodrupchen Rinpoche had been invited to join a large group of Tibetans and their Western attendants at a Chinese restaurant in midtown. I was a native New Yorker who knew my way around the city. I played guide, attendant, and diligent servant not just to one venerable holy man but to a greater domain of spiritual virtue that felt electrifying and worthy. Tiptoeing around the outermost edge of this new and vibrant universe kept me happily engaged and good at my responsibilities.

Our host for the Chinese luncheon was the majestic Dilgo Khyentse Rinpoche. At six feet eight inches, he was tall for a Westerner, but among the Tibetans, his anomalous height enhanced his legendary bigness of all things: unsurpassable big-wisdom mind, big compassion, big delight in all phenomena, bigheartedness, big radiance of warmth and love—a dharma king. And his bigger-than-life physicality was the perfect manifestation of his unparalleled rank. In contrast, Dodrupchen by size, modesty, and inclination hid his light, and unless you were sensitized to spiritual qualities or had been tipped off, you might miss his gifts altogether.

Dilgo Khyentse Rinpoche was traveling with his grandson, Rabjam

Rinpoche, an amusing nine-year-old who throughout the luncheon squirmed in and out of his grandfather's generous lap. At the end of the meal several black limousines appeared, and Dodrupchen Rinpoche and I were ushered into one. In another twenty minutes, the cars pulled up to a high-rise on Central Park West. We squeezed into elevators and then stepped into a well-appointed apartment overlooking Central Park. There stood Trungpa Rinpoche, again in a dark suit, remaining in place as the rest of us passed single file before him. Then we left. We were told that Dilgo Khyentse Rinpoche just wanted to pay a surprise visit, which did not last more than ten minutes, and no one sat down. I escorted Dodrupchen back to Cornelia Street, looking for meaning in yet another unexpected encounter with Trungpa, but nothing took hold, and over the years my encounters with him would be just as brief and erratic.

Having arranged for Dilgo Khyentse Rinpoche and his entourage to stay in a brownstone in Brooklyn, Vivian pressured me into having a private interview with him. In those early years of Tibetan masters visiting the US, the devout alone, at least in New York City, could not fill the interview slots. Vivian did her best to explain to a skeptical neophyte the benefits of being in the presence of a great enlightened mind. In our gullible enthusiasm, language often outflanked our naïveté, for really all most of us could do was imitate those who might know better than we did. At the time of my interview, one other person was waiting in the antechamber, and I watched him with lowered eyes, wondering if he had more history with this kind of meeting—or just appeared to. This initiated my friendship with Lex Hixon: an ethereal presence in those days, straight, tall, Nordic pale, slight, and luminous as a vertical fluorescent tube.

As it turned out, Lex knew a lot about interacting with spiritual exemplars of every faith through his radio show *In the Spirit*. This hugely important broadcast in New York City not only introduced new players of prominence in the emergent spread of Buddhism, Vedanta, and Sufism through groundbreaking interviews, but in addition to these unknown Asian voices, Lex also interviewed Western clergy with broad-minded approaches to their own traditions, such as Brother David Steindl-Rast, and Father Thomas Keating who, influenced by Theravada meditation, founded Centering Prayer. With an ecumenical heart, Lex dodged the politics and sectarianism of institutional religion, and stayed tuned to the parallels and core qualities of all authentic wisdom teachings. Furthermore, he did this at a time when many of his devout listeners had come to assume that any wakeful spirituality that may have once been valued in America had been steamrolled to death by material excess. *In the Spirit* offered an optimistic reappraisal.

I would continue to know Lex in different dharma settings over the years as he and his wife, Sheila, played a critical role in weaving together patches of Buddhist activity that helped seed dharma fields in this barren land. By the time of our first encounter in the antechamber, this included their patronage of my frail charge from 1968, Domo Geshe Rinpoche.

The brownstone that Vivian had rented for Dilgo Khyentse's visit was a few blocks from Junior's on Flatbush Avenue, a world-famous eatery renowned for its New York cheesecake. Vivian had the grand idea to introduce the Tibetans to a New York experience by arranging for them to pile into Junior's one evening for hamburgers and dessert. The large, noisy diner, all neon and plastic, had never before hosted a party of bald brown men in bright orange blouses and maroon gowns with an average height of five feet four inches, and in their midst one unwieldy giant, who even then walked—as he did when he entered the restaurant—with his elbows resting on the shoulders of two of his tallest monks, and his thinning white hair pulled back in a bun. Once settled into two long rows facing each other, with Dilgo Khyentse Rinpoche at the head and plates of hamburgers and fries set before them, the monks began the meal chant, heads bowed, palms together at the heart. If the dissonance made anyone uncomfortable, it would have been me, self-consciously wondering what the staff made of these guests, feeling protective of them, not wanting them to be made fun of. The Tibetans themselves looked right at home and were soon carrying on the way Tibetans do in social gatherings: making jokes and cracking each other up. I knew of this penchant for slapstick from my days in Kathmandu—for example, pulling a chair out from under someone about to sit down. Ha-ha! But in my bifurcated distinction between the sacred and the profane, I had erroneously assumed that boisterous Tibetan humor would not extend to monastics.

Tibet was not Shangri-La, not a perfected, ideal prototype of human exceptionalism. It would take a while for Westerners to figure that out, and the Tibetans, blown out of their medieval fortress by the Chinese, also had to figure that out. Prior to 1959, most Tibetans knew nothing of some place called *the West* and had little reason to doubt the preservation of their heritage. Even the earliest concerns of prescient, reformist Tibetans did not project a Chinese takeover that would include the wanton destruction of monasteries or brutal torture and killing. Americans might have known something of the recent and ongoing destruction of this Himalayan region, but those drawn to meeting the visiting lamas imbued them with the romantic mythology of old Tibet.

By the time of the American bicentennial, the proliferation of Tibetan teachers touring the United States had transformed the landscape of Buddhism in America. Tibetan outfits alone mirrored the colors of hot sauce and spices—reds, maroons, turmeric, mustard yellow. Compared to the altars of Zen and Theravada lineages, Tibetan shrines appeared gaudy with too many flowers and incense that smelled too sticky and sweet, and were crowded with offerings appropriate for Halloween trick-or-treaters: orange-and-yellow corn candies, silver-wrapped chocolate kisses, and packaged Oreo cookies. The anticipated arrival of high-ranking *rinpoches* and their retinues resembled the Ringling Brothers Circus arriving at Madison Square Garden: the resonant horns and drum rolls, the procession of performers, the clowns, the handlers, the ringmaster, the colorful costumes and flamboyant stage settings, the shiny and elaborate décor, and the hushed anticipation of transcendence.

Dharma Diversity

The growing variety of Buddhist traditions from Asian countries had never before coexisted with the degree of plurality fostered in the United States. In 1974, a group of fledgling Buddhists in Cambridge, Massachusetts, arranged a debate between the Korean Master Seung Sahn, head of the Providence Zen Center in Rhode Island, and Kalu Rinpoche, a highly esteemed Tibetan lama. The meeting took place in Mirabai Bush's bedroom on the top floor of a house owned by David McClelland, the Harvard psychology professor who had brought Leary and Alpert to the university. Long after their expulsion, the house remained a hospitable gathering place for young seekers and their innovative experiments. At the time of the debate Mirabai had recently returned from India and from being with Neem Karoli Baba, the Indian guru immortalized by Ram Dass.

Debate is an honored practice in both Zen and Tibetan Buddhism, and the encounter had been anticipated as revelatory proof of the essential unity between distinct Buddhist traditions. According to Mirabai, the two masters sat opposite each other on the floor: the rotund, smiling Seung Sahn in the gray robes of his Korean Zen school, and the gaunt, intense Kalu Rinpoche in his maroon robes. Right off the bat, Seung Sahn reached into his robe and pulled out an orange. Holding it in the palm of his hand, he thrust it toward Kalu Rinpoche and insistently demanded, *What is this?*

Kalu Rinpoche turned to his translator, heard the words in Tibetan, and said nothing. Seung Sahn—in the assertive manner of a Zen master trying to provoke a student into recognizing the essential, ungraspable, indescribable *suchness* of phenomena—repeated the gesture and the words, all the time keeping his eyes on his silent opponent. Seung Sahn made several more attempts to engage Kalu Rinpoche by using the classic Zen strategy of pushing the mind beyond its conceptual boundaries. *What is this?* Kalu Rinpoche said nothing. Finally, the Tibetan master turned to his translator and wondered aloud, *What's the matter with this guy—hasn't he ever seen an orange before?*

Teachers in different traditions did not know what to make of each other, and many perpetuated sectarian biases that had taken hold in Asia. Teachers from the Theravada traditions of Southeast Asia emphasized the foundational teachings of Shakyamuni Buddha, proclaimed by proponents as the only pure and unadulterated form of Buddhism. A friend took me to meet a venerated teacher from Sri Lanka who had been gathering people for informal afternoon talks in the drab basement of a Unitarian Church in the East Thirties. Once again, I had to be instructed on etiquette, this time to make sure not to touch the monk or extend a hand to shake his, for he was strictly forbidden to touch females, even in their infancy. In the course of his talk, he mocked the Mahayana aspiration *to save all sentient beings.*

Did you ever hear of a more silly vow? he asked. No, I had not. In fact, it was so silly, so over-the-top ridiculous that its obvious unattainability in any literal sense was precisely what made it reasonable. I knew this from experience. When I was about six years old, my parents took Hermine and me on a special summer excursion to the Bronx Zoo. In the petting zoo for kids, we got into pens with lambs, piglets, and chicks. It was a happy day, and when we came to a wishing-well fountain, my parents gave us a penny apiece to throw in and make a wish. Perhaps it was the cheerfulness of the day or the relaxed affections that can flow more easily between humans in the presence of animals, but something compelled my wish to encompass the whole world. It started small, before letting go of the penny, with thinking of what I wanted—what doll maybe, or food, or flavor of ice cream. But that did not feel big enough, and I began to wish for good things to happen to my parents and my sister and to the animals in the zoo and to the trees and the people in the park until I could not name or label or identify one more thing or category, and it became a good wish for every being and thing. And every wish since that day—whether blowing out birthday candles or lighting votive offerings or holding the end of a chicken breastbone—has followed that same arc. I did not convert this wish into a vow and never, as a child, attempted to figure out how this might work in daily life, but in my lasting memory the wish came forth with such natural ease that it seemed to have always been there, as intrinsic to my body as my heart. So, when I heard this teacher refer to how silly a vow of this magnitude was, I thought he might find me silly if he knew of my wishes, although they have never felt silly to me.

There was, however, a lot of silliness among the converted Buddhists with regard to sects. *Thera* means elder. Theravada, the tradition of the elders, was a corrective to the term *Hinayana. Hina* means low or weak, and *yana,* vehicle; Hinayana was the lesser vehicle—the smaller vehicle for those of lesser capacities—but only from the Mahayana perspective. *Maha* means larger, more inclusive. Some Mahayana Buddhist teachers have insisted on sticking with the pejorative *Hinayana,* and even those who used the politically correct *Theravada* could not help but reveal their dismissal of Southeast Asian traditions. New American students bought right into these prejudices, advertising their Buddhist credentials by becoming standard-bearers for petty sectarianism before they hardly knew a thing about any form of dharma.

The Asian teachers often did not know what to make of us either. Tai Situ Rinpoche, an eminent Tibetan master, has spoken of his surprising encounters during his first teaching tour of North America in the mid-seventies. When he was only five years old, Tai Situ was shepherded away from the Chinese takeover of Tibet by an eighty-year-old attendant, and he grew up in a Tibetan exile community in Himachal Pradesh, in northern India. In those days that area did not get a lot of hippie traffic, and Tai Situ Rinpoche's experience of Westerners led him to imagine a North American population of well-kempt citizens with ironed clothes, cameras, and tennis shoes. In 2016, I attended teachings that Tai Situ Rinpoche gave in Bodh Gaya during which he recalled that on his first trip to North America he walked into a rented hall on the West Coast to teach. On peering out, he saw a sea of men and women with long, loose hair, some with white cloth wrapped around their lower bodies, barefoot and decked out in beads and hoop earrings. He had seen people like this in the yogi enclaves of the southern Himalayas and on the ghats of the Ganges. Tai Situ Rinpoche happily concluded that he was surrounded by hundreds of Milarepa replicas. How marvelous! It did not take long before a hand shot up, and a yogi lookalike asked, in a belligerent tone, *How do you know this stuff?* Tai Situ Rinpoche concluded, *Milarepa would never have asked that question. At that moment, I understood that I had gotten it all wrong. I just didn't know.*

Dudjom Rinpoche

In 1976, the preeminent Vajrayana master Dudjom Rinpoche visited New York City accompanied by his wife, their three grown children, and several attendants. Dudjom's translator was the young, skinny, Cambridge-trained tulku, Sogyal Rinpoche. The downtown poet John Giorno had been a student of Dudjom's for several years by then, having first met him in Darjeeling. With Vivian as his accomplice, John had rented a posh brownstone in the East Seventies between Park and Lexington Avenues, which would double as residence and teaching venue. I signed up for a weekend seminar.

Dudjom Rinpoche moved slowly and in such a relaxed manner that the speediness of the Americans around him suggested mental agitation, not efficiency. His thinning hair, tied in a bun at the back of his head, was dyed black by his adoring wife, and he spoke with the soft rasp of old age, although those who had known him as a younger man described a similar hoarseness. Once again there was a learning curve in terms of form, bowing, placement of texts, flowers, and serving. Once again, the arrival of a VIP lama provoked a jockeying for position, disagreements on who held the authority on what to do, what was correct. I remember the luxurious silver-striped wallpaper in the parlor where the teachings took place, and a ring with a spray of diamonds worn by Dudjom's glamorous wife, and a bunch of sincere Western newbies, most of us too ignorant to know how ignorant we really were—self-important and dazzled, trying to get it right and hoping not to look too foolish.

Those in the know suggested that to even glimpse an embodiment of buddha mind, manifested by Dudjom Rinpoche, assured realization of one's own buddha-being in a mere seven lifetimes. This whispered veneration served as an imprimatur of insider spiritual wisdom. I had no confidence in my ability to realize an awakened mind, and with my scant capacity for formal studies the possibility of gaining so much by just keeping my eyes open sounded like a terrific deal. Other participants might have been on their way to becoming accomplished translators, scholars, practitioners of merit, dharma teachers, or monastery administrators. I identified more with Tibetan peasants elbowing their way to the front of the crowd to receive the blessings bestowed by glimpsing a living god.

My clearest memories of that weekend relate to meeting both Rick Fields and Harold Talbott. Each became an important friend, and their presence in Dudjom's world helped ground my cautious curiosity. On the Saturday lunch break a dozen of us crammed into an Italian restaurant. A cheerful camaraderie prevailed over the single long table, with people switching seats to strike up new conversations. Rick Fields's small frame and broad smile projected exuberant charm. He had been studying with Trungpa Rinpoche, and had already started research for his classic narrative on the history of Buddhism in America, *How the Swans Came to the Lake*.

On being introduced, Rick said, *I think we were siblings before we were born.* I thought to myself, *This is the dumbest pickup line I have ever heard,* and said nothing. Rick recalibrated. *No, really. I think our parents lived together before any of us kids were born.* He then recalled a chapter in my parents' lives that I had never known. In the mid-1930s, both our fathers had been school teachers and union organizers, and with our mothers had shared a top-floor loft on Twenty-Second Street, east of Broadway. The painter Elaine Fried lived on the first floor and was then being courted by her future husband, Bill de Kooning. Relatively young and on the move, my parents landed on Twenty-Third Street shortly before I was born. Some six years later, my father and de Kooning shared adjacent studios on Tenth

Street, and I don't know where Elaine moved to, but in the immediate aftermath of their separation Bill ate a lot of dinners at our house.

Al and Reva Fields moved to Queens to raise their three children. They had named their only son Frederick Douglas Fields after the remarkable abolitionist. From the restaurant's pay phone, I checked Rick's story with my mother. With his description verified, I warmed to the sibling allusion, and over the next twenty years, until his death from lung cancer at age fifty-seven, we remained close friends.

I had known of Harold Talbott from reading *The Asian Journal of Thomas Merton*. Harold had been studying with the Dalai Lama in northern India when a former mentor, Dom Aelred Graham, suggested to Merton that for his forthcoming tour to Asia, he tap Harold to be his guide to the Tibetans. The journals collected for Merton's last book were written in 1968 during the months leading to his tragic death in Thailand. In it, he recalls his utter shock on learning that his affable young guide was not in the least troubled by the American war in Vietnam. In turn, Harold was bewildered by Merton's antiwar activism. The war presented Harold with no more reason to rebuke America than any aspect of feudal or theocratic Tibet gave him pause to reconsider his religion of choice. Eventually Harold did shift his views on the war, but political events were still just waves on top of the deeper waters where his commitments, affiliations, and devotions were not to be disturbed by political mayhem.

Harold was born in 1936, ten years ahead of the engulfing counterculture and into an upper-class military family that combined political clout with Anglo aristocracy and café society. His father had been secretary of the air force under President Eisenhower, and from the get-go Harold's little lungs breathed in power, privilege, and wealth. During his junior year at Harvard he converted from Protestantism to Roman Catholicism, undeterred by the church's condemnation of homosexuality, although he was openly gay.

Soon after he was received by the Catholic Church, Harold took off for the Abbey of Gethsemani in Kentucky where he proudly announced to Father Louis—aka Thomas Merton—that he wished to join the monastic brotherhood. As he recounted much later, Merton took one look at this eager queen—as Harold put it—placed his hand on his shoulder, and said, *My son, this is not the place for you.*

Despite his sexual and religious orientations Harold never rejected his background and never eyed Buddhism from America's outer periphery. Rather, he leaned toward the refined sensibilities of an older generation of Transcendentalist-influenced Boston Brahmin connoisseurs of Eastern art and philosophy.

To arrive at Buddhism through rejecting our cultural heritage created the perfect conditions for projecting onto Buddhism a pristine universe in which all the ills of money and materialism, racism and sexism, warfare and wealth had been purified by collective spiritual values. To maintain this happy fiction, the less we knew about Buddhist cultures, the better. And Tibet, with its curtain of snowy mountains and its celluloid version of Shangri-La, offered the perfect blank screen, which we turned into a split screen: secular on one side, spiritual on the other; war on one side, peace on the other. Good, bad; right, wrong; true, false.

Harold's capacious oratorical gifts offered a view that held the sacred and profane within a singular nucleus, undivided for conceptual conveniences. He was tall and lanky, and in a talkative mood, with his legs crossed and hands flying—and with an inflection made legendary by the likes of Gore Vidal and William Buckley—Harold could flamboyantly paint an alluring vision of human greed and ignorance, anger and jealousy, all intertwined with longing for meaning, acceptance, and freedom, fusing and mixing and integrating all the impulses toward spiritual awakening with the habits of perpetual despair. In his spontaneous discourses on world history, the whole range of human endeavor emerged from one cosmic core in an ongoing eternal dance within every individual life and within every culture. With lightning speed, he traveled between Egyptian pharaohs and French emperors, royal courts and dharma kings, theocracies and democracies, and swerved from the plush red ermine-lined cloaks of Roman cardinals to the embroidered Chinese finery of Mandarin princes. He could talk about the route that Alexander the Great took to India and the ideas that traveled the same route back to Greece, and then compare the Greek philosophers to the Indians and the spread of those ideas north, east, and west—all fueled, in his mesmerizing telling, by the search for meaning and money, transcendence, power, territory, doing good and doing bad, paid for the way big exploits are always paid for—on the backs of day laborers.

Several years after I met Harold, I visited him at his home in the seaside village of Marion, Massachusetts, on the western edge of the Cape Cod Canal. It was my first visit to this quaint remnant of a bygone era, and after parking the car, I walked in the shade of leafy trees, checking the house numbers. It was a warm summer day, and the windows of the historic houses were wide open. Suddenly Harold's voice shattered the genteel quiet. Speaking on the telephone, and attempting to rectify a scheduling conflict, he loudly lamented, *I simply cannot decide whether to have lunch with Jackie O or His Holiness the Dalai Lama.* Once settled inside, I chided Harold for only pretending not to know his preference. By the time the visit came to an end, I understood that his ambivalence was genuine, and then I began to know him.

Yeshe Nyingpo

The year following Dudjom's stay on the Upper East Side, John Giorno raised money for a down payment on a townhouse on Sixteenth Street, west of Union Square. Yeshe Nyingpo (*yeshe* means wisdom, and *nyingpo* means heart or essence) would serve as a dharma center and residence for Dudjom Rinpoche, his family, and his retinue. At varying times this included Sogyal Rinpoche, as well as Tulku Pema Wangyal, Tulku Thondup, and Dudjom's son from his previous marriage, Thinley Norbu Rinpoche.

Over the next few years, I spent a lot of time at the Tibetan center. I had moved into Hermine and Bob's apartment in the West Village when they relocated to Tribeca, which meant a fifteen-minute walk to Yeshe Nyingpo, and a forty-minute walk along the Hudson River to my job with Richard Serra. According to Richard, I arrived at his Tribeca loft every morning after picking up his mail at the Canal Street post office and then routinely tossed it unopened into the trash can. I remember tasks that required a little more finesse. On many mornings, I walked Inook to Richard's loft on Duane Square, and on many late afternoons I walked north to the Tibetan center where I often cooked dinner for the family.

For meals, Dudjom Rinpoche sat at the end of a rectangular table and faced the small windowless kitchen. His wife sat to one side, with their family and guests gathered around. I had been a vegetarian, but once I started to fulfill the requests for red meat, I began eating leftovers: pot roasts, meat loafs, beef stews with the more fat the better. Per Vivian's instructions, white rice was never exchanged for brown, which steamed itself to sticky perfection in an automatically timed Chinese rice cooker.

After serving the meal I retreated to the kitchen to start cleaning up, but not without peeking out to gauge my efforts and watch Dudjom Rinpoche pick up his fork and put down his fork, watch him place his napkin on his lap, see him delight in his daughters. This was my first experience of living dharma, and it looked nothing like any ideas I had ever entertained about enlightened beings. To watch him was like looking at the sky. A quality of utter transparency prevailed, which is not to say that he was explicitly knowable but that he was without affect. There was no place within his aura to land; nothing about him engaged me in terms of my own sense of self, of who I was or where I was. There was no reaching out to invite you in—as one might expect from conventional encounters. There was nothing to adhere to, nothing sticky, nothing to inquire about, no *information* that one might use to know another. Wiping his mouth with his napkin or bringing his spoon to his mouth or turning his head toward someone talking was never accompanied by an extra gesture: an eye roll, a raised shrug, a sign of approval. His mind did not appear to follow the movements of his hand. His ears might take in sounds from different directions, but his mind did not appear to race around between the sources of each sound, so that, for example, he seemed to just listen—without bringing to bear any preconceptions about the source of the sound.

Everything about Dudjom Rinpoche was utterly natural. But what allowed me to take note of his exceptional behavior was the very absence of what we call *ordinary*—which turns out to be quite contrived: the way we size each other up, trying to figure out the other by dress, speech, bearing, using projections and biases, trying to understand who we are to the other or who they are to us. Generally, these responses make their way to the surface, in the form of tension around the lips or eyes, or in gestures—a protruding elbow, a shoulder shrug, a raised brow. Mental activity, supposedly invisible, turns out to be anything but. Dudjom's mind did not mask movement but appeared free of the compulsion to follow thoughts, to constantly move toward or away from sense objects. His eyes might move from one object to another, his ears might move from one sound to another, but his mind did not seem to follow. The photograph of Thich Quang Duc suggested that his mind had not followed, or identified with, the sensation of pain. Watching Dudjom Rinpoche through the opened crack of the kitchen door felt like falling through space.

I could now identify the conceptual mind as the source of suffering, with its propensity to repeat and recycle the same old versions of who we are and where we're stuck, stories that bind and glue though attachment and identification. And I had some faith—more than anything known from experience or information—that the key to liberation lay with the release of these spinning, reiterated stories. But it was still all about *my* mind. Dudjom Rinpoche allowed for an encounter with a big mind, sky-like mind, all-encompassing mind. My mind—Helen's individual small mind—could not comprehend that mind. To meet *mind*, in the embodiment of Dudjom, I would have to drop Helen, in the embodiment of Helen. I was far from being able to do this, but just being in his presence invited this possibility, and I could intuit how rare a gift this was.

What color is your mind? Dudjom Rinpoche asked in my first private interview. He asked with gentle curiosity, sounding as if he genuinely assumed that I might have an answer. He asked, as we might ask of each other, *How do you feel today, dear?*

What color is my mind? I had no idea—not about the color, not about who I was with, or who I was. He sat in an upholstered wing chair on the first floor of the Sixteenth Street brownstone. I sat on the floor with my butt on my heels. *How do thoughts enter your mind?* he continued. *Do they come from the left side or the right side? What shape is your mind?*

I had never entertained these questions, never imagined them. My mind went blank and I couldn't say anything. The interview came to a close. I had prepared a question, now long forgotten, but had not asked it. I stood up, bowed, and as I backed away, he motioned for me to come forward. Through the translator he said, *You should put that shirt on your shrine and pray to it.*

I looked down. On the front of my T-shirt was a silk-screened image of Milarepa, his head cocked to one side, his hand raised to his ear.

Being around Dudjom Rinpoche proved that waking up was not sacred fiction, not a fairy tale from the ancient India of Shakyamuni under the Bo Tree. Realizing the true mind, or what D. T. Suzuki had called *sky-like mind,* undistorted by concepts and memory, was truly possible—at least for Tibetans born in rarified spiritual altitudes, recognized as *tulkus,* or reincarnate masters, who had been raised to fulfill the highest expectations of their lineages, who had spent years in solitary retreat in mountain caves and had received rigorous, demanding training in monasteries and institutes of advanced learning. For a Western woman coming upon dharma after decades of only knowing the mind that talks to itself, developing confidence in liberation from the tyranny of thoughts did not come easily. And I didn't have a clue that my messed-up mind was already enlightened—the optimistic understanding shared by Zen and Tibetan schools, which hold that we do not practice in order to attain the awakened mind but to awaken the sleeping buddha-being within that is the birthright of every sentient being.

I was invested in the faraway Buddha, in seeing the Buddha *over there.* The vision of unattainable, mountaintop golden buddhas, living and dead, in all their glorious remove, was an easy fiction to slip into, promoted by the sacred texts of various schools, by iconic imagery, and often by esteemed masters within the very traditions that urged you to see yourself as having the same mind—*in essence*—as the enlightened buddhas. Trungpa Rinpoche constantly cautioned his students against idealizing the guru and putting him on a pedestal, but they did that anyway. We all put our teachers on pedestals. How could we not? They spoke of realities that no one in our own culture, laity or clergy, had ever mentioned. In the case of the Tibetans, they emerged from a landscape that was as shrouded in mystery as the teachings themselves. Without their status elevated by thrones and silks and fawning minions, who would have listened to them? In tenth-century India, Naropa, the refined abbot of the Buddhist university Nalanda, walked away from his high seat to seek out the elusive adept Tilopa. After an arduous search, he found the wild-eyed, eccentric yogi stark naked and eating raw fish guts by a river in Bengal. Who among us would have studied with a bum like that? Imagine the exquisite level of dharma sensitivity that Naropa had already attained to recognize in Tilopa the master he needed to perfect his understanding.

Mingyur Rinpoche frequently repeats—perhaps precisely for the benefit of students like me—that during his childhood, as many times as his revered father told him that there was no difference between a buddha and an old dog, he could not believe it; and when his father said, again and again, that all beings are blessed with an inherent enlightened mind, he could not accept that *all* actually included him.

There are many inventive ways of holding the dharma at bay. Among the Westerners around Yeshe Nyingpo in the mid-1970s were a couple of Hunter Thompson wannabes who referred to Dudjom Rinpoche as *the man* and who attended teachings *to score the dharma*. One woman agonized over jettisoning her season opera tickets for the evening teachings and spoke of both in identical terms: a beloved spectacle, on stage over there, to be gazed upon from coveted seats, an occasion to dress for and by which to be transported to rapturous realms.

Michal Abrams was a different story. By the time I met her, she, like Harold Talbott, had already spent years in the Himalayas studying with Tibetan teachers. She had a reputation for being a dedicated and erudite student and was treated respectfully by the lamas. Her white face, framed by unruly black curls, often appeared tight with determination and sometimes with rude annoyance. One day a group of us were on the stoop at the entrance to Yeshe Nyingpo, where we hung out to smoke cigarettes. Suddenly Michal gripped the metal railing, pawed the ground like a high-strung filly, and declared, *I want to get enlightened!* Despite the melodrama, her intention felt authentic.

A few evenings later, Michal and I left the center together and walked west on Sixteenth Street. I explained that I had been thinking about what she had said. *I can't say that I want to get enlightened,* I told her, *and I also wonder why that is.*

She shot back, *You don't suffer enough.*

We parted company at the corner of Sixth Avenue, and I headed south, feeling dejected. One more thing to feel bad about: *I don't suffer enough. I can never get enlightened.* It's true, I thought, nothing really awful had ever happened to me. I hadn't felt safe either in my family or in the world, but neither my parents nor a sibling had died when I was little. Despite my father's wrath, I had never received more than the occasional, compulsive whack with his rolled-up newspaper, which always left him feeling worse than I did. My mother was too anxious to breastfeed, but I hadn't starved. I was never raped, never lived through war or knew homelessness or saw someone I loved strung up on a street pole and shot the way Holocaust-survivor friends of my parents had. *Wait a sec . . . something's not right. The Buddha did not describe suffering as a pile-up of bad things that happened to you, and whoever's pile is biggest suffers the most. He defined suffering in terms of misperception and ignorance, and in his understanding, we don't get to blame anyone—including ourselves. What was Michal talking about?* I had asked myself if I wanted to get enlightened and live in a boundless universe in which I was not the epicenter. The truthful answer had been *no*. On the other hand, what if I had asked, *How'd you like to be free of mental anguish, shake off some sadness, dispel bouts of terror, live with less disapproval and remorse?* That was an attractive invitation, but it didn't sound like enlightenment. More like psychotherapy—the same conundrum that I had faced with Arica two years earlier. By now it was easier to see that I didn't wish to deal with psychological issues and hoped that aspiring, in my fashion, to elevated plains would render the more quotidian habits of neurotic behavior irrelevant. It took a long time to apprehend that the Buddha's First Noble Truth addressed the need to accept suffering, move into it, and close the separation between the one who experiences suffering and the perceived source of the suffering, and then examine its transitory, malleable, fabricated qualities and see how they were kept in place by my very own mental habits. Running away will never work. Perhaps that's what Michal had meant: not that I had a deficit of suffering but that I had yet to look at it, befriend it, embrace it. In that sense, she would have been right.

At Yeshe Nyingpo, a classic teaching tale was printed in tiny type and distributed in a stapled booklet. It delineated the distinction—from the Tibetan perspective—between the early, middle, and later schools of Buddhism: in the midst of a parched desert a succulent cactus appears laden with beautiful fruit. Practitioners of Theravada—the path associated with the basic teachings of the historical Buddha—identify the fruit as poisonous and make a detour to circumvent danger, thus protecting themselves by avoidance. Practitioners of the Mahayana—associated with views that came to prominence some four hundred years after the historical Buddha—identify the fruit as poisonous but eat it, knowing that every action has an antidote. The practitioner of Vajrayana eats the fruit, recognizing that in the absence of dualistic perception, all appearances arise from mind—and therefore poison can be transformed into ambrosia.

Many of us were heirs to outrage and wished to see ourselves as lotus-eaters fully prepared to transform poison. We were not new to the wilder shores of social taboos. Seeking alternatives in the Vietnam era, we embraced an ethos that had emerged in protest and enhanced our moral fortitude by rejecting conventions. We had transgressed sexual mores, experimented with drugs, food fads, new music and art, and now, a radical new spiritual path. We wanted to be cool Vajrayana yogis, sky dancers in the realms of bliss and wonder. We were invested with rebel spirit, wary of authority, individualistic as cowboys and proud of it, seesawing between an invisible, idealized old Tibet and the hippest, coolest outposts of Manhattan.

Feigning world weariness was the stock-in-trade of playing cool, but letting go of our self-created worlds, of the stories we lived by, the lies we told ourselves and each other, turned out not to be so easy. Padmasambhava, the eighth-century tantric master who brought Buddhist dharma from India to Tibet, said, *My view is higher than the sky, yet my attention to actions and their effects is finer than flour.* I don't believe any of us took this to heart. We treated each other carelessly, gossiped viciously, acted out petty jealousies, vied for attention from the teachers, had secret sex, judged, and waited in ambush. We might have wanted out of *the* world, but not out of *our* worlds.

Looking back at the fledgling Tibetan center, I see an odd assortment of Westerners new to Buddhism who wanted to change ourselves and change the world. We had the uninformed zeal of converts, too naïve and too enamored of our new religion and our own efforts to intuit the thorny thickets lying in wait. We wanted everything to be better than it was, including ourselves and each other. I don't believe that any among us at the time knew how bruising this path could be—or yet understood how much getting messed up was a critical part of it. Paradise, it turned out, existed right in the middle of your own shit, and if you didn't find it there, you might miss it altogether.

With Dudjom Rinpoche, I took refuge for the first time, a ceremony that functions as a formal initiation into the Buddhist path. One becomes a child of the buddhas, a follower of the teachings of Shakyamuni Buddha. Perhaps Dudjom Rinpoche assumed that his new American students knew more than we did. Perhaps everyone knew more than I did. I don't remember receiving teachings about refuge or how it might be used, and I did not give its true meaning much thought. *I take refuge in the Buddha, I take refuge in the Dharma, I take refuge in the Sangha.* I was joining a group of cool downtown people, perhaps as close to becoming a member of a club or a tribe as I would ever know. The words remained disconnected from any deeply personal investigation of what it meant to *leave home*—the traditional description of taking refuge.

In ancient India, inspired laity literally left home to follow the Buddha, leaving behind—as did Siddhartha Gautama, the Buddha-to-be—parents, spouses, and offspring. Over time, some Buddhist schools evolved specifically to address the needs of the laity, while others accommodated married clergy. Yet married or celibate, the mind of *leaving home* rests with turning away from worldly pursuits of happiness; turning away from the delusion of permanence and toward the understanding that not one thing in this entire world system is permanent; turning away from identifying yourself as a solid, fixed, immutable being, and turning toward experiencing the fluid, temporary, constantly changing manifestations of what we call *personhood*. Taking refuge means to turn away from samsara, the everyday world of confusion, and turn toward nirvana, the world of clarity.

In 1977, a ritualized version of leaving home felt like a perfect fit for those of us who had already turned our backs on society. Every convert Buddhist that I knew had been against the war in Vietnam. In some cases, family ties had been so sundered that there was no physical parental home in which they were welcome. The US government was regarded with disdain and mistrust by the new Buddhists. We already snubbed picket-fence models; we scorned American money dreams and uptight puritanical sexual taboos. It turned out that none of these social repudiations approached the true meaning of leaving home. Basically, we renounced one version of samsara in favor of another, and seamlessly bypassed the home of our habitual addictions and proclivities—the comfort zone that unconsciously accepted and recycled afflictive behavior. I definitely was not ready to leave behind those ego-cherishing versions of myself that were, in my ignorant view, of critical importance to how I saw myself—even if they did make me crazy. The challenge had been presented first by psychedelics. The difference—and it was huge—was that now the invitation to work with a radically new version of mind was presented within a context—within historical dimensions and by venerated elders. That made the path trustworthy but not easy. For the preeminent role that mind-expanding drugs played in introducing dharma to the West, one Tibetan lama labeled LSD *an American bodhisattva.* Nonetheless, despite the benefits of drugs and meditation, the habitual patterns that worked to keep the ego-self in place turned into formidably tenacious monsters.

When I took refuge with Dudjom Rinpoche, any ideas I might have held with regard to giving up worldly refuges added up to no more than skeptical aspirations. I would never say that I wished to be rich. How vulgar. Yet apartments with fireplaces that overlooked Gramercy Park floated through my fantasies, as well as expensive hippie fashions made from Indian silks, or fringed buckskin jackets. I still fantasized about taking refuge in motherhood. I had continued my tormented suspicion that my late-term miscarriage was of my own making. The most horrifying possibility was that I might not have wanted to be a mother. That would make me more a defect of nature than the miscarriage itself. Again and again, socially sanctioned concepts of happiness took precedence over actual experience. I could not understand why I was not more averse to worldly pursuits, as my experience had already exposed the fallacies of conventional promises. In retrospect, I see that I continued to underestimate the depth and strength of habitual patterns, and how much discipline and constancy it would take to uproot them. Thinley Norbu used to tell me, *You love that white dog more than you love Buddha.* I never disagreed.

A Bardo Retreat

In 1977 John Giorno organized a weeklong residential retreat at a Mahayana Buddhist temple in upstate New York, near Cairo. The temple primarily served Buddhists from New York City's Chinatown who arrived by the busload every Sunday. Having taken the Mahayana vow *to save all sentient beings,* they brought living creatures purchased in the markets for release on the temple grounds, and subsequently shells of old box turtles that had been saved from the soup pot littered the woods.

For this retreat the refined, soft-spoken Tulku Pema Wangyal offered teachings on the *bardos*—the intermediate states, most famously between death and rebirth. For Westerners, bardo teachings provoke questions about reincarnation. In the transmission of Tibetan Buddhism to the West, this subject has presented such an obstacle that many teachers have had to assure us that we can benefit from Buddhism without believing in life after death. During this retreat, many hours of each day were spent lying on the floor of the temple shrine room, which was kept in darkness by makeshift curtains, and listening to instructions that guided us through the stages of dying—the dissolution of sense functions, the dissolution of the elements, the laboring of the breath. It sounds so serious. It was serious, and yet sessions were regularly interrupted by someone unable to contain their mirth, and soon the whole floor would be shaking with laughter. This hysteria-infused effect of bardo teachings had certainly never happened in old Tibet. Then again, this is how the dharma seeped into mainstream America: the perfect teacher, the profound teachings, and, from a long look back, a room of idealistic seekers—innocent, sincere, and ridiculous: on our backs in rehearsal for the only certain event of our lives, and we couldn't stop giggling.

These teachings were traditionally taught to young monks in maroon robes who had already spent years in monastic training. In 1977, a group of adults long steeped in the American denial of death had carved out this retreat time from jobs, family responsibilities, and social outings. A comical element was bound to filter into a darkened room where people lay on the floor and pretended to die. Every religion depends on ritual and theatrics to set the stage for transformation. Yet Tibetan Buddhism can be particularly dramatic—for which it has earned a reputation in the Western world for being *Catholicism on acid*. Then again, for seven days we had agreed to step out of a society in which the subject of death and dying had been banished. I had never seen a dead body, except in India. Many of us had never sat by the side of a dying person or even attended a funeral. Lucky for us, many Tibetans have a charitable sense of humor, and perhaps they understood more about our nervous laughter than we did. Perhaps they also knew more about the challenges we faced than we ourselves recognized. After all, they were in America and experiencing something of our lives while we knew so little of theirs. For all our giggling, our questions about form, and the skepticism about the continuity of mind beyond death, it was left up to us to figure out how to integrate these teachings into daily life, to apply them as best we could outside of the traditional confines of monasteries. For that we had no road maps.

I can't say that the retreat brought me any closer to being comfortable with physical death. Yet long before I began a meditation practice, some inchoate sense of living underneath myself, submerged, insulated, led to often repeating—silently and only to myself—*I hope I'm born before I die.* In the bardo teachings, death comes first; then birth: allowing for death in the form of letting go, of dissolving the cycles of neurosis and patterning, releasing fixed ideas that we hold about ourselves and our world, so that we can greet each day, each moment, with the fresh, delighted eyes of a newborn. It helped too that Thinley Norbu's exhortation *to relax your mind* was beginning to make a little bit of sense.

Relax Your Mind

From the time of his first visit to New York City, Dudjom Rinpoche's son Thinley Norbu reiterated a traditional Tibetan prescription for a mind addled by preconceptions and contrivances: *Relax. Relax your mind.* How beautiful—so soothing, so simple, and such an easy alternative to the stringent disciplines of meditation, recitations, visualizations, and prostrations. Relax, aided perhaps by a glass of wine or a little marijuana. Relax: play, pillows and sunshine, beaches, dinner parties, movies. *Relax* might have been the best translation, but the American context differed so radically from the lexicon of Tibetan dharma that the meaning got mangled.

In the most refined mind-teachings *relax* encourages release from the restrictive self-imposed boundaries that keep the mind spinning in habitual loops. Relax. Let go of the tight wires that bind the self-centered mind to its familiar fabrications. Let go. Open up. Allow for new possibilities. Relax with fear and uncertainty. Relax without wanting to change a thing, relax without striving, judging, shifting. To glimpse reality as it is, relax. In some lineages, this is a ten-thousand-year project. Tibetan Buddhism promises a shortcut, but that short? *Relax* short? Let go of the reference points. Rest. Stop finding fault or feeling discomfort with this very moment. All our anxieties and agitations always boil down to dissatisfaction with what is happening right now. *Relax.* This moment is OK. Make peace with now. Welcome yourself.

Stop spoiling reality by trying to fix it. Stop tinkering. *Relax* encapsulates the essence of meditation—letting go of the known constructed realities. Let go, rest, let it be. Relax, die, allow for rebirth, allow for renewal, take a break from what you think you know, ease into not knowing, into freshness. Know nothing. Be nothing.

As I continued to pursue awakening practices, I came to understand that no instruction for liberation would ever be more profound than *Relax your mind*. And nothing I have ever done would demand more courage and trust. I say this because forty years after first hearing this, I undertook practices in which *Relax* was the primary, core instruction, and I needed every minute of less demanding practices to develop confidence and ease with this possibility.

PART FIVE

CONVERGENCES AND FRACTURES

A Cabin in the Woods

Camping alone with Inook after splitting up with my husband was never repeated. Friends in Cape Breton had arrived at a consensus that the campsite was too isolated, perhaps a little dangerous. For the next five summers, I lived in a cabin that was built for me on Hermine and Bob's land. Philip did most of the carpentry aided occasionally by Richard Serra, whose own house was nearby, and Rudy paid for the materials. It measured twelve by sixteen feet, with views of the seaway, no indoor plumbing, running water, or electricity, but perfect nonetheless. To take a shower, I walked down to the cove below and stood under the cold waterfall. I no longer craved a haven to hide in, but got one anyway.

I moved into the cabin in August 1977. Then I became so enamored with it, so thrilled to call this little hermitage my own, so mesmerized by the view, so pleased with myself for making my way through the woods at night with my white dog and a flashlight, and at the same time stunned, overwhelmed by gratitude for the friends who had made this possible, especially Philip—who spent hours carrying lumber down the little path, sawing, measuring, hammering. So stunned that it made my appreciation hard to process, and my expressions of gratitude awkward. All of which conspired to keep me kind of stuck there. I just couldn't leave. Rather than experience this attachment as a contradiction to taking the refuge vow in the home-leaving ceremony with Dudjom, I interpreted its monastic simplicity to perfectly accord with the vows, especially as I did not even own the land it had been built on. By the middle of October, the weather drove me away. And then I still felt too rooted in Cape Breton to leave and moved half a mile up the road to Richard's wreck of a farmhouse, the house that neighbors said was haunted.

This predated the renovations made by Clara Weyergraf, the German art historian who became Richard's wife a few years later. Yet even then the house had electricity, indoor plumbing, a telephone, and a coal-burning stove. I was enjoying the upgrade when Richard telephoned to ask me to consider returning to New York to work with him on a new project. He had been invited to submit a proposal for a site-specific sculpture by the Pennsylvania Avenue Development Corporation (PADC), which had been assigned to administer the design of what became Freedom Plaza. This prime piece of Washington, DC, real estate sits adjacent to Pennsylvania Avenue, a few blocks from the White House. The PADC included architects and landscape designers who would assemble for meetings in Washington under the leadership of Carter Brown, then director of the National Gallery. I accepted Richard's offer without ever imagining the sly, stealth presence of dharma in the White House that would come of it.

Dharma at the White House

For the PADC commission, Richard determined to study the site from every angle, from the windows of buildings that overlooked the site, including the old post office and the United States Treasury, and from construction platforms placed in the middle of the avenue that extended thirty feet into the air. I obtained permits for the lifts from the city government with the stipulation that we only work from six to eight o'clock on Sunday mornings, under the protective custody of the police, who closed the streets to traffic.

Two lifts were placed on Pennsylvania Avenue, and Richard moved swiftly between them, always carrying a notebook. With his craggy good looks and belligerent jaw, he stood thirty feet in midair, peering into the morning light with the fiery resolve of Ahab on the deck of the *Pequod,* absorbing the measure of every angle, corner, width, and height of each form within his sight.

The architect Robert Venturi, a member of the PADC team, submitted a proposal that included two steel pylons. In addition to this shameless appropriation of the sculptural language of Richard's own work, the pylons framed the US Treasury Building. At the following meeting, and with photocopies that I had located at the public library on Forty-Second Street, Richard compared Venturi's design to Albert Speer's architecture in which similar columns glorified the Third Reich by their strategic framing of government buildings. Venturi's pylons had not drawn attention to the White House or the Lincoln Memorial or any historic symbol of democracy or political freedom. His design focused attention on money, materialism, capitalism, and greed.

Is that really what you want to glorify? Richard asked.

That put an end to Venturi's pylons, but Richard's proposal wasn't getting any traction either. Richard has a deserved reputation for playing rough, yet for the nation's capital he had examined the site with deeply felt sincerity and had articulated an aesthetic clarity that had eluded his colleagues. And when least expected he could show remarkable restraint. At the last PADC meeting to which his presence was requested, the architect Denise Scott Brown asked Richard if, in place of his rolled-steel rectilinear plate, he might consider a more mollifying design: *Would you consider a fountain, Richard?* He kept his eyes down and said quietly, *I don't do water.*

Two years after the PADC debacle, Richard was invited to the White House to attend a gathering of artists and art administrators. Clara was in Germany waiting for her US legal residency papers and concluded that reentering the United States might jeopardize this process. Richard invited me to join him, joking of our triumphant return to the capital.

To John Giorno, my invitation to the White House warranted Dudjom Rinpoche's attention. Tibetans place great faith in planting karmic seeds, even if the results might not manifest for years, decades, or centuries. It is the working of karma: positive intentions enhance possibilities for positive results. Giorno, an outrageous, transgressive, gay figure of ultra-cool art and poetry circles, was simultaneously an old-school traditionalist when it came to dharma orthodoxy, and he was one of Dudjom's most genuinely devout students. John viewed my visit to the White House as a supreme opportunity for bringing blessings from a dharma king, an enlightened living buddha, to the headquarters of American power and international sovereignty. In effect, this continued the dissemination of the dharma as it had always traveled: from India to Tibet, and to China and Sri Lanka and Southeast Asia and Korea and Japan, with pilgrims, devotees, and lackeys moving anonymously through corridors of power, negotiating for patronage and salvation.

I arrived at the White House wearing a new champagne-colored organza mid-calf shirtwaist with a mandarin collar, and carrying a beaded purse I had borrowed from my mother. The purse contained a *gau*—a portable shrine favored by Tibetans that I had first seen around Tenzin's neck in Kathmandu some twelve years earlier. Tenzin, who had given me my first mala and, calling me *Lotus Girl,* had told me to take Buddha beads to America. I wore this mala, invisible under my dress, although a red protection cord—a strand of thin string blessed and tied around my neck by Dudjom Rinpoche—was visible at my throat.

The elaborately embossed silver gau measured about two by three inches and had a window in it through which a deity could be seen—and could see out. John handed me the gau wrapped in white silk, having had it blessed by Dudjom Rinpoche with aspiration prayers, mantras, and incense. John then suggested that at every opportunity I hold the purse as high as possible and rotate my hand from the wrist to disperse the blessings far and wide.

Vice President Walter Mondale and Mrs. Mondale hosted the subdued event. At one end of a formal reception hall a quartet played classical music. We strolled around, trying to pretend we belonged there. The only guest I knew was my mother's first cousin, Harvey Lichtenstein. By then Harvey was ten years into his long tenure as executive director of the Brooklyn Academy of Music, during which he single-handedly—more or less—and ingeniously redrew the cultural map of New York City. It was Harvey's mother, Jenny, who had introduced her brother Max—my grandfather—to her coworker at the garment factory, the grandmother who had spent most of her life in an insane asylum. Harvey had always known the secret of my mother's mother, and for this reason, my mother had held him at bay. By now, we all knew this fraught history, but it sat between Harvey and me with unacknowledged discomfort. Meanwhile, I kept the purse pressed against my chest and intermittently swung my arm open from the elbow in imitation of the insouciant glamor of 1940s movie stars.

With no announcement, President Carter made a spontaneous appearance. Guests angled for a front-row position. All eyes were on the president, leaving the gau free to radiate its magic, and when it came my turn to shake the president's hand, it was easy to brush the purse along his sleeve. The secret mission had been a source of amusement to me, certainly not shared with Richard. That such subversive intentions had eluded notice played right into my childhood fantasies of life as a secret agent. But for all the self-cherishing dramatic appeal, I had no idea what might come of this.

In old Tibet, according to legends, enlightened masters flew through space and transferred their consciousness to ravens and dogs, using omniscience to generate benevolence and bestow blessings. Thinley Norbu said, *In old Tibet, everyone knew how to fly.* I took as a given that I did not know what a liberated mind could do, where it could go, what it could achieve— how far the mind could travel beyond what the eyes saw, what the ears heard. I could not say whether world peace would be more swiftly realized because of Dudjom Rinpoche's aspirations, or if his blessings could help subvert America's romance with violence, or if Buddhist teachings could help tame the United States or be a force for peace or racial equality or help us treat each other with more kindness. Could Buddhism help America become America? I hoped that it could.

After President Carter's walk-through, I left Richard in the reception hall and descended a wide marble staircase to use the powder room, as it was designated. The corridor was surprisingly empty, save for two handsome young honor guards, one Black, one white, standing sentry at either side of the bathroom door, decked out in caps, fitted white jackets with gold buttons, and white pants. I passed through, assuming that the bathroom sentries were standard White House protocol. To the left were three stalls, to the right, three sinks set into a green marble counter, and above them, one long, rectangular mirror. The door to one stall was closed.

A peculiar phenomenon that women experience when urinating relates to sound. A woman who has peed into a water-filled toilet bowl with an adjacent stall in use might think she is still peeing when actually it is only the sound that has not stopped, but it is coming from the next stall. Such was the case at the White House, so that after the occupants finished fussing with underpants and pantyhose, two stall doors opened at once. As we stood at our separate sinks, I looked into the mirror and discovered that the sweet moment of merged identities had been shared with Lady Bird Johnson.

I focused on faucets, heart racing, then soap, and the habit of hand motions at a sink. My temples throbbed. I peeked up at the mirror: *I voted for your husband,* I said silently. *My first time voting for a president. That meant something to me. Sixty thousand Americans dead, millions of Vietnamese. Was he sorry? Did he cry in his sleep?*

We dried our hands. Refreshed our lipstick. She looked like a nice lady. Dyed black hair, lacquer sprayed. Jeweled choker. She smiled into the mirror. Her wide mouth made for a generous smile. I smiled back. She stepped out first and walked ahead, closely flanked by her honor guards.

Fifty paces back I waved my beaded purse wildly in a gesture big enough to discharge cannons of anger and hope. I waved to wake that motherfucker from the dead, waved my blessed amulets to dispel the betrayals of my country and waved them so that I too might be tamed by Dudjom Rinpoche's prayers for pacification. I joined Richard upstairs, and we left the White House in time to catch the last flight to New York.

In *Crazy Wisdom,* a documentary about Chögyam Trungpa Rinpoche, one of his earliest American students, Jim Gimian, tells of a dialogue that took place in about 1973. Amid rampant talk about the Vietnam War, a young man asked Trungpa to talk about aggression in America. He replied, *I want to talk about the aggression in this room.* Photographs suggest the aggression in that room was embodied by women and men with tender gazes, flowing hair, beads, and ribbons. And their guru asked them to look at their own aggression. The aggression in this room, in your mind, in my mind. This aggression that cannot be explained or justified by the Vietnam War. Let's talk about this aggression that has no point of origin and cannot hide behind beards and beads.

During the war, anger provided credibility. The more anger you expressed, the more passionately you cared about justice, about dead Vietnamese babies and villages destroyed by napalm. Anger was the Purple Heart worn in our mouths. We denounced war but venerated rage against the war, especially from campus firebrands. We could call for peace, chant *Make love, not war,* flash the *V* sign, and offer flowers to riot squads. But we did not know how to *be* peace—how to inhabit a steady mind, calm in the midst of turbulence, not buffeted between what we did and did not like, between good and bad, between aversion and attraction. We didn't know how to confront anger without being angry, so that for all our good intentions, we increased the collective density of anger in the atmosphere.

I had never entertained the possibility that in order to disarm anger on the outside, first you had to deal with your own. It's like the flight attendant on an airplane giving instructions for the emergency use of oxygen masks: *Put on your own mask first before trying to assist others.* The Buddhist message that arrived at the height of the Vietnam War was that lasting freedom could be realized by taking responsibility for our own states of mind—*under any and all conditions.* Look at the Dalai Lama. Look at Gandhi; at Martin Luther King, Jr. We had the capacity to free ourselves from the destructive mind states of aggression, anger, and revenge. *Don't use an unjust war to justify your angry mind.* No situation, we were told, inherently, immutably determines its reaction. We act as if it does. In the midst of America's most divisive war, Asian Buddhist teachers insistently suggested that the righteous moral satisfaction that we enjoyed from protest was another way to aggrandize our own egos. In so many words, the teachers kept telling us: *Actually, we Buddhists have been doing these mind-training practices for thousands of years. And you Westerners might consider learning something from us, because honestly you are all so crazy and speedy and uptight and busy and aggressive.*

A House Blessing

In the summer of 1978, I arranged for Geshe Kundrup, my Tibetan friend from Quebec, to visit Inverness and to perform some version of a traditional Tibetan house blessing. Fortunately, the day was sunny and dry, because many more guests watched and listened through the opened windows than could squeeze inside. I built a makeshift shrine with pyramids of oranges and apples, cookies, candies, and bottles of fruit juice. Geshe Kundrup appeared to have a magical supply of rice in his hands, for while reciting incantations in Tibetan, he repeatedly opened his arms wide in a gesture of all-encompassing munificence, similar to the pope's blessings from the balcony of the Vatican, and then tossed white rice in every direction. When rice covered the inside surfaces, the lama led all of us outside to circumambulate the cabin, during which he continued to chant and toss more rice into the surrounding woods. I don't know what anyone thought about the ceremony. Tibet? Maroon-robed lama? Yet without doubt it aspired to be of radiating benefit to me, my friends and neighbors, and to the creatures and spirits of the land and the sea, and everyone seemed happy to be there.

There was also a backstory: When Jim and I finalized our decision to divorce, the one person that I had difficulty telling was Geshe Kundrup. His role as priest and religious authority made me feel ashamed. I had never taken my marriage vows seriously. In my world divorce was so common that my mother used to joke about which man she might claim as her ex-husband, because she was the only person she knew without an ex, and both my father and Biala had two. Yet associating Geshe Kundrup with a spiritual world of profound moral depth made the vows—now broken— sacred for the first time. Only with Geshe Kundrup, a most gentle and forgiving man, did I feel that I had betrayed a supreme law of the universe, not just trespassed on convention. I anguished over the letter that I sent to him telling him about the divorce. Two years later, arranging his visit to Inverness was to invite him to purify my space—inside and out. The afternoon was a housewarming, a cabin blessing, and an exorcism.

Jasper, Meet Thinley Norbu

In accord with President Nixon's policy détente with China, the type of Tibetan refugee community with which Geshe Kundrup was affiliated did not exist in the United States. Except for a few Westerners like me and Jim, his world remained primarily circumscribed by the traditions and needs of his community. This made his circumstances very different from those Tibetan teachers who were moving through Europe and the Americas independently. Generally, they traveled at the invitation of patrons, and their initial itineraries and expenses were arranged in advance. For return visits, as well as for buying property and building centers, the organizational requirements often fell to devout students.

For John Giorno, while the White House embodied secular supremacy, other commanding positions could also help Tibetan dharma flourish. About a year after seeing me off to Washington, DC, with blessings from Dudjom Rinpoche, John had another bright idea. At that time, Jasper Johns had a house in Rockland County, about fifty miles north of New York City. A cabin just across a stream had been rented by Julian Lethbridge, also a painter, and for a certain stretch I often used the cabin when Julian wasn't there. I had known Jasper through my parents, and he and John Giorno were old friends. John, with unbounded enthusiasm, decided that Jasper should meet Thinley Norbu Rinpoche. Connecting hot spots of emanating energy would help nurture this refined seedling in coarse American soil.

One day, John drove Thinley Norbu from New York City to the cabin where I was staying. It was midsummer, with the stream shallow enough for us to walk across barefoot to have lunch at Jasper's. Things did not go well. Thinley Norbu's relentless silence suggested that he got the message that this meeting was important—at least to John; that he was being dragged out like a show pony, that he was supposed to be a diplomatic emissary from the most cultivated spheres of dharma to art world eminence. He refused to play. He sat sullen, displaying none of the humor and charms that both John and I knew well. Jasper was Jasper and unfailingly polite. John talked enough for all of us, fast and a little hysterical. I remained embarrassed and uptight the whole time, and was relieved to be back across the stream in Julian's cabin. John was well-intentioned. His attitude toward the lamas was always impeccably respectful. Nonetheless, I appreciated Thinley Norbu's obstinate integrity; and how dharma was disseminated would have to proceed with a little more discernment—for now perhaps something closer to a deity wrapped in blessed cloth, and hidden in a beaded handheld clutch.

Lamas in the Big Apple

Dudjom Rinpoche never showed concern about whether it was hot or cold, or whether he was in Nepal or New York. He showed no interest in figuring out America, or learning English or how to run a nonprofit, or addressing cultural differences. His delight in whatever paraded before his senses seemed completely fulfilling—a hidden yogi sitting on the park bench, fully content to feed pigeons and watch the children play. Meanwhile, the younger Tibetans, with their homeland lost and their teaching careers ahead of them, had an inquisitive appetite for exploring every nook of New York. Some had already learned English in India. Sogyal Rinpoche, who was then around twenty-eight years old, had attended Cambridge University and spoke like a don. They all wore maroon robes, with little to suggest which ones had taken monastic vows of celibacy and which were in householder lineages, and the pursuit of young women by men in skirts had moments worthy of *A Midsummer Night's Dream.* One blond beauty took a monk newly arrived from a monastery in India to the rowboat pond in Central Park on a summer afternoon and reported that when they stopped at the center of the Japanese bridge, with a slight breeze blowing against his robe, she had asked, *What makes you so sexy?* And he had said, *The wind.*

Flirtations enlivened Yeshe Nyingpo, even with Dudjom in residence, and more so in his absence. When it came to urban adventures nothing was too frivolous or profane. The young lamas were up for all of it—Greek statues of naked men and women, Mesopotamian jewelry and medieval armor at the Metropolitan Museum of Art, dinosaurs and dioramas at the Museum of Natural History, Coney Island, the supermarkets, the pet stores, and the sex shops on Times Square—although those excursions were led by guys, I think. I never knew of any women who accompanied them, although following an evening of dharma teachings, I participated in a jaunt to Plato's Retreat, the legendary sex club in the basement of the Ansonia Hotel. Five of us—two American women, an American man, and two Tibetan lamas took a taxi to the Upper West Side.

Plato's Retreat was billed as the most phantasmagoric experiment in sexual ecstasy the world had ever known, at least for clubs that were both legal and public. Half-wrapped in towels, we opted for the lounge chairs by the pool, where the music blared and the lights stayed low, and from there watched various body parts—arms, legs, bums, breasts, penises—break the water's surface in masses of writhing tentacle-style entanglements of naked limbs surging, splashing, and squealing. Liberation, 1970s American style. Surely Tibetans who grew up in monasteries were not familiar with public displays of pan-gender group sex. I had never been to anything like Plato's Retreat but knew that such places existed. So I had to wonder why I was the most shocked and uptight among us—not that the Tibetans weren't amused, but what the heck were they seeing, registering? Stories had circulated across the Himalayas from yogi enclaves in India that depicted meditation gatherings in forest caves that explicitly relied on sexual bliss to transcend the conventional boundaries of mind. Perhaps they thought this was the Western version.

I was probably trying to look like I had been there a dozen times before, but I was quickly closing down around the possibility of being groped by strangers. I understood that this freedom from convention was not the liberation that spiritual texts pointed to. But I was not sure if fear of spiritual liberation did not overlap with fear of sexual abandon. If this discrete, uptight, skin-bound self continued to resolutely resist merging indiscriminately with everything right now, right here, then what reason did I have to think that it might change in a safe, clean meditation hall with floral arrangements and lit candles?

I had read about Plato's Retreat in magazines, so I knew something of what to expect. But I could not just leave my prudish ideas about sex, privacy, and nudity in the dressing room along with my clothes, even if I had wanted to—which I most definitely did not. Even if I had had dreams of sexual ecstasy with multiple anonymous partners, I would not have identified those visions as being as real as the sex club. They were *just* in my mind, and the chasm between my conceptual, culture-bound mind and boundless, sky-like mind was immeasurable. The lamas on this excursion were not in Dudjom's league, but they had already spent decades exploring shifting realities: dreamscapes, hologram imagery, conditioned and unconditioned perception, the insubstantiality of form, the inseparability of form and emptiness. Perhaps Plato's Retreat registered as one more consensual hallucination. At least that was my projection, for they seemed shockingly unperturbed. The American man jumped in the pool stark naked. He beckoned for the rest of us to come in, but the two lamas never fully undressed, having left their underpants on beneath towels wrapped around their waists; the other woman and I did not leave our lounge chairs.

Hanging out with the lamas, while never again in such risqué circumstances, could be rollicking and ridiculous, with two, three, four people palling around, enjoying the day—and always with opportunities for learning. They never failed to help a stranger when they could: giving money to beggars, buying soup for the homeless, helping a bag lady lift her cart to the sidewalk, assisting a mother struggling to get her stroller up the subway steps. Every act of kindness was carried out with the total absence of role—the compassionate Buddhist monk role. American Buddhist centers were already beginning to burgeon with earnest bodhisattvas whose vow to save all sentient beings included the self-congratulatory scouring of city blocks for candy wrappers and tossed beer cans. But the lamas' proclivity for helping seemed instinctually selfless.

An elderly stooped lama who spoke little English asked me to take him to visit a family in Brooklyn. He handed me an address scribbled on a torn piece of paper. After an hour on the subway we arrived at a six-story tenement in which several Tibetan families had apartments. The lama had been summoned by the parents of a teenage boy. The mother, visibly upset, spoke in Tibetan and kept pointing to a fish tank that appeared to be the harmless home to a couple of fancy-tailed goldfish and two seahorses. The father stayed in the kitchen. The boy kept his head down and stared at the floor, looking like any American teenager. That was the problem. He had become so American that he had thought nothing of nourishing his seahorses with live feeder shrimp. The lama listened intently. Then the mother waved me into the kitchen, leaving the boy and the lama alone.

The lama did not look happy on the return trip. One generation out of the Himalayas and already the kids were violating the most sacred Buddhist principle: not killing. The teachings emphasize compassion for *all* beings—no exceptions. By then I had heard the words hundreds of times. Oh yeah, I had read all about compassion. I had seen images of deities that manifested the compassionate heart-mind of the Buddha, I had recited vows to generate compassion for *all* beings—cats and dogs and bag ladies and homeless beggars, American soldiers and their Vietnamese victims— *all*, no exceptions, never, ever but . . . feeder shrimp? I felt compassion for the lama on the subway back to Sixteenth Street, for his troubled countenance and his confusion about this strange new land. I felt teary watching him and thinking about the rescued box turtles and the many times our group of flamboyant intellectual converts had witnessed a lama helping a stranger, and this monk's long trip to and from Brooklyn; and thinking that the driving virtue of Mahayana Buddhism—to save all sentient beings—was not a metaphor.

Wind River Retreat

June 1978. John Giorno arranged for Thinley Norbu Rinpoche to lead a residential retreat at a dude ranch in the Wind River Valley in Wyoming. The ranch sprawled across a valley floor and butted up against a striated wall that turned from tawny brown to mauve at sunset. Past the entry gate a ramshackle barn stabled a dozen horses, with their paddocks extending into dry brush. The long driveway continued to a house where the owner and her young daughter lived. Thinley Norbu, his eldest daughter, and his wife who had joined him from Bhutan stayed in a house nearby. A common-area lodge held large rooms for dining and the dharma talks. About twenty-five of us lived in rustic cabins spread away from the main buildings in various directions. Vivian and I shared a cabin and for one month cohabited cloud-cuckoo-land where mythic Tibet met the American West.

Whenever possible, I rode horses through pine woods and around crystal mountain lakes, just as I had always wished for in my girlhood dreams of riding zebras—or horses—away from my family, away from concrete canyons, away from intellectual discourse. We made campfires and organized cookouts. Thinley Norbu instigated various tag-team games and delighted in witnessing the masks of constructed personas get cracked open by physical exertion. Then he would remind us: *Watch your mind.* That was always Thinley Norbu's instruction, and he would use any situation anywhere and anytime in an attempt to introduce us to ourselves. Like other students, I sometimes received these lessons in late-evening phone calls. I might pick up the phone to the sound of his crooning compliments. I would take pleasure and pride in his descriptions of my silky hair and diamond eyes, then once I was hooked, I would hear, *Only one problem: You are so fat.* Total deflation. Up, down, then *Watch your mind.*

Watch your mind. Then what? Then take responsibility for it. Responsibility? I was a responsible citizen. I voted. I paid my bills. I took care of my dog, I helped my friends. Responsibility for my mind? What did that look like?

On other occasions, Thinley Norbu might question me about a dharma text or principle. And then he would say, *You really have good understanding. You are so smart. You are my most intelligent student.* Turns out, I was actually the dumbest person he had ever met. *Watch your mind. Direct your wild-horse mind rather than allowing it to ride away with you.*

By then I had some begrudging acceptance of just how wild and indulgent my mind was. But in Wyoming, where the retreat location matched the Wild West of girlhood fantasies, it proved irresistible to revert to that dream in which freedom, wildness, and wilderness got all mixed up. I wanted nothing more than to get on a horse and let it ride away with me.

The average horse at the ranch dwarfed Tibetan ponies. Big sky, big horses, big America, and . . . *Look, Rinpoche, those are moose licking the salt blocks in the pasture—moose, the biggest members of the deer family in the world. And that menacing yowling at night comes from coyotes, the trickster gods of native lore.* On group excursions to nearby Dubois, urban retreatants bought cowboy boots and sampled checkered shirts with pearly snap-buttons. We visited a hideout where Butch Cassidy had reputedly laid low, and gleefully explained to our Tibetan guru that this notorious outlaw became a beloved American hero for his cunning avoidance of the law. *Aren't we terrific, Rinpoche? That's who Americans cheer for: the underdog, the unblessed, the outlaw on the lam and hugging the edges.* No wonder that Dilgo Khyentse Rinpoche, after his first tour of the United States, despaired that there were no places of pilgrimage in this vast land.

The retreat came to an end. Enough of prostrations and chanting and dharma teachings. I delayed my return to New York and took off on a weeklong riding adventure into the southern end of Yellowstone National Park with the cowboy who ran the ranch.

Family Problems

Somewhere around 1979, Dudjom Rinpoche left New York to return to Asia, and Thinley Norbu Rinpoche remained at the center. Within months, the sangha fractured. Two camps divided between father and son. Thinley Norbu—contrarian, playful, and brilliant—had always spoken about his stepmother and stepsisters with such contempt as to earn him the nickname *Cinderella Rinpoche*. He ridiculed their Bloomingdale's shopping sprees and glamorous hairstyles, pantomimed their sashay walk in high-heeled shoes, and mimicked how they carried their designer handbags. We showed adoration and sympathy by laughing. Yet even at its most amusing, his scorn confounded us. Surely, he could not really have the same wicked stepfamily issues as the heroine of our cherished folktale. These eruptions must be for our edification, not a genuine expression of banal human characteristics such as hurt, anger, or jealousy. His own mother still resided inside Tibet. The Americans around Yeshe Nyingpo had known nothing of this family's troubled history, though we later learned that it had generated decades of gossip among the Tibetans.

One afternoon at Vivian's apartment on lower Fifth Avenue, four or five of us were discussing the family matter with Tulku Thondup, a young lama-scholar who often stayed at Yeshe Nyingpo. We had looked for explanations everywhere but in our own families or in those we knew with stepparent hostilities or sibling rivalry. *This was a dharma family. Enlightened beings were not supposed to be starring in the same stupid soap opera episodes as we were. They were not on earth to teach us about petty jealousies and the anguish of humiliation and disrespect, and how even loving family members can innocently leave each other wounded.*

Tulku Thondup advised us to take advantage of identifying with any behaviors of the guru that we could. What a gift. We could not identify with the boundless, empty, luminous mind of Dudjom Rinpoche. We were too uptight and self-conscious to help bag ladies with their burgeoning carts and were still picking and choosing the objects of our goodwill, totally missing the mark of an altruistic heart. So, if we could identify with emotional difficulties, well then, how lucky could we get? According to Tulku Thondup, *We always want to identify with the most realized aspects of the masters, but actually, at this stage, they are out of reach.* He suggested that we identify this discord as a rope that had been lowered to help us climb to the top, and told us stories of great masters who shared family problems, starting with Shakyamuni. When the Great Sage disappeared into the forest to seek the truth, he abandoned his wife and infant son, and broke his father's heart. Naropa and Atisha, two of Tibet's greatest adepts, also rebelled against their families' succession plans. The dispute within Milarepa's family led to mass murder before he became Tibet's most heroic saint. *OK, OK, we get it. All families are fucked up.* And then too, as a Tibetan lama in Kathmandu said with a shrug, *Thinley Norbu Rinpoche likes stormy weather.*

It turned out that the image of the rope had been used again and again to reassure disciples that their teachers' behavior could always be turned to their own advantage. Apparently, this was not another case of new-to-dharma, rigid American morality. And Tulku Thondup's advice to look at our own minds was compelling, since that's the only effective laboratory that we have access to. It also did not answer our questions. We were so greedy. We had perfect teachings, but we also wanted perfect teachers and perfect dharma centers.

Falling Apart

Wealthy students of Thinley Norbu's bought him his own center in upstate New York. John Giorno remained active in Yeshe Nyingpo. Vivian Kurz and Michel Abrams entered a traditional, cloistered three-year retreat in France. I spent most of 1980 under the covers, unable to go toward one camp or the other. I had moved into a small loft on West Twenty-Second Street. Every morning I put a long coat over my pajamas and walked Inook to Madison Square Park, then returned to bed, telling myself that I was very tired. I have only the vaguest memory of minimal income from intermittent freelance editing jobs. Clara had moved from Germany to live with Richard in New York and took over my work with him. I would see friends, converse, smile, all the while falling apart.

On several occasions within the paralysis of that dystopic year, I even appeared as an appropriate candidate for different business partnerships. One proposal came from Jan Hashey, a woman of diverse talents with long, straight, strawberry-blond hair and big-framed black glasses. Looking equally elegant in Farmer Brown overalls or Prada, Jan could sweep into a room with unbowed élan and laugh like a crow. Around this time, she had been making terrific large paintings of brown bowls, but having become a single parent she needed to earn a living.

We met at the Cupping Room at the corner of West Broadway and

Broome Street and sat in the front room at a table for two. Jan proposed that we go into real estate together. Soho was on the verge of exploding with residents in the money business, and the post-Warhol art world, including the artists, was eager for show-offy lofts. As we ate our lunch and entertained this scheme, the string of the mala given to me by Tenzin suddenly broke. One hundred and eight beads rolled down my chest and away from the table. I jumped down and started to collect them, padding around the restaurant floor on all fours in between chairs and legs. Jan must have been appalled. Had I been her daughter, I would have been commanded back to my chair. By the time I resurfaced, the die was cast: selling lofts was not my calling.

At around the same time, Paula Cooper talked to me about starting the first hotel in Soho, which seemed far-fetched. But in 1968, she had opened the first gallery below Houston Street with an exhibit to benefit the Student Mobilization Committee to End the War in Vietnam. She had been told that nobody—especially anyone who could afford to buy art—would venture into that desolate warehouse neighborhood. By the time she proposed the hotel, a hundred galleries had followed her lead.

I had worked for Paula briefly in 1976. She had rented a gallery space in Los Angeles for three months and had planned to exhibit the artists in her New York gallery, among them Elizabeth Murray, Jennifer Bartlett, and Joel Shapiro. I had recently returned to New York from Canada and had no work. I found Paula's glamourous, gorgeous looks a little intimidating, but she was so warm and friendly and promised to walk me through how to talk to collectors on the plane ride from New York to LA. Before leaving me there on my own, she arranged for me to take driving lessons to make the freeways less terrifying.

I met important West Coast collectors and accepted dinner invitations to their extravagant homes and admired their valuable collections. I served chilled white wine in the little garden behind the gallery and escorted collectors around the exhibitions solemnly discussing the work as best I could, and palled around with Elizabeth Murray, who had a one-year teaching job at California Institute of the Arts—known as CalArts. We had met the year before at Hermine and Bob's, and had become fast friends with the discovery that we were both reading Ronald Clark's biography of Albert Einstein. In California, we went to the beach in Santa Monica with her son, Dakota, and to wild parties in Venice. Occasionally, Paula came to visit, sometimes with her two sons, and with all the kids we went to Universal Studios and Disney World. It was a fabulous three months during which I did not sell one piece of art. In light of the hotel proposal, it seems that Paula did not hold this against me. As it turned out, her costly short-term excursion into the LA art scene had constructive long-term repercussions for her artists.

Offers of jobs indicate that I was perceived by others as competent, even if that description doesn't compute with my memory. I also know that when I wasn't spaced-out and daydreaming, I could be tough, analytical, competitive, and aggressive, personality traits associated with sound business instincts. There was one catch: making money held no appeal. Despite my ambivalence about motherhood, I had assumed that this role would define my life and did not know how to construct a life without it. I had no community of dharma friends and lacked the determination to seek a new situation on my own. I assumed that sooner or later I would fall backward or stumble into an exit from inertia. In echoes from long ago, I waited to be rescued. Even though the immediate catalyst for this situation hinged on the split in the dharma community, it was impossible to feel anger toward either camp. I knew about being angry, how comforting it could be, how it made me right and the other wrong. Its absence left a pervasive but spineless muddle that felt like a dense blanket—gray, damp, too heavy to lift. I missed the heated, clarifying force of anger.

I spent hours every day during that year lying in bed with rigid, paralyzing fear, and was frequently visited by images of family members who had suffered from mental illness. When I was about six, my mother stopped talking for a year or two and could not be in the house without another adult. Her sister, my aunt Minnie, had been in and out of mental hospitals, and Minnie's daughter rotated between the street, halfway houses, and hospitals. There was no illness named for my mother's mother, who had been taken away to an asylum, or for my father's mother, who had spent days in bed, too dysfunctional to cook or clean. I could experience anger and imitate my father's volatile eruptions; I could feel hurt and sullen and imitate my mother's silent withdrawals—behavior patterns that had influenced my personality—but I refused to see myself as hostage to genetics. And maybe . . . maybe I just needed to remain mute and immobile as a chrysalis, to stay still and pray to be reborn. Although I could pull myself together for social situations, that was not enough to fool my sister who, after a year, dragged me to a therapist. In retrospect, Hermine did not *drag* me to a therapist. Not having agency fueled my story. Once I started therapy, things shifted rapidly. I undertook a freelance editing job, and through my friend Larry Shainberg, began exploring new options for Buddhist practice.

PART SIX

WAVES AND WINDOWS

Zen in America

A Protestant friend who grew up in Cleveland once said of her ex-husband, an editor at Grove Press, *I married the New York Jewish intellectual that I wished to be.* She was not married to Larry Shainberg but might have wished to be had she known him. A published author, a house on Cape Cod, a well-appointed residence in downtown Manhattan, walls lined with books, professorial eyeglasses, Columbia lit grad, an aficionado of coffee beans and basketball. But not homegrown. He came from Memphis, Tennessee, and spoke with a southern accent; not a full-blown drawl of elongated vowels, but an amiable twang. When hosting parties, he was partial to barbecue sent from his hometown.

Larry and I first met in the mid-seventies when, amid the American bicentennial celebrations, he had written a cover story for *The New York Times Magazine* on the opening of Dai Bosatsu, Eido Shimano's new Japanese monastery in the Catskills, and where he explored his own interest in Zen. Two years later, following a scandal about Eido Roshi's affairs with women students, he cut his ties to Dai Bosatsu and subsequently tried to interest me in his current infatuation, a Korean master of both Zen and the martial arts who had a dojo in the West Village.

With spontaneous wit and analytic intelligence, Larry can be both annoying and endearing in his insistence that friends share his enthusiasms.

In 1979, while I was in the doldrums about the fractious disputes at Yeshe Nyingpo, he persuaded me to attend a New Year's Eve meditation at the dojo where he had been studying with the Korean master, followed by a lavish buffet at his loft on Wooster Street in Soho. At dinner, the master sat on a couch with students milling about in various attitudes of submissive adoration. After people had finished eating, they sat on the floor holding their empty plates until a woman made her way through the seated bodies to collect them. As she approached the master from one side, he thrust his plate at her without even a glance in her direction and continued talking without acknowledging her—a display of arrogance that ended any interest in him I might have had. I understood that one seeker's guru was another's charlatan, but I never returned to the dojo and soon after, for reasons of his own, neither did Larry.

The following year, Larry became newly enthusiastic about an American teacher, Bernie Glassman, then known by his dharma name, Tetsugen Sensei. (*Sensei* is Japanese for teacher; and Tetsugen is the dharma name given to him by his teacher, Maezumi Roshi.) A Brooklyn-born applied mathematician turned Zen adept, Glassman had recently arrived from Los Angeles and set up shop in the Riverdale section of the Bronx, one of the most affluent neighborhoods in the New York area. With support from Riverdale residents Lex and Sheila Hixon, the Zen Community of New York (ZCNY) had purchased Greyston, a Gothic Revival stone mansion. Designed by James Renwick, the architect of St. Patrick's Cathedral, Greyston looked out over manicured lawns sloping down to the Hudson River and beyond that to the dramatic cliffs of the Palisades in New Jersey. The setting was grand—and for a Zen center, somewhat grandiose.

I began taking the interborough bus to Riverdale on Sunday mornings for Glassman's public talks, intrigued by the incongruities: a brilliant Jewish-Buddhist Zen teacher in a wealthy, conservative, Anglo-Protestant enclave, and an odd collection of plebeians, including a schoolteacher, a nurse, a railroad employee, and an editor of Russian journals. In addition, a few monastics with shaved heads in robes had, like Larry, broken off their affiliation with Eido Roshi and were all residing in genteel splendor amid their curious and wary patrician neighbors.

The Sunday talks took place in a spacious ground-floor parlor room with high ceilings, oak-paneled walls, and heavy pocket doors that opened into a similar room. Glassman sat cross-legged at the head of the room in formal, layered Zen robes, while the rest of us faced him, seated on cushions on the floor or on folding chairs with seats upholstered in red velvet. In one of the first talks I attended, Glassman reiterated the classic Zen version of Shakyamuni Buddha's awakening: the newly enlightened Buddha, seated on a grass mat beneath a bodhi tree, looks up at the morning star and exclaims, *How wonderful, how wonderful! All things are enlightened exactly as they are.*

Inevitably, as if on cue, someone in the audience asked, *What about the Holocaust?*

That too, Glassman replied.

His imposing quietude slowly absorbed the agitation provoked by his answer. He could not have been a stranger to the question. Envisioning extreme examples of suffering is a familiar response to first hearing that *things just as they are* cannot, by their very nature, be problematic. This was the hard-won lesson I had learned—or more accurately, had apprehended—in retelling the story of my miscarriage during the Arica program. What defines *problematic, painful, wrong* exists within all the ideas and attitudes, the personal and cultural beliefs that we project onto an event, but those problems do not inherently exist in the unfolding of those frame-by-frame actions that comprise the event itself. I certainly hadn't stopped blaming others for my unhappiness, and I still saw situations—personal and political—in terms of right and wrong, perpetrator and victim. Yet the Arica experiment had provided a glimpse of how the mind constructs suffering, and this, augmented by my Tibetan studies, brought Glassman's enigmatic response within the realm of reason.

As I first learned from D. T. Suzuki, Zen teachers have offered millions of words on the ineffability of the enlightened view, yet at that moment Glassman chose to communicate through silence.

What about slavery, tsunamis, sexual abuse, warfare, poverty?

That too.

Glassman's big, dark eyes remained soft and receptive. Most impressively, he didn't rush in to explain that the Buddha would have never condoned Nazi atrocities. He remained gently resolute, allowing the discomfort in the room to make landfall on its own. That our conclusions about suffering come from mental constructions of our own making and not from an object of perception could be a bitter-tasting pill.

Glassman did not try to counter what may have been interpreted as the Buddha's indifference to, say, the Holocaust. The Buddha did not proclaim that *everything is enlightened just as it is* and then walk into the forest and disappear. This American Zen teacher could have pointed out that the Buddha stuck around; that he did not agitate for the overthrow of the caste system, and his role was not that of public advocate for social justice. Yet one step at a time, he turned the Indian Brahmanic apple cart upside down, eventually even admitting women to his community. But I liked Glassman's handling of the awakening story. I liked his gutsy delivery of hard truth to an audience sitting politely on red-velvet-cushioned chairs in the parlor of a fancy mansion, blindly steeped in American political ideology. Despite the uplifting refinements of Riverdale's aristocratic setting, Shakyamuni Buddha's wisdom is actually so inhospitable to treasured conventional assumptions, and can land in your gut with such wrenching implications that, to a Western neophyte like myself, it seemed that only the power and truth of the dharma could account for how it took hold at all, either in ancient India or the contemporary West.

By the time I met Glassman, Zen activity in the United States had been galvanized by American teachers and their students replete with entrepreneurial skills, enthusiastic devotion to their newfound faith, and personal ambition. It could not have been otherwise. We convert-Buddhists were like starry-eyed immigrants from the old country, so eager to start again, so willing to idealize the new and leave behind the sorrows of poverty and persecution. But we brought with us our personal neuroses, our habitual stories and justifications, our longings and ambitions and confusion—and none of that automatically dissolved in the country of the new.

Like other immigrant challenges, the struggle to adapt to the dress codes and language and food tastes of Zen could become a preoccupying cover-up for not dealing with the subtler levels of dislocation and the fear of letting go of the self-centric props. Matters of acculturation could dominate discussions among the residents for weeks, even years. One Japanese teacher denounced his American dharma heir for introducing English into the daily liturgy. In the absence of regulated monastic robes, controversy erupted over appropriate clothing in the meditation hall. Communities became embroiled in food fights, painstakingly assessing the aftershocks of replacing pickled seaweed for breakfast—a Japanese monastery staple—with scrambled eggs, or removing soy sauce from the condiment tray for oatmeal in favor of maple syrup. During one silent meal, a troubled young man screamed: *I am not Japanese! Why the fuck am I eating with chopsticks?*

The writer Natalie Goldberg tells a story about her Japanese teacher, Dainin Katagiri Roshi, abbot of the Minnesota Zen Meditation Center from 1972 until his death in 1990. For his dharma talks, Katagiri Roshi often took one word that epitomized a theme and then exuberantly repeated it again and again, although his pronunciation of English could make enigmatic Zen totally incomprehensible. Once, following a talk by Katagiri at the San Francisco Zen Center, a group of old Zen hands sat around musing on what English word he had been repeating. According to Natalie, the group was joined by a student who was a businessman and thought what the roshi had said was obvious: *economic success.* Katagiri had been repeating, *The whole world depends on economic success,* the businessman explained. The students knew that Katagiri had been trying, with affecting diligence, to comprehend his adopted country; now, perhaps, he had come to accept what most of them had rejected. Not everyone was convinced, however; the explanation just didn't make sense. Someone finally went to Katagiri for clarification. What he had been saying was, *The whole world depends on egolessness.*

Born in 1939, Glassman started practicing Zen in Los Angeles with Taizan Maezumi Roshi in 1968, the year that lives in infamy for the riots, demonstrations, and assassinations that shattered America. Contrary to the subversive lifestyles of many convert Buddhists, Bernie Glassman, twenty-nine years old and married, had a day job at McDonnell Douglas, the aerospace corporation. While the barrage of political catastrophes often felt like meteors crashing into the earth's surface, Glassman got up each morning, put on a suit and tie, and went to work designing shuttle systems to travel between Earth and Mars. At the time he became a monk, in 1970, McDonnell Douglas, under contract to the Unites States military, was sponsoring his doctoral work in mathematics at the University of California, Los Angeles.

The possibility of studying with an American held a compromised appeal. Fascination with Tibetan exoticism had functioned as a way to hide out, to wear a Buddhist mask. I had shunned overt displays of Tibetanism, such as attending teachings in Tibetan-style dresses or wearing traditional coral-and-turquoise jewelry. Still, I had used Tibetan cultural forms to inhabit a fog of otherness that was one of my many strategies for drifting off. With an American teacher, the absence of cultural static was threatening. How much was I willing to expose myself—or even to try?

In the fall of 1980, Rudy Wurlitzer, Elizabeth Murray, and I registered for a *sesshin*, a one-week meditation retreat, at Greyston. By then Rudy had written scripts for Hollywood—among them *Two-Lane Blacktop* and *Pat Garrett and Billy the Kid*—and had published several novels. Following the peripatetic style of many American seekers, he had left Arica and traveled to India to spend time in the Pune ashram of Bhagwan Rajneesh, later the controversial—and allegedly criminal—leader of a community in Oregon. That didn't last either. Rudy had been friends with John Giorno, and on returning to New York, he got involved with Yeshe Nyingpo and then, like me, pulled away when the sangha fell apart. After her Catholic girlhood, Elizabeth had retained a wary attitude toward institutional religion. I had been telling her about my visits to Greyston for the Sunday talks, but none of us had ever considered anything as radical as a Zen retreat. Rudy drove us from Manhattan, and we arrived at the imposing Zen mansion pleased with ourselves for signing on to this rigorous quest but apprehensive about sitting silently in cross-legged posture eight hours a day for seven days straight. Actually, we were scared to death. In accordance with old-school custom, newcomers were expected to follow along with no instruction and as little overt looking around as possible.

Zen training employs various methods to intensify ego-killing. Among the most effective is the required adherence to a rigorous schedule: a time to wake up, a time to sit, a time to stand, a time to walk, to chant, to eat, to go to bed. No time to ask, *Do I want to do this, or should I?* Involuntary arrival at the right place at exactly the right time lends credibility to comparisons between Zen training and military boot camp. It can also affirm the image of robotic Zen *zip heads*—as they were called by loquacious free thinkers like the author Alan Watts. Yet I learned that if one submits to the schedule, it functions as a sharp-edged sword of compassion that cuts off the monkey-mind's most familiar and inconsequential cycles of anguished chitchat.

The Tibetan practices that I had been doing did not include long hours of sitting still. Zen felt uncompromisingly stark: no decorations, no pretty pictures, no visualizations, no mantras, no inspiring echoes of enlightenment—just you and your crazy, fucked-up mind in a bare room. During that first *sesshin*—and many subsequent ones—my mind did not stop fidgeting. The *Platform Sutra of the Sixth Patriarch* speaks of "the mind that abides nowhere." This is the mind liberated from identification with a body, free of a historical story, free of memory and habitual patterns—a mind that has no *me* at its center. Despite fleeting moments of egoless presence, the possibility of that *me* actually disappearing prompted frantic, obsessive attempts to lock it in place. I sat through that first retreat with a mind that acted more like the flea than the dog, grasping at this thought and clinging to that one, flitting from one ego life jacket to another. I could hear Thinley Norbu's voice: *Watch your mind.* Watch your mind racing, wriggling, trying to be anywhere but here, trying with each futile attempt to escape the present moment.

Elizabeth bailed after two days. She packed up her black gym bag and returned to Manhattan by taxi. Rudy and I finished the week—in our fashion. After the dawn sitting on the last day, conspiring through sign language and notes, we met in the parking lot and drove to a diner for breakfast. Neither of us could submit to the schedule 100 percent. We had to mess it up, even with a smudge, on the very last morning. After breakfast, we returned for the formal closing of the retreat. Rudy never returned to Greyston, while I felt that just getting through the long week, however fitfully, deserved further exploration. On Sunday, February 15, 1981, I moved from my loft on West Twenty-Second Street to a second-floor bed-room in Greyston, joining about fifteen other residents.

Given my recent year of debilitating depression, moving to Greyston was an invigorating shift, but I still had doubts about whether running away wasn't a greater motivation than anything I was going toward. I was still haunted by not having children. I had not had any significant roman-tic relationships since my divorce, and Greyston showed no potential in that department. I was not giving up a promising career to pursue Zen. I was not giving up anything at all, not anything I valued. From friends, I learned that my withdrawal from what they considered an enviable engage-ment with the world of art celebrities qualified as a sacrifice, but I already knew that that was not my world. I had no clarity about whether this move would answer some pivotal questions or just delay them. Fortunately, I stuck with an intuition that I was stumbling toward something true.

Community life at Greyston centered around early morning and eve-ning meditation and liturgical service. I adhered to the schedule as if my life depended on it. Maybe it did. It was certainly a welcomed palliative after my year of inertia. Zen at Greyston in 1981 felt emergent, heady, roil-ing with possibility. We sat silently at the intersection of ancient wisdom morphing into new forms of emptiness. The six American monks who lived and worked at Greyston functioned as an authoritative ballast to the revolving door of practitioners more interested in short-term experiments. When the house was not in silence, there were intense conversations about Zen history, its migration from China to Japan, and the doctrinal distinc-tions between Soto and Rinzai, Zen's two main schools. In addition, there were classes on Zen texts, as well as talks that took advantage of the non-residential membership. Larry Shainberg spoke about Samuel Beckett and Zen; Nancy Baker, then a professor of philosophy at Sarah Lawrence and now a Zen teacher, talked about Zen and Wittgenstein. The author Peter Matthiessen, a senior student, often joined the residents from his home on Long Island; in addition to his renown as a writer, his patrician heritage and erect carriage lent Glassman credibility with the neighbors.

I thought of us residents as utopian visionaries, the advanced guard of tectonic shifts in cultural values, beacons of an exalted alternative. We were making ourselves better people who could make society and the world a better place. Like the students around Dudjom Rinpoche, we were motivated by good intentions, however ignorant and idealized. We were cultivating Buddhism in America, and even as we were spiritually immature, our personal needs and ambitions mixed with authentic aspirations for ourselves and others.

A Solo Retreat

When I first moved into Greyston, Larry was doing a private retreat, inhabiting a room on the top floor. Occasionally I saw him on the stairs or in the kitchen. He always kept his eyes down in Zen fashion, and we never acknowledged each other. Inspired by his commitment, I arranged with Glassman to do a similar retreat that summer. Over a period of six weeks the sitting schedule increased to eighteen hours a day. I joined the communal schedule for early morning and evening practice. Talking was confined to meeting with Glassman every few days. No reading or writing allowed.

Having instigated a plan designed to dissolve the monkey-mind, I watched the monkey stockpile artillery. Several fixations rushed in to assure the monkey of its dominion in the jungle of my mind; foremost of the fixations was the schedule itself. Between the dawn and evening sittings, I could wander in and out of the zendo on my own, take a break, sit on the gracious wide veranda and look out at the Hudson River. But how long should I sit, walk, rest, sleep—for *exactly* how many minutes and in exactly what sequence? That was the most pressing issue I needed to discuss with Glassman, and I initiated it at every meeting. One day he asked, *What's with the schedule?* I could not answer. Yet his question exposed its obsessive grip, and in the coming days I came to see that fixating on specifics of time measurements functioned to keep me—my life, my identity—intact, frozen, so that nothing could soften into unknown and uncontrollable territory. The ticktock of minutes was like the rigidity of jail bars, confining my mind to the comforting familiarity of its prison-striped psyche.

What's with the schedule?

Liberation is terrifying, that's what's with the schedule. I'm scared. I'm too vulnerable, too messed up to do this. I need my fabricated identity, need to be swaddled and protected by it, to be held together like the jumble of bones inside this bag of skin.

I sat in the zendo watching the movements of the monkey provoke both attraction and resistance—watching myself going toward and away from relaxed, sky-like spaciousness. I wrestled with the merciless attraction of things that kept me spinning in loops of insatiable desire—a new outfit, a new lover, even an emerald ring that had belonged to my first boyfriend's mother. I had coveted it and wondered if I would have inherited that ring if I had married him. As the retreat went on, my mind fluctuated with varying degrees of openness, calm, agitation, boredom, and fatigue. One stifling afternoon in July, Glassman walked into the zendo and found me slumped against a wall, my limbs akimbo. He said nothing and walked out.

In addition to the schedule, two other themes made themselves at home in my discursive mind: my father on his deathbed and the television serial *Dallas*. My father had been diagnosed with prostate cancer, and the doctors had given him a year. I also wanted desperately to know about J. R.'s latest scheme and Sue Ellen's congenital despair. I invented entire episodes of *Dallas*, and when I interrupted them to acknowledge that the story had transported me away from where I was, I berated myself. When I stepped back to watch myself thinking about my father, I was more forgiving: *This is serious. My father is dying. Death is a big deal. I'm going to sit here and face this sad, momentous event.* My father's dying justified talking to myself; *Dallas* did not. One was real life; the other make-believe. This channel is better than that channel.

One afternoon, alone in the zendo, I suddenly experienced J. R. and my father as equidistant. One was not closer to me than the other. At that moment thinking about my father had no greater emotional impact than thinking about *Dallas*. They were two stories unfolding in midair, constructs of memory and projection, weightless and disembodied thought bubbles with an equal capacity to float away in the vast expanse of space from which they had emerged. If I let them. But equating my dying father and J. R. of *Dallas* was too shocking, too uncomfortable. I could not stay with it. My heart sped up as I struggled to prioritize a flesh-and-blood relationship over a television show, and to reinhabit a conventional view of what was important and what wasn't. Then I returned to an incident that had occurred with Dudjom Rinpoche two years earlier.

Dudjom Rinpoche had been giving an afternoon teaching at the Sixteenth Street center. An artist who lived nearby had arrived uncharacteristically late and during the question period had said, *Rinpoche, this morning I was home watching a movie on television. In the movie, I saw a man take out a gun and shoot another man. This afternoon, I left my house to come here, and on my block, I saw a man take out a gun and shoot another man. What is the difference between these two events?*

Dudjom Rinpoche shook his head. *No difference,* said the translator.

No one moved or spoke. *No difference.* Perhaps Rinpoche did not understand the story. Or we did not understand him. Maybe he did not understand the word *television.* The stunned silence was broken by a young woman who ventured to gently explain, *Rinpoche, in the television version the man who gets shot can get up and walk away. He's an actor. He's not really dead.*

Dudjom Rinpoche chuckled. How funny was that.

Sitting in the zendo with the improbable insight that J. R. and my father existed nowhere but in my mind, I replayed this incident with Dudjom Rinpoche, as I have continued to do for decades. The story of one man shooting another—one on the street and one on a TV screen—placed both events in precisely the same relationship to any mind that might toggle back and forth between them. Interpretations that explained the relative differences between the two events conformed to consensus reality. They made sense. Perhaps making sense was more important than whether or not something was true. I was not ready to allow the images of my father and *Dallas* to dissolve into the equivalence of the man who got shot on the television and the man who got shot on the street. It was time to get off my cushion, to reconstruct Helen, to be the devoted daughter of a dying father. This sadness was mine to cherish—my socially sanctioned sadness, my psychologically sane sadness.

Later I came to see that the perception of parity, while not exactly false, was nonetheless lopsided. The history and conditions by which my life had intersected with the story of my father and the story of the TV show were planets apart. The parity had its own truth, but so did the relative experiential relationships, and they too had to be acknowledged with the weight of their own significance.

Tomatoes had been planted in a fifteen-foot strip along Greyston's stone back wall. The vines were beginning to topple, and during the last week of my retreat I made a project of tying them up. I twisted fibrous twine around drainpipes, looped it through the rusted grommets of defunct shutters, and lashed the vines onto makeshift stakes. The irregular lattice looked rough, but it worked. On examination, I thought: *This design is just like my mind—undisciplined, a little crazy and crude, yet inventive and sturdy.* That seemed just fine: I was fucked up *and* perfect *and,* most important, acceptable. I had not known many moments of knowing that I was 100 percent OK just as I was. The tomato grid made me laugh, and I delighted in looking at it. At the end of the retreat I concluded that a little practice goes a long way. I began smiling a lot and feeling great affection for the other residents. To my astonishment, within just six weeks, everyone had transformed into softer, kinder versions of themselves, less intimidating and friendlier.

Provincetown

After the retreat, I left Greyston to see my parents in Provincetown. I had stopped spending summers on the Cape after high school, though I had continued to visit for summer weekends—visits that did not have a good history. I vowed that this time would be different. My father's cancer was in remission. He had been in good spirits and had prepared for my visit by reading D. T. Suzuki. Many of his friends, including the composer John Cage, had attended Suzuki's lectures on Zen Buddhism at Columbia University in 1950. My father adored Cage, but while the composer's immersion in Zen was a source of amusement to him, my own evoked a more mistrustful response. Still, I was touched by this effort to better understand what I was up to, and thought it boded well for my visit.

My parents' nineteenth-century white clapboard house was on Commercial Street in the West End. It sat fifty feet behind a carefully tended rectangular lawn. The approach, through a wooden gate and along a brick path leading up to the front porch, looked quaint and picturesque. Inside and out, the house had the elegant simplicity of Shaker aesthetics. No curlicues. The rough edges were confined to familial relations. Soon after I arrived, my father began discoursing on Zen's disturbing nihilism.

My aunt Biala once told me that when she was five years old and my father eight, he asked her, *How many gods do you think there are?* My aunt knew of one God, but figured that since God was good, the more the better. She held up her opened hand to indicate five. My father walked away in disgust. All these years later, despite his progressive modernist convictions, he had remained an Old Testament Jew, and no religion was preferable to one without God.

Two years after attending Suzuki's lectures, Cage invited audiences to his signature piece: *4'33"*, the span of time during which no sound came from the stage. Musicians sat holding instruments without moving, and David Tudor sat still at his piano. Soon enough, sounds filled the theater: shouts of disapproval, disappointment, accusations of money wasted. *Booooooo.*

My parents had taken me and Hermine to an afternoon performance to celebrate my birthday. Hard to imagine that they conceived of this as an appropriate present for a ten-year-old, but it must have been the only way that they themselves could attend. I can't claim that it was a fun birthday outing, but I never forgot the performance and am always reminded of it when working with sound meditation, a practice that requires staying steady with sounds that have been conventionally labeled pleasant—birdsong, cosmic hums, gentle waves—and with sounds that we preconceive to be unpleasant such as traffic, sirens, barking, retching. We can follow the habitual swings of the mind between attraction and aversion or . . . try to let go of preconceived distinctions between music, sound, and noise and learn to rest with bare awareness and *just listen.*

During the performance, my parents did not join the increasingly loud outrage, but I have no sense of what they made of it either. In 1967, my father and Cage traveled around the States together as part of a program, Contemporary Voices in the Arts, that brought together art and technology. On his return, my father recounted an exchange between them. They had been walking by a lake after dinner, and John had looked up at the night sky and exclaimed, *How beautiful!* To which my father had said, *John, I thought you believed in one taste.* My father reported that they had both laughed. But he told the story as if he had just one-upped not only Cage but all of Zen. I don't know where my father had encountered the term *one taste,* but it seems that he mistakenly assumed that it denied particularity.

Without denying distinction, the term points to the essential emptiness of all phenomena—which then manifests in innumerable and distinct forms, as distinct as the sounds that erupted during the performance of *4'33"*; and which were as empty in essence as the sounds of Beethoven's Ninth Symphony; or the sounds that the audience came expecting from a John Cage concert. When we discussed what he was reading in D. T. Suzuki, it was clear that my father had confused emptiness with nihilism—a common misinterpretation in the West.

D. T. Suzuki translated *shunyata* as emptiness—sky-like emptiness—but he also described shunyata as fullness. Because sky-like mind is empty of boundaries, restrictions, concepts, biases, and language, it encompasses the universe and everything in it, including Yahweh, including cancer, illness, and death, including family love and discord. *Big-sky mind* encompassed the unconditional love between us that my father and I had long held in the privacy of our hearts. Face to face, that longing—and that love—remained trapped, defended by arrogance, mistrust, and self-doubt. We were both so stubborn and proud. If big-sky mind could accommodate this visit—and all the mangled versions of love and hate within it—maybe I too could accommodate the visit by not taking angry walks on the beach or disappearing into fantasy but instead staying present and open, allowing for a more spacious reality than the one that played in the old tapes that crowded my head. But the visit was already slipping off the rails. Once again, I became the sullen, willful younger daughter in need of being straightened out. In response, I began to withdraw, separate, and shut down. Yet even watching myself contract and recoil, and acknowledging this inability to stay with discomfort, anger, and aversion, signaled a newfound willingness to look at my behavior. In part, seeing this came into focus through an incident that had recently taken place in the zendo.

One evening a week, Glassman gave a dharma talk. The residents were joined by other students, primarily from Manhattan. On this particular evening, the zendo was packed and Glassman spoke about Sogaku Harada (1871–1961), an exceptional Zen master who determined to rid careerist

Zen institutions of calcified, rote holiness. Then Glassman spoke about Harada's favorite student: a layman, a poet, and a drunk. His name, I believe, was Ito-en. As I remember the story, Harada identified this eccentric Zen genius as the only disciple who surpassed his own understanding, and he had allowed him to live in a small hermitage behind the main temple.

The hermitage stank of the dried fish that hung from the rafters. Empty sake bottles, newspapers, and poems written on rice paper littered the floor. One afternoon, through the window, Ito-en glimpsed Harada Roshi walking toward his hut to pay a visit. According to Glassman, *Ito-en was completely embarrassed and hid in a corner behind a shoji screen.*

A hand shot up in the back of the zendo. A psychotherapist who came to Greyston regularly from her townhouse on the Upper East side asked, *Sensei, how can a Zen man of such accomplishment be embarrassed?*

Soshan! roared Glassman, using her dharma name, *I said Ito-en was* completely *embarrassed.*

I was dazzled by Glassman's spontaneous response. Yet to relate to it in a personal way, I again resorted to memories of LSD and to the experience of completion with myself. Even the intuition of a divided self had only emerged in its temporary absence. And only with psychedelics did the layers of fabrication get peeled back, and only then was there no me watching me, no self-conscious witnessing of consciousness. A deep contentment came with the dissolution of that agitated, worrisome undercurrent that something which we cannot name or know is missing.

When my mother worked at the Lighthouse she arranged for me to spend a high-school summer working with blind children. One little girl, four years old and blind from birth, walked around all day tapping her closed eyelids, her small hands fluttering continuously. It looked as if she was trying to awaken this dormant body part that she knew to be missing.

At the time of this visit to Provincetown, I was still tapping my hands against my eyes. It wasn't just my parents who had been waiting for my life to visibly cohere. I too hadn't let go of conventional benchmarks: marriage, children, career. There were still no signs of moving toward any shape that might qualify me as an adult with meaningful ambitions. While my parents made clear their mistrust of my choices, the zendo was the one place where I never felt I was wasting my time. Sitting for hours in silence felt like a more deeply rewarding and intimate way of being with others than conventional socializing, and I discovered that silence brings forth compassion in ways that conversation cannot match. This was true even as I spent entire sitting periods designing dresses or making up menus or soap opera episodes. I was grateful not to be in bed, rigid with depression, but I also wished, especially during summer visits with my parents, that I could magically transform into a patient, kind, helpful, and happy person who would make the benefits of meditation practice so glaringly obvious that no one would question the efficacy of my choices. I had hoped that meditation would make my problems disappear. It never works that way. However, I had begun to see that what I thought were my private miseries were part of a bigger landscape that extended far beyond individual psychological issues. Even if the internal noise while I was on the cushion was deafening at times, meditation was operating like earthworms aerating packed dirt: tiny pinpricks of light were beginning to penetrate layers of obscuration.

I had come to Buddhism with no idea that my attempts to create a meaningful life had been plagued by fundamental misunderstandings of how life worked. My failure to find happiness had not been just the result of my inability to transcend a damaged and unforgiving ego. The very self that had set my agenda for happiness, that had pursued glittering attractions and created expectations, did not exist in any of the ways I had assumed. This cherished, conventional way of identifying the self through patterns of behavior, through desires and aversions and emotional states, turned out to be as much a figment of my imagination as Tarzan's Jane. That my personal understanding of accomplishment had merged so seamlessly with the powerful forces of consensus reality only made its delusional aspects more difficult to discern, but not any closer to reality.

On LSD, I had experienced a sense of completion—moments of a mind emptied of definition, and completed by the empty nature of everything else. The emptiness inside had found perfect harmonic resonance within the world at large; but I needed the context of Buddhism to trust that the quest for understanding beyond the limits of selfhood was a worthy and beneficial exploration of reality, not just a recreational day trip with no lasting value. During my years at the Zen center, meditation practice became a form of hands tapping at my blind eyes; but slowly, I tapped with increasing faith in the possibility that they might actually be opened.

A Peace Offering

In 1982 my father's cancer began to invade the bone. As a kind of peace offering between us, my parents accepted an invitation in early spring to have lunch with the Glassmans in Riverdale. For many years my father had been applying mathematical systems to his paintings, in particular the Fibonacci sequence. Given Glassman's background in math, I had hoped to steer the conversation toward an area of mutual interest. All I remember now is the dialogue that set my father up for one of his last great belly laughs before he died five months later. Glassman had talked about his upcoming trip to Japan with Peter Matthiessen. My mother, a voracious reader, was a big fan of Peter's, especially of *The Snow Leopard*, in which the quest for the elusive cat could be seen, on another level, as a metaphor for a journey toward awakening.

Just after saying goodbye, as I was backing the car out of the Glassmans' driveway, my mother asked, *Why are Peter Matthiessen and Glassman going to Japan?*

Mom, I said, *we just spent two hours with Glassman. Why didn't you ask him why he's going to Japan?*

Why should I ask him? she answered. *He already knows why he's going to Japan.*

Ascending the Mountain

The trip to Japan related to Glassman's *Shin San Shiki*—the Ascending the Mountain Ceremony—which is when a new abbot is installed. Ascending to this role, and replacing Maezumi Roshi as abbot of ZCNY, was scheduled to take place a few months later. Paying homage to the monasteries in Japan and to the roshis and administrative dignitaries of his Zen lineage prefigured this ceremony, which would culminate at Greyston. Peter, his most senior monk, would accompany Glassman as his attendant.

On a warm Sunday morning, the sixth of June, two hundred and fifty guests lined up to participate in an outdoor procession intended to replicate the new abbot's traditional approach to the temple. Replete with banners and drums, this tiny manicured haven of privilege within the disorderly borough of the Bronx enjoyed a taste of medieval Japan, with black-and-white simplicity transformed into a colorful pageant, and Maezumi Roshi leading the way in a robe of majestic purple.

After the procession and before the elaborate brocaded shrine, Glassman, in a scripted liturgy, dedicated the merit of the occasion to the harmony of all beings, world peace—*and the successive presidents of the United States*. For the American version, this last line had been changed from *the emperors in Japan*.

I was not the only one there to register a silent gasp. Ronald Reagan had come into office six months earlier. For those like me who had entered the dharma gates through the counterculture, the constitutional separation of church and state implied the separation of Buddhism and normative social values. The mistrust of the establishment cut deep in reconfiguring a moral universe. Our newfound enthusiasm for an American dharma did not include President Reagan. In Japan, the emperor had bridged heaven and earth, summoning celestial benedictions on behalf of the earthborn. Ronald Reagan had been a grade-B Hollywood actor who had costarred with a chimpanzee named Bonzo.

Zen centers in the United States had been expanding more through Jack Kerouac than through powerful patronage. Our emperor was that handsome heartthrob who envisioned the antiauthoritarian rucksack revolution, and inspired thousands of Gary Snyder/Japhy Ryder wannabes to sit down in lotus posture, and who died in his mama's house in Florida from alcohol, age forty-seven. We had followed the subterranean footsteps of homoerotic misfits, venerators of hobo rail riders, and other outcasts who might make a poet in philistine America feel less like a lonely freak. No one had invited Ronald Reagan to the zendo.

My Father's Death

Following the abbot installation, I spent my father's last months with him in Provincetown. He had stopped receiving treatments. Hermine and Bob had rented a house at Beach Point, just outside of town. Hermine had read an article in which Norman Cousins claimed that laughter had helped cure his cancer, and she had arrived on the Cape with a stack of Marx Brothers movies. We set up a projector in my father's studio and invited friends to join us. *A Night at the Opera, Duck Soup, A Day at the Races.* We laughed until tears streamed down our faces, though my father continued to decline. Friends came through all summer to say goodbye. In the evenings, my mother and sister and I gathered in a small apartment upstairs within earshot of my father's room. About once a week, Larry Shainberg arrived unannounced from his house in Wellfleet, bringing quarts of ice cream. He and my mother frequently talked about literature, conversations that also included raucous laughter, partly because of Larry's impish humor and partly because at the end of heavyhearted days at my father's bedside, nothing released intense anguish more than a roaring guffaw.

At the end of these evenings, Hermine returned to her husband and son; I returned to sitting with my mother at the kitchen table. I had arrived on the Cape with as much concern for her as for my father. Care for him demanded attention. What meds to give when. Carrying food trays up and down the stairs. We would keep him at home to die. Nurses came to help with bathing and, at the end, with morphine injections. My mother's choices were dangling right before her eyes, and none offered much comfort. She had moved in with my father from her childhood home fifty years ago. He had been her vocation, the name of her county.

Hermine's devotion to my father was less compromised than my own. I had learned to accommodate his shaming criticisms, while not having outgrown their effects. But we made a good team, Hermine and I, getting through this great demise. Growing up, I had assumed that my father's adoration of his firstborn meant that she had the easier row to hoe; by now, I recognized that our polarized roles within the family had burdened each of us in distinct ways, and that both identities were equidistant from a more complex mix of ragged contradictions.

In *Ambivalent Zen,* a memoir that Larry Shainberg published in 1996, he wrote that on first meeting Kyudo Roshi, the Japanese Zen master who would become his primary teacher, Kyudo asked if his parents were still alive and if he was taking care of them. Kyudo Roshi explained, *Must gratitude your parents. They give you most precious gift. If you not gratitude parents, you not gratitude Buddha.*

In contrast to Kyudo's advice, the therapist that I had been seeing in New York and had continued to talk with on the telephone during those months had explained that I owed my parents nothing. According to Buddhist teachings, as reiterated by Kyudo Roshi, I owed my parents everything. The Buddhist view did not negate my anger, but by now I had drawn a line between anger and blame. As I understood it, to blame others denies taking responsibility for your own emotional state. Blame indicates not maintaining a vigilant watch over your mind. This affirmed the lesson from Arica, namely that every event is inherently neutral and that negative responses are not bound to the situation but can be modulated, even liberated, through awareness. The practice removed the focus from the bad other, the awful circumstances, the evil and violent perpetrator. Bad things will always happen, things that are unkind, hurtful, unjust, but there is always the choice to hold tight to the experience or allow it to go. For a long time, I nurtured my anger, watered it, and turned it toward the sun like a houseplant, all the while feeling justified and righteous. Until I was ready to let go of being the victimized daughter of a tyrannical father, I could not discern that my anger could be diminished. Blame could be a balm—so soothing, so seductive. But it did nothing to release anger.

To my therapist, not blaming my parents for my fears, my insecurities, my lack of confidence, my low self-esteem, indicated my refusal to embrace the kind of rejection that was warranted by their behavior, and expressed infantile bondage to my father's authority. There did not seem to be any room in this view for—as Buddhist liturgy puts it—*the gift of this precious life*. Parents have given their bodies in service to this life. And then, if you're lucky, they also give you their care, their love, and their protection. According to the optimistic Buddhist understanding, each of us comes into the world with the potential to wake up. And this potential cannot be diminished or destroyed, even when someone experiences abandonment, loss, or abuse in their childhood. These wounds need to be unpacked and acknowledged, and psychotherapy can be an immense help; trauma can create powerful obstacles to self-liberation, but it is not an immovable roadblock, and it is not intrinsic to our basic composition. As I had learned in the Tibetan refugee camp, we can become bigger than our suffering. Blaming others, I told my therapist, keeps the arrows lodged in our own bodies. And we'll never get rid of them if we deny responsibility for keeping them in place. Turning inward helps us ferret out not only the source of our despair but also the source of its relief. The Buddha's First Noble Truth on the nature of suffering teaches us that suffering itself is the key to liberation. My therapist didn't buy it. Neither of us changed our minds.

During that summer, I asked a young Tibetan lama what I could do in the future when a practice called for visualizing my father. He laughed. What a hopeless knucklehead I was, so attached to materiality, still making primitive distinctions between life and death. I would never learn anything, never understand the essential deathlessness of all phenomena.

I also had several phone conversations with Glassman. I had been sitting zazen by my father's bed and needed to clarify what it meant to be one with everything, because my father was dying and I did not want to die. *Don't be too literal*, Glassman had said. *You and your father are not one, not two.*

According to Tibetan bardo teachings on death and dying, the essence of mind—awareness or consciousness—continues beyond the death of the body. In general, it takes about three days to complete the separation of the mind from the body following the final exhale. I asked my mother if we could keep my father's body at home for a few days. In the Jewish tradition, burial occurs as soon as possible. This was my mother's preference, which she tried to couch in terms of religious sentiment. But she was not religious and the least sentimental person I have ever known, and she sheepishly acknowledged that getting the body into the ground quickly addressed her anxieties. She wanted it over and done. My father's death on Labor Day weekend provided a compromise. The gravediggers for the Provincetown cemetery were on holiday, and the undertaker agreed not to come to our house for a day. I spent the night sitting in my father's room. The next day I accompanied his body to the funeral home. I was not convinced that he was completely dead and did not trust his care to the morticians. As we left the house, I saw that my mother had already rearranged the furniture in the living room.

At the funeral home, the thermostat in the procedural room was set to near freezing. Work had been completed on another corpse, an elderly man with thick salt-and pepper hair, dressed for the special occasion in a brown wool suit and looking completely at home in his new surroundings. On an adjacent metal table my father lay faceup, bald and naked, vulnerable as an abandoned newborn. His blood had drained to the underside of his body, turning it bruised blue, and his penis was engorged with pooled blood. I wanted to wrap him in a blanket, to put a forgiving cloth between his skin and the sterile steel slab. I wanted to protect him from the cold of the room and to shield his modesty. More than anything, I wanted him to know something of the serenity emanating from the dead stranger in the brown suit.

My father went into his coffin dressed in dungarees and a denim shirt, along with a pail full of sand, pebbles, seashells, and the translucent carapaces of horseshoe crabs. I slipped in a small wooden Buddha that I had brought back from Japan. The consternation around his eyes never softened before the coffin lid closed, and the lowering of the pine box into the ground suggested that it never would.

The poet Stanley Kunitz and his wife, the painter Elise Asher, spent summers in the house adjacent to ours, separated by a walkway not more than twenty feet wide. All summer Stanley had advocated for a prominent obituary, needling my mother about preparing notes, photos, and dates. In his estimation, this public notice would define my father's place in history. While his suggestions were received with only slightly veiled contempt, a lengthy obituary was nonetheless announced on the front page of *The New York Times* and included more nice things about my father than the paper of record had ever printed during his life.

I returned to Greyston while Maezumi Roshi was visiting. The prominent obituary had impressed him, which annoyed me as much as Stanley's preoccupation with legacy—my father's and his own—had annoyed my mother. The following day, Maezumi and Glassman together conducted a memorial service for my father. I held to some grumpy conviction about karmic benefits, but I was no more pleased to have my father in the zendo than when Ronald Reagan had showed up at Glassman's abbot installation three months earlier.

By then my father had entered the zendo many times in my own wandering thoughts. My engagement with Zen had inspired a fresh appreciation for a certain period of his work. He had become known in the 1950s for his abstract expressionist paintings. By the mid-sixties he needed to paint his way out of repetition. He approached the canvas in search of new forms, experimented with different pallets, applied rhythms from math and music. Once he abandoned signature abstraction, he never fit a slot, never again inhabited a brand, and his career never recovered. Even one of his own gallery dealers had lamented, *What a shame that he moved away from abstraction.* Yeah, well . . . an alternative would have been to exit repetition through suicide, as Mark Rothko did in 1970. The day of Rothko's death, he and my father had run into each other on a street corner in midtown. Rothko had asked my father to come with him to his studio, which was nearby, but my father wanted to get back downtown to his own studio.

In his journal, my father noted that Rothko had looked disconsolate, but my father had continued on, thinking about how depressing it must be to get trapped by style.

The paintings of my father's that I revisited through Zen were dark gray, as monochromatic as a Zen meditation hall. Gone were the emotional colors of ego-abstraction. The allusions to figures had been painted out, but he maintained the attention to gestural detail that he had brought to his earlier work. And in a striking departure from abstraction, he had imposed an impersonal grid. With my immersion in Zen, I experienced the grid as having the virtue of a vow with greater freedom to be explored through restriction than through unrestrained choice. But while he admirably painted himself out of his signature style, he continued to suffer from the same cycles of anxieties and emotional turbulence that had routinely ensnared him.

The View from the Kitchen Window

In 1983 I returned to Cape Breton and impulsively bought a house. I had no intention of ever owning a house. I had not been looking for one and can still remember the offer coming out of my mouth, strained and squeaky, as if I had just swallowed a ventriloquist. But this wasn't just any house: it was both exceptionally dilapidated and exceptionally beloved, and a lot of people wanted it.

It measured twenty-two by twenty-six feet, with the same proportions as a Monopoly house, and it sat on a steep hill overlooking the St. Lawrence Seaway, making for an unobstructed view at the exact level of the horizon. The road leading to the campsite where I had spent summers with Jim was off this same road, and at that time, this house was still lived in by Duncan Angus Rankin and his sister Mary Catherine, who had been born here and grew up in this house with their six siblings. Duncan epitomized old Cape Breton—a rangy, ruggedly handsome hard worker and a heavy drinker. He had worked in the mines and in the woods, had fished and farmed, and had a flock of sheep that regularly clogged the road, creating a pastoral idyll for us urban visitors, and annoying any local trying to drive through. In contrast to Duncan's gregarious ways, Mary Catherine was exceedingly shy, keeping her head down and talking rarely. Toward the end of their lives they moved closer to Inverness, and sold this house to Lloyd and Cissy O'Conner. Their primary residence was near town but their marriage was on the rocks, and Cissy had been spending a lot of her days at the decrepit old house.

The house sat halfway between my cabin and the end of the road, and Inook and I passed it frequently on our walks. I had heard that Cissy had put the house on the market, but immediately withdrew it whenever an offer was made. She was also the beloved grade-twelve history teacher who never missed a chance to voice her virulent dislike of Americans. One afternoon, as I passed below and looked up the steep hill, I saw her sitting outside, leaning against the front wall. We waved. I yelled up, *I hear you're selling your house*. She yelled back, *You want to see it?*

Sure. Why not? I had never been inside before.

It felt uninhabited. Abandoned. No signs of used dishes, clothes, books. Scant furnishings, crude chairs, bare shelves, layers of tattered linoleum on the floor. The table in the kitchen had an indentation at the edge of one side facing the water. *That's where Duncan Angus used to sit with his elbow on the table and his head in the palm of his hand*, explained Cissy.

A tall woman, big-boned and sad-eyed, she walked me from the kitchen to an empty back room, and to its side, a room that featured a toilet, the sole bathroom fixture. I tried to show polite interest, but I only wanted to look at the view through the kitchen windows, to see the outside from the inside: all sky and water. Vast. Beyond vast. Mind-stopping vast. Original space. What's there before we fill the big screen in the sky with our own personal projections.

My knees wobbled. I steadied myself against a doorjamb and that's when this weird, thin, unrecognizable voice said, *I'd like to buy your house*.

Of course she knew that I was American. She said she'd discuss the offer with Lloyd. Not promising, as I don't think she had discussed anything with Lloyd for a very long time. The asking price was $16,000 USD. The mountain land had been paid for by the sale of an artwork that my father had given to me. I had just sold that land for $11,000, and I would borrow $5,000.

Then she asked me about living alone in the cabin. What was that like? A woman alone in the woods. She invited me to sit at the kitchen table.

She asked about driving from New York to Nova Scotia. Alone. *What was that like? How long did it take? Where did you stay? Were you afraid?* I gave short answers: yes, no, both. What did she really want? Only later did I learn that she was getting ready for a road trip herself, a long one, alone, and far away from her family and friends and from Inverness where she had lived all her life. But no one knew this at the time.

You're Buddhist, right?

I said, *Yes.*

She asked if Buddhists believed in the afterlife. I hesitated, concerned that further negotiations might hinge on this answer. Then I truthfully explained that I did not have a clear understanding of what that meant. She asked if I believed in reincarnation. Again, my answer was ambiguous but no different than what I would say to anyone at that time. I couldn't say definitely one way or another. I did not believe or disbelieve. I could only conclude that I did not know. She then explained that in her vision of heaven, she would be reunited with those of her loved ones who had died. And I knew that more than anyone, this vision had fervently, passionately focused on her beautiful teenage daughter who had died in a tragic car accident a few years earlier.

The conversation had run its course. Her anti-Americanism had been nowhere in evidence. This was a Thursday. I asked if I might come back the next day with a friend who could help assess the structure. We set a time. The house was obviously falling down, but this allowed for a way to return, and besides, it seemed like the grown-up and responsible thing to do. The next morning, I returned with Richard.

Richard entered the basement through a wooden door flat to the ground outside the house, and crawled around with a flashlight, making his way through the pile of large rectangular quarry stones that had collapsed from the sides. He emerged with an optimistic report: the foundational beams were in good shape. It turned out that they were completely rotten, and had not been reinforced or replaced since the house was built in 1875. I don't know whether this miscalculation was based on hubris, or was Richard's way of not discouraging me; I only know that for his own work, thankfully, he depends on professional engineers.

By the time of the second visit, I had secured a possible loan, and I had learned that a traveling lawyer would be in Inverness the following week. I told Cissy that if she and Lloyd wanted to go through with the sale, we could meet at the lawyer's office on Wednesday. By the end of the day, between me and Richard, word spread. Not that Helen was buying Duncan Angus's house—which is what it's called to this day—but rather, *Poor Helen, she got duped just like everyone else. And she's an American. Cissy will never sell her that house.* On Saturday morning two guys that I had known for years came to the cabin to warn me, to explain that Cissy had this pattern, and they didn't want to see me get hurt. Their concerns were touching, disturbing, but not altogether discouraging.

For the next day, a Sunday, I designed a plan for optimal distraction. Before leaving New York, I had read in *The Vajradhatu Sun,* the newsletter for Trungpa Rinpoche's community, that a piece of property outside of Pleasant Bay, about sixty miles north of Inverness, had recently been purchased for the purpose of starting a Tibetan Monastery. I had inherited my father's 1968 Pontiac station wagon, a huge red bruiser, and to pass the time on this day of waiting, Inook and I set out for the highlands to check out this curious report. It was a miserable, foggy day, and we crawled along the Cabot Trail, finally arriving at an odd-shaped yellow house toward the end of the Red River Road, almost as isolated and remote as the house I had hoped to buy, and also facing the St. Lawrence Seaway. A brown and white goat shivered on the small covered porch. A Western man wearing Tibetan monastic robes invited me in. I suppose I asked about plans for the monastery. I suppose he was happy to share them. I don't think he had many visitors. But I had spent the drive and the teatime wondering about whether the purchase of the house would go through, and it would continue to preoccupy me on the slow drive home. Yet I never forgot the visit, the first of what would become many over the years, and I never forgot the goat sheltering against the front door.

I visited with Cissy the following afternoon. More people from town warned me. On Wednesday, Cissy, Lloyd, and I met with the lawyer. Papers were signed, money paid, the deed transferred. I was already forty years old, yet ownership of something called *a house* felt like playing dress-up in my mother's shoes, a little too big, a little too adult. However derelict, a house is not a cabin. I had no idea about what I had just done. I owned a falling-down house. Now what? Over the next few days I returned to the house and sat at the kitchen table with my elbow in the indentation made by Duncan Angus, and stared out the window. Then I knew why this house had called to me—even as the big empty view vaporized ideas about ownership or adulthood or self, and there would never be enough hours in a day to gaze into it.

On my return to Greyston, the community was in the throes of the first of Glassman's iconoclastic maneuvers. He had finally convinced a wary board of directors that in the United States, business offered the most effective conduit for the dissemination of Buddhism. He began putting his efforts into starting the Greyston Bakery in a neglected section of Yonkers, about ten miles north of Riverdale. He told us that if we wanted to study Zen with him, we could volunteer to work at the bakery. Within a matter of months, he rarely showed up in the zendo, which provoked heated debates. At the extreme, this break with tradition continued the American legacy of forging new, creative paradigms, making him the perfect leader to pioneer Zen in the New World; alternatively, he was an immature posturer who did not embody Zen dharma but rather Glassmanism. I recognized some truth in both versions—which changed nothing about my days at Greyston.

In addition to buying a house, in another exploration of adulthood following my father's death, I began to write a series of profiles of American Zen teachers within Japanese lineages. I had moved out of the Greyston mansion, joining several other students in an apartment complex a few blocks away. Each morning in the dark I walked to the zendo and then returned to work at my desk. I took afternoon walks with Inook along the railroad tracks by the river's edge and returned to Greyston in the evenings, often to cook dinner for the residents as well as eat there myself and to join the evening zazen sessions. I was sitting about four hours a day, and this rhythm, with its tidal flow between being with others and being alone, created a deeply satisfying daily life, even as it took place within an emerging community that was already falling apart. Occasionally I traveled to conduct interviews for the book: to Hawaii to meet with Robert Aitken Roshi; to Cambridge, Massachusetts, to meet with Maurine Stuart; to California to see Kwong Roshi; to New Mexico for Richard Baker; and to Yonkers, to talk with Glassman.

A New Morning

Somewhere around 1985, I took note of waking up each morning with enthusiasm for the coming day, a state that I had never known before. I still spaced-out in the zendo and indulged in distractions; was still often reactive, angry, and self-preoccupied; was still entertained by gossip and my own opinions about everything; yet old friends I would see in Manhattan asked if I was in love, and I knew why they were asking. One dark winter morning, walking to the zendo at about 4:15, I suddenly thought, *I am not depressed.* The recognition was startling. As far back as I could remember, I had woken up with a sensate dread so deep in my bones that its absence left me looking for it.

I didn't dare call this happiness. All I knew for sure was the absence of weight, a weight lifted off my shoulders. An iron box no longer pressed on my heart. The recognition left a euphoria that lasted for days. I looked around as if I had been transported to a new neighborhood and did not know where to buy a cup of coffee. Everything looked exactly the same—and at the same time different.

Cycles of highs and lows returned. Since that time, I have known periods of depression, of enervating despair, of feeling that everything in my personal life and in the world is hopelessly messed up. But the paralyzing depression during the year before I moved to the Zen community never returned. The weight of sadness that had kept me lying motionless for hours and days never again kept me in bed for even a day; and that's been a change to feel good about.

The tomato garden may have played a role in this shift. For decades, the irregular lattice kept reappearing in my mind, and I could never figure out why. Then just a few years ago, it appeared again during a conversation with Vivian Kurz over dinner in an Italian restaurant in Chelsea. Vivian was speaking about *essence love,* the term that the Tibetan teacher Tsoknyi Rinpoche uses to describe a complete, unadulterated experience of well-being. Essence love is subtler and somewhat more refined than happiness—more attuned to the contented calm of deep ocean waters than the jaunty inconsistency of waves. Tsoknyi's emphasis on an embodied experience of well-being evolved after more than twenty years of teaching in the West, and offered a prescription for Westerners like me whose focus on self-knowledge favors intellectual analysis over emotional revelation. Tsokyni developed this emphasis after concluding that his Western students, while dedicated to understanding erudite points of theory and logic, were not making critical changes in behavior. Their dissatisfactions and frustrations and complaints had not diminished. Dharma had pervaded their heads, but in his view, without essence love, critical shifts in how they related to themselves and to others could not be accomplished. True compassion for others could not radiate without a basic, profound, embodied experience of well-being, he said. Only with the recognition that we really are OK just as we are can we expand this primal experience of fundamental goodness. And only then can we develop love and compassion for others. Without essence love we cannot flourish and will remain closed-hearted inside our little shells, hindered in how we live and how we love.

The tomato lattice reflected a jumble of imperfections. It was actually kind of ugly. Had it been a face, it might have been blemished by acne or scarred by smallpox. It had also been completely acceptable, perfect just as it was. A reflection of my OK mind, my OK body, my OK rough-edged personality. I had not acknowledged many moments when I felt *I am OK, right now, just as I am. I am unconditionally OK.* I was always quick to see what I lacked, how I was broken, what needed to be improved or fixed, and to prioritize the importance of any deficiency over any virtue. Within this habitual mindset, I could not even notice—or give credibility to—those innumerable fleeting moments when in truth I felt just fine. The lasting impact of the tomato grid did not come from just a fleeting experience but from the fusion of experience and recognition. It was the recognition, the acknowledgment of what was happening when it was happening that imbued this fleeting moment with lasting consequence. Moments of sensory bliss, like those occasioned by sex, food, meteor showers, ocean sunsets, or the appearance of wild animals—ordinary-extraordinary moments that stop the mind, break the spinning, muttering, talking-to-itself mind—had passed without recognition and therefore had come and gone without changing my perception. Once in Cape Breton I was going into town from my house, which includes going over a mountain, and just past the top, as I started down, I came upon a large black bear standing completely still in the center of the road. It was May, the time when the bears come down from the highlands to catch fish and eat new shoots. The bear stood in perfect profile to the road, and it happened to be an exceptionally beautiful bear, its back flat and straight, not rounded at the butt as they can be sometimes, and if its front legs were bunched forward at the shoulders, I could not see that. It held its head high, nose straight forward, its coat glossy in the daytime light, a bear in its prime. No cubs, maybe a male. I stopped and watched for several minutes until it meandered away. My mind stopped. So much so, and with such a lasting imprint that today, some ten years later, I see that bear standing still in that same spot whenever I come down the mountain. The stopped conceptual mind became a memory of an experience, but it was only incrementally more helpful to understanding the nature of mind itself than when Dudjom Rinpoche had asked, *What color is your mind?* Recognizing yourself as fundamentally OK is, in Tsokyni's description, the first step. Or, as Shunryu Suzuki Roshi told his students: *You are all perfect just as you are . . . and you could use a little work.*

Maezumi Roshi

In the midst of writing profiles of American Zen teachers, I was drawn to studying with Maezumi Roshi. The Asian Buddhists that I had encountered were not consistently exceptional, but they were at ease in their own dharma skins in ways that eluded most Westerners. Their dharma felt so thoroughly digested that nothing of it stuck in their throats. Meanwhile, their earnest young heirs were still ironing their proudly displayed robes onto shiny American personalities. From 1984 until Maezumi's death in 1995, I flew to Los Angeles each Christmas Day to participate in the year-end retreat at ZCLA. For two weeks in the summer, I joined the long program at ZCLA's rural Mountain Center southeast of Palm Springs. Just watching Maezumi sit down on his zafu made the cross-country flight worthwhile. He moved with exquisite economy, not using his body to take up more space than was needed or less than was required. I learned this from breaking the rules. Zendo ethics called for—to use the Benedictine term—*keeping custody of the eyes*: protecting the mind from distractions and commentator jabber by keeping the eyes lowered. In the zendo I watched Maezumi sit, stand, and bow. I watched him lower his body to the cushion as he bent one leg at the knee and kept the other straight out before folding it onto the opposite thigh to assume the lotus position. I watched him arrange his robe, at once precise and relaxed, keeping custody of the mind that is gathered and at ease.

One summer at Mountain Center, having been especially inspired, I decided to continue past my two-week plan. The only available telephone was in the center's office, housed in a funky trailer and not always in service. Rearranging plane schedules, securing a ride to the airport, and rescheduling dates for pet care and work obligations took the better part of a day. The next morning, bursting with self-satisfaction, I explained my decision to Roshi. We were facing each other in his interview room. Roshi looked at me as if I were the most pathetic creature on the planet and said, almost inaudibly, *That is not our way.*

One of the most quoted sayings in Zen literature is: *The way is not difficult for those who do not pick and choose.* I had heard this many times, but that morning it sunk in for the first time.

For more than ten years, and always during the individual formal interviews that take place within the community meditation sessions, Maezumi Roshi had asked me, *Why don't you become a nun?* I always gave the same answer: *Roshi, if I ever become a nun, I'll join the Carmelites.*

Like many of his compatriots, Maezumi had difficulty enunciating the *r* and *l* sounds. And he seemed never to remember that this exchange had evolved into something of an annual ritual. His next question always sounded like, *Whassa Cowmowhite?*

Real nuns, I would explain, *who are removed from secular activity, living lives of contemplative, cloistered silence. They don't mix it up Zen style, having sex, making babies, living in the world with shaved heads and holier-than-thou clerical robes.*

He would smile, nod, say *I see,* and ring me out of the interview room.

A Winter in Cape Breton

In autumn 1988, I planned to spend the winter at my falling-down house in Cape Breton. Inook was on her last legs, painfully unsteady when she squatted down to pee and poop. I could easily lose her before spring. A guy I knew from the other side of town called one day. A part-shepherd pup had been hanging around the bulrushes by the pond near his cabin. They'd just stop by for a visit. No obligations. This is how I met Moses, the love of my life. Mostly German Shepherd, but with the high, long legs of a wolf, about six, maybe eight months old, still with huge paws, and comically unacquainted with interiors. He moved across the kitchen stepping onto whatever was in front of him, making no distinction between the floor, a chair, the stove, table, or the wood pile. But unlike Inook, who contin-ued to fade and remained utterly indifferent to his presence, he wanted to please, to learn, to be good, to get praised, so he was easy to train, although he was not fixed and occasionally wandered down the road.

For a couple of months, I would be joined by the American nun Pema Chödrön, the director of Gampo Abbey, the Tibetan Buddhist monastery north of Inverness that I had first visited while waiting to see if I could buy this house. As a place for meditation retreats, the abbey worked well, but administrative details, personal meetings, and the disagreements endemic to intentional communities left the director with little time for practice. We had become friends a few years earlier when she first moved to Cape Breton from Boulder, and that winter she arranged to do a retreat at my house from the middle of February until the middle of April.

By the time Pema arrived, Inook had passed on, and Moses and I were sharing the house with a winter weasel, also called an ermine, all white except for the black tip of its tail. I had gone to the Department of Wildlife to borrow a live trap but the ranger explained that if I did not have chickens or small cats, that this wonderful animal was mostly carnivorous—unlike squirrels who eat the rafters—and I'd have no trouble with rodents. He suggested that I keep it around by feeding it raw beef. Soon the ermine was eating better than Moses and was smart enough to appear only when Moses was outside. Then it would come out of hiding and eat chopped meat from my hand. Little did it know that ritual delicacies were on the horizon.

Before the retreat started, Pema spent hours constructing *torma*, Tibetan offerings made from flour and butter and dyed in bright colors. Once the preparations were completed, she circumambulated the outside of the house, accompanied by mantra recitation and the burning of juniper. I followed behind, and in this way, the house was ritually sealed. Once Pema stepped back inside, she did not leave again for the duration of her retreat. No one was allowed to enter, not even the snowplow driver whose route ended at my house and who had grown accustomed to having a rum toddy by the wood-burning stove before turning around. About every ten days I followed the plow back into town to shop for groceries.

Pema lived upstairs in an attic space, an open room with eaves that sloped down to the floor and two small windows at each of the peaked ends. Although I had banked the house with fir boughs and hay bales, frigid winds came up through the floorboards, and the winds that howled outside squeezed through the corner joints in piercing whistles. I kept the wood stove stoked all night, and the heat from coal in the old cook stove was worth the oily dust that covered the kitchen. The gravity-fed water system proved incompatible with winter dwelling, and the hoses froze almost daily despite being wrapped with insulation. The kitchen commonly

turned into a forest of black rubber tubes hanging from hooks in the rafters to thaw out into buckets before I dragged them back up the hill and
rehooked them into a holding tank, only to freeze again.

What's called by the locals *the Big Ice* had come in by the time Pema's
retreat started. The St. Lawrence Seaway does not freeze, but ice floes from
the north jam into the coastline so that as far as the eye can see—some forty
miles out—the seaway itself looks frozen. A clear sunrise over the ice turns
the sky pink and mauve, and dramatic reds and purples move in at the end of
a cloudless day. On a still, clear day after a hard snow, the world transforms
into a crystal palace. The glare off the ice made my eyes ache and required
sunglasses in the kitchen. In March, seals came onto the ice to have their
pups, and I watched through binoculars.

At arranged times, and with preapproved food choices, I carried meal
trays to the attic and placed them at the top of the crooked stairs, then
took back to the kitchen used dishes along with whatever underclothes
and socks had been left for washing. When I heard Pema come downstairs
to use the only bathroom, I hid in my study off the kitchen. Every once
in while a loud, clunkety-clunk sound came down the steps, and I learned
that I would find one of the torma offerings that the ermine had removed
from the shrine.

For seven weeks, we did not exchange a single word or once make eye
contact. While I marvel to recall our discipline, between the two of us it's
only me who has a penchant for breaking rules. But there was one commu-
nication, of sorts. I kept the telephone in my study and any conversation
took place with the door shut and a blanket over my head to muffle the
sound. One day, I got a disturbing call about Moses. I don't know what
Pema heard. It must have been something like, *Oh I am so sorry, I promise
that will never happen again, the children must be so upset to have lost their
cat, oh this is terrible, I am so sorry. . . .* The next time I went up to the attic
to retrieve the dishes, there was a note on the tray, *For Moses,* along with a
red protection cord, which I tied around his neck.

As the days went on, I became familiar with the sounds in the attic: the
chanting, accompanied by bells, gongs, and a two-sided handheld drum;
periods of silence, then chanting again. The sacred sounds reverberated

throughout the house like prayer flags strung from trees. Silence after the noon meal. Perhaps a nap. Maybe a piece of torma rolling down the steps. The days began to lose their mooring to the known world, and every sound and movement, and the work needed to maintain the routine, intensified my attention: the precious nun; the isolation of the house at the end of the road; the ice-packed sea; the chance of a flue fire or slipping on ice; the threat of not being able to walk through heavy snow down the long driveway to the road where the car was parked, or not being able to back the car out of a snow bank. With my senses on high alert, everything felt new, astonishing, and alluring, and nothing felt safe.

The extreme environment outside and my wide-awake senses made every gesture consequential. Paying attention was about survival, not an injunction to stay present in a warm, protected meditation hall tracking the mind that wanders. Paying attention to the stove, to how much dry wood was inside, to how much snow was piling up against the front door; paying attention to putting my foot down on the ice, to driving along the empty road with groceries from town. After about ten days into the retreat, all I wanted was for this sacred activity in the attic to continue uninterrupted. I had neither the aspiration nor dedication to do what Pema was doing, but I could be a mindful attendant. Everything I wanted was right here in this little Monopoly house. With my custodial responsibilities and eating leftover meals alone at the kitchen table, my small universe became bigger and bigger until on clear days, with each branch encased in ice and prism light dancing on the horizon, it seemed that luminosity itself might loosen the house from its earthbound moorings and lift it into the sky.

PART SEVEN

THE *TRICYCLE* YEARS

When the Swans Almost Drowned in the Lake

For several years prior to that winter in Nova Scotia, Rick Fields and I and a few friends on the West Coast had been talking about starting the first nonsectarian, independent Buddhist journal, a newsstand publication. The only Buddhist publications were house organs that served their own communities with notices about marriages, births, deaths, and a dharma talk by the teacher, maybe a little history of the lineage. Here in America, the land of plurality, we imagined a single forum for different schools. Buddhism was flowering; our exuberant idealism was boundless. We were children of the sixties, agents of change and proud of it. We dreamed out loud, joked around, shared our projections of what shape this enterprise might take. But before we got anywhere close to a workable plan for a real publication, the first of many Buddhist scandals surfaced. When the tremors started, we didn't know if Buddhism in North America had stabilized enough to weather the storms or would get blown out to sea. By this time, Rick's book on the history of Buddhism in the West, *How the Swans Came to the Lake,* had been well received. Rick now joked that the sequel might be *How the Swans Drowned in the Lake.*

By the mid-eighties, earnest young Americans had become middle-aged critics of their Buddhist teachers. Accusations of inappropriate sex, alcoholism, and the mismanagement of funds sent shock waves through communities in the Zen, Vipassana, and Tibetan traditions. Both accusers and defenders staked their views to orthodoxy. Accordingly, mere mortals, especially from the land of uptight white Puritanism, could not judge the behavior of enlightened teachers. No one denied that Americans were up-tight and moralistic about sex. But adherents on the other side claimed that this argument was a red herring. Forget puritanical repression: inap-propriate sex, lying, and drinking violate the Buddhist precepts, and this meant that a teacher could not be enlightened.

Until then, attempts to understand enlightenment had been approached with respectful understanding of the innate inability of the conceptual mind to comprehend the mind beyond concepts. Quite suddenly, enlightened be-havior was measured according to behavior that we liked or not, or that met with our approval or disapproval. Outrage gathered steam under the rubric of sex scandals, although specific incidents suggest that the most volatile reac-tions resulted from lies told to cover up the accusations. Feelings of betrayal left communities fractured and angry. Alcoholism and extramarital affairs got mixed up with more ambiguous considerations, such as the nature of enlight-enment and what enlightened experiences counted for, if anything, in terms of behavior that we did not like or that did not fit our ideas of what enlight-ened behavior was supposed to look like. Maezumi Roshi, married with three children, casually revealed that he was having an affair with a senior student, also married. Although he seemed peculiarly unprepared for the infuriated response, the disclosure became the flash point for long-simmering denun-ciations. Apparently, he had had affairs for some time and had been a heavy drinker. From my biannual visits to his center, I had not learned this.

According to a Tibetan proverb: *The best guru is one six valleys away.* Maezumi Roshi would be a good example of the six-valley measure, at least for me. At the same time, many senior students had worked with the chal-lenges of Maezumi's behavior, and perhaps their capacity to accommodate conduct that did not fit the model of guru perfection taught them more than anything I took away from this complicated teacher. I only know that no new information about Maezumi made me doubt his ability or his commitment to introduce me to myself; and I had no inclination to join the demand that he relinquish his role of teacher. Yet this did not dispel the confusion about how he could behave in ways that created such deep anguish for his family and his community. Under pressure from his students, he signed up for a residential rehab program but let it be known that this was not because he himself wished to be *rehabilitated*—a word that he could not pronounce. It was difficult to imagine that a mismatch of this magnitude would work—and it didn't.

In 1984, Richard Baker Roshi's affair with a married student at the San Francisco Zen Center introduced a new dimension of disruption. So far, heated confrontations had been confined to the communities, but Baker's successful courtship of the media as he expanded Zen activity in the Bay Area had made him an easy target, and when his star plummeted, his story was the first of the Buddhist scandals to enter the mainstream press.

Then came the crisis that involved Trungpa Rinpoche's American heir, Thomas Rich. Trungpa Rinpoche died in 1987, leaving his designated regent, known by his dharma name, Ösel Tendzin, in charge of the Shambhala community. Traditionally, a regent held the master's seat until the new reincarnation of the master grew into his role as lineage holder and leader. Ösel Tendzin had been diagnosed with the AIDS virus and had knowingly engaged in unprotected sex, accounting for the death of at least one partner. Apparently, Ösel Tendzin had convinced himself that receiving dharma transmission granted him immunity from the virus. By all accounts he was a brilliant teacher, making it more baffling to comprehend hubris of such tragic dimensions.

It was also reported that Ösel Tendzin had been surrounded by an inner circle of fifteen or twenty followers who had conspired to keep his illness and sexual activity secret. The revelations landed like dynamite. In dispute was the thorny question of the teacher's authority, in this case both Tendzin's and Trungpa Rinpoche's. For many students, Trungpa embodied the most treasured Vajrayana orthodoxies attributed to the enlightened guru, and these extended to unquestionable omniscience. That placed Trungpa beyond the capacity for error, infallible as the pope, and included his choice of Tom Rich as Vajra Regent. For the faithful, even the transmission of a deadly virus held unknowable, potentially positive outcomes; this made Trungpa's selection of Rich sacrosanct, and nothing could alter that. Others demanded that the organizational hierarchy immediately strip Rich of any status and authority. After Rich's death from AIDS in 1990, debates continued regarding his legacy within Shambhala.

At the Zen community in Riverdale, Glassman discouraged idle chatter, and I do not recall any open discussion about Maezumi or Baker, although nothing stopped the gossip. The Vajra Regent quagmire had a dimension of a different order. Someone had died. This occurred in 1988, in the midst of the AIDS epidemic. Those in the Vajra Regent's inner circle were worldly and educated and knew the risks. The devastating effect on Zen students in New York testified to the singular impact that Chögyam Trungpa had on Buddhism in America. Everyone had paid attention to Trungpa Rinpoche. This wasn't just anyone's dharma heir who had messed up so spectacularly. Glassman called for an open discussion.

I would like to think that I could never be ensnared in collective delusions that sanctioned harm to others. I never questioned that had I been a young German in 1933, Nazi propaganda would not have seduced me into Hitler's youth movement. But who knows. In 1978, in obedience to a charismatic cult leader, nine hundred people downed the lethal Kool-Aid in Jonestown. I might imagine that my intuitive good sense offered protection from such poisoned ideologies. But plenty of times I experienced myself going along for the ride, and the fact that the ride did not end up in Jonestown—or Ösel Tendzin's backyard—could seem more a matter of luck than discernment. I had met the Vajra Regent in Halifax in the mid-1980s and had found him arrogant and vain, but many men in his community had struck me the same way. When the crisis occurred, some of those same men stood by him, while others did not. I also knew people who defended his rank to the end and who came across as so reasonable, so lively and intelligent, that I might otherwise have sought their friendship.

While the scandals preoccupied convert Buddhists, all the house newsletters were under the aegis of the director or abbot of their respective communities, precluding any discussion of the turmoil they were in. And the brotherhood of male teachers precluded any other community's publications reporting on the scandals. The time had come to reconsider an independent journal. We would no longer be energized by idealistic and entertaining dreams of a pan-Buddhist collaboration but by an exigent need for an independent forum that could explore the dominant concerns of diverse Buddhist communities across the country. And if the swans were destined to die in the lake, at least let their obituaries be written by sympathizers, not by cynical journalists in the mainstream press.

Since the 1960s, new Buddhist communities had promoted the preeminence of their own traditions. I had already moved between the Tibetan and Zen traditions—as had Rick Fields—and I never subscribed to the superiority of one over the other or participated in the snide cracks about the other school, but I had held both in higher regard than the Theravada communities, one of which had its own sex scandal around the same time. This never blew up in the public arena, but the fact that scandals had affected all three major schools in the United States—Tibetan, Zen, and Vipassana/Theravada—placed us all in the same boat. Doctrinal differences looked petty and irrelevant by the overriding conclusion that none of us had any idea how to bring this sacred tradition into this profane society, that we did not know what a spiritual teacher was, and that we didn't actually have any idea of what dharma meant or what it meant to be practitioners. Our expectations had been so high and the disappointments so deep. And nothing could have been more salutary for calming the frenzied excitations of convert Buddhists than a swell of shared disenchantment.

Rick Fields had been in Boulder editing *The Vajradhatu Sun*, the house publication of Trungpa's community. Rick was furious and squarely on the side that strongly condemned the Regent as well as those who had colluded in keeping his illness and irresponsible sexual exploits under wraps. It was also a matter of journalistic integrity to him that *the current situation*—as it was called—be discussed in *The Vajradhatu Sun*. According to Rick, he was prohibited from doing this by the board of directors of the Shambhala community and subsequently quit his job.

Rick and I were on the phone several times a week. He was shaken to the core and just trying to process the information. Several months later, I suggested that we revisit the possibility of starting an independent Buddhist magazine. In addition to the needs within the Buddhist communities, both of us were going through personal transitions and willing to consider any outlandish scheme. Rick needed to make money, and I needed to get out of Riverdale. The Greyston Seminary had been sold in 1988, and the last of the residents had moved to a down-and-out section of Yonkers near the bakery.

Given that Rick and I lived thousands of miles apart and spent a lot of our time on the phone gossiping, nothing happened quickly. We also became implausibly enthusiastic about starting the first independent newsstand Buddhist journal from the American heartland. *Let's forget the pompous European-facing East Coast, with its uptight academic reach and intellectual pretensions! Let's forget the more obvious choice of the Asian-facing West Coast, with its granola work ethos and trippy hot tubs! Let's go to white-bread Kansas City or St. Louis or Des Moines or Milwaukee. Let's raise this Buddha baby among wheat fields and cornflakes and work the halcyon flat-lands,* which we had never visited and where we knew no one, had no contacts, and had no help to start. For me, this harked back to visions of the Midwest that had formed around Helen Boyd and had taken me to the University of Cincinnati; but then I remembered that I had cried myself to sleep there, and anyway, as a place to start a Buddhist magazine, it was a dumb idea.

In 1989, *Zen in America: Profiles of Five Teachers* was published by North Point Press. It was well-received, functioning for quite a few people as a bridge between an armchair interest in Zen and seeking out a teacher or way to practice. Personalizing real American lives with their habitual patterns, their dedication and homegrown adjustments to the tradition, provided a useful addition to Asian mountaintop masters, whose lives— not to mention their wisdom—had so often felt out of reach. It did not have the breadth and historical depth of Rick's *Swans,* but *Zen in America* bolstered my own confidence in working with words, and lent credibility to Rick and me teaming up to start a magazine.

The book also continued my childhood attempts to understand the ways that disparate sociocultural forms bump up against each other, come together, move apart, where two edges zip together or get stuck. It also provided a workable model for the magazine that became *Tricycle,* playing with the juxtapositions, alliances, and contradictions of different Buddhist traditions and how they bumped up against each other in this new pluralistic territory, and against the pervasive panorama of the contemporary world.

What strikes me now is how this book testifies to the enormous growth of Buddhism, and specifically of Zen. Not wishing to rely on a personal selection of teachers, I had created a workable category: American teachers who had been trained in the Japanese Zen tradition and had established their own centers. In 1984, this came to a grand total of seven. Two declined to be included. Today, this same category numbers in the hundreds—although the proliferation of teachers who now use the titles of *sensei* and *roshi* have diminished the status that these titles once signified.

I was in Cape Breton when a box of books arrived from the press. My summer friends had already left, but I decided to have a book party anyway. No one needed to know what I was celebrating and besides, among either summer or local friends, there was no genuine interest in Zen. The evening went on too long, too late, and with stragglers sitting around at the end trying to sober up enough to drive home. It was not a particularly joyous occasion, but I have one memory that I still cherish: a baby, maybe eight months old, crawling on the kitchen floor. That's because this baby now has two little boys of his own, and they are the fifth generation of a family that I have known for over fifty years. In an atmosphere that can so easily dissolve conventional measurements of time, and in the absence of situating my own life within past or future generations, I enjoy this counterpoint, the specificity of these little bodies growing old, again and again.

When I returned from Nova Scotia to New York, it was not to Riverdale, but to my old loft on Twenty-Second Street. A few weeks later Rick visited from Boulder. We worked at the kitchen table, some three blocks west of the building where our parents had lived fifty years earlier. We took a road trip to talk to friends about our project: a nonsectarian Buddhist magazine that would be distributed like mainstream magazines, with paid advertisements and subscriptions. This had never been tried before, and nothing in the tried-and-true business models to start a magazine, let alone a not-for-profit niche Buddhist magazine, suggested that it could ever work. Every statistic favored failure. One cautionary report claimed that 90 percent of start-up magazines that had been funded to the tune of several hundred thousand dollars in investment capital never published a second issue. In my pig-headed fashion, I took this as one more reason to disregard conventional wisdom—and am glad that I did.

Neither Rick nor I had any money. I had been living off the rent from my loft on Twenty-Second Street, but once I moved back, I needed another income. Rick's situation was compounded by chronic debt, and by having a girlfriend at the time who threatened to leave him if he did not get a job. Our project did not portend solvency. After about a year, he confessed that he had interviewed for *a real job*. I was devastated—and angry, thinking, *How dare you string me along for a year and leave me in the lurch!* He was the one with journalistic experience. I didn't know anything. I had once worked at Marvel Comics. Twice a week I had gone to the Madison Avenue office to pick up the fan mail, which I answered from my apartment on East Fourteenth Street, sending out blue cards to the boys and pink cards to the girls. Occasionally an extraordinary packet would arrive, always from a young boy, with an entire story drawn out in sequence, and I would get Stan Lee to sign a note to him. But I learned nothing about publishing and nothing about working in an office. Slowly the prospect of going forward without Rick had me repeating Bernie Glassman's refrain about starting a bakery with no expertise: *If you put your mind to it, you can do anything.*

Most important was my newfound willingness to fail. After years of meditation, I might wish to proclaim eureka insights about the essential nature of mind, or the intrinsic unity of wisdom and compassion, or transcendent moments of emptiness. My celebratory measure was a willingness to fall flat on my face. My father's death had been a big help in releasing me from a fixed identification with failure. And meditation further encouraged seeing behavior as fluid and transitory, not always stuck in habitual definitions. In the morning, I might feel like a failure; in the afternoon, I might feel like a success. Neither one defined me. Failure became just another experience, fleeting and insubstantial. It was no longer a label of immutable deficiency. Freed of thinking of myself as a failure, I was free to fail.

And if I did fail, so what? Glassman had a student named Nuncio, a Jesuit seminarian turned Wall Street broker. Nuncio had his own Zen teaching: *The So-What Sutra*. To any statement or thought, be sure to add, *So what*. I am rich and powerful: *So what*. I am small and puny: *So what*. I am unloved and miserable or happy: *So what*. I am thinking of starting the first newsstand Buddhist magazine ever. I might fail spectacularly. I don't know what I'm doing. *So what*.

Tricycle: The Buddhist Review

Lex and Sheila Hixon provided funds to hire Lorraine Kisly, a professional magazine consultant. Without Lorraine, *Tricycle* would never have left the starting gate. My loft on Twenty-Second Street doubled as the office; the kitchen table became my desk. I started working with volunteers, shamelessly trying to cajole anyone who had an interest in Buddhism into giving time, expertise, money. To my surprise, both young volunteers and job applicants cited Kerouac's *The Dharma Bums* to reference their own interest in Buddhism.

After many attempts, I finally convinced the acclaimed graphic artist Frank Olinsky to help with the design. To my eyes, this alone compensated for my audacious wheedling. For the first cover, Frank chose an improbable image of His Holiness the Dalai Lama. In 1989 the Dalai Lama had received the Nobel Peace Prize, crowning his status as an international celebrity, easily identified by his maroon robes, shaved head, and smiling, bespectacled face. Frank's choice, a black-and-white portrait by Herb Ritts, featured a three-quarter angle shot of the Dalai Lama, his head tilted back slightly and his face turned away from the camera. The image captured a timeless, layered serenity. He looks both more vulnerable than usual and more enigmatic. He is not wearing glasses, not smiling, and looks more contemplative than charming. A maroon border framed the photograph, and the cover framed the editorial approach: an unfamiliar presentation of a familiar subject; a respectful but quirky approach to content; a contemporary presentation of ancient wisdom.

We had anticipated a first print run of five thousand. By the time we went to press, that number had increased to seventeen thousand. Lorraine had carefully constructed the design and language of the first direct-mail solicitation, explaining to me, *It's easier to sell the sizzle than the steak.* The preorders paid for the first print run. The second would depend on donations, as would every subsequent issue for the next fifteen years, making fundraising a stressful and unexpected part of my job.

Spalding Gray interviewed the Dalai Lama for the inaugural issue. The paths of the revered Buddhist leader and the avant-garde monologist crossed in a hotel suite at the Fess Parker Red Lion Inn in Santa Barbara, California, on April 8, 1991. While the cover design received unequivocal kudos, the interview did not. Spalding asked the Dalai Lama about his daily meditation and his dreams; about flying, sexual desire, and death and dying. I was in the room during the interview and saw that His Holiness was totally delighted with such fresh and off-script questions. But many readers found them offensive and disrespectful, thereby characterizing me, the editor-in-chief, as woefully inept and inappropriate—an embarrassment to the fledgling Buddhist community. Among the harshest critics were influential scholars and Buddhist teachers—the very men who had identified themselves as orchestrating Buddhism in America and who had been the happy, if blinkered, heirs of a doggedly patriarchal tradition. They could not quite believe that their complete control of the Buddhist discourse in America had been punctured by, against all odds, a woman. They shook their heads, despaired, and gossiped. In turn, I learned just how conservative, conventional, and parochial educated convert Buddhists could be. My own interactions with friends in dharma communities had not prepared me for this. To some extent, I think the negative response was elicited by the exposure of the dharma on the newsstand, of wanting to make a good impression, like dressing up for a job interview and playing it safe by adhering to convention. This was especially true of the academics, and this was not Spalding Gray's style. Mine either for that matter. I already knew of the congenital misogyny in the Buddhist communities that perfectly reflected the society at large, and which was reinforced by the historic patriarchy of Buddhism from its origins in India to its spread throughout Asia. Accounts of women in the historical record were the exceptions. Fortunately, among my friends, there were also exceptions. By then Rick had a full-time job in Berkeley, a monthly salary, and medical benefits, and was generous with constructive criticism while his support never wavered. Lex Hixon marked up every line of each issue and then got me on the phone for a diligent page-by-page critique, with the understanding that no matter what, he was in my corner.

The first issue was not the first time that the magazine drew fire. That came earlier, with the name. Throughout the spring of 1991, Lorraine Kisly worked to put in place contracts with printers, distributors, and a subscription fulfillment service, as well as to secure advertisements—all for a magazine that we could not name. Carole Corcoran, a lawyer and another pro bono snare, often showed up at the loft close to midnight after her own office day ended. She would arrive looking ghostly tired, climb the rickety wooden stairs in professional high heels, and systematically review new contracts. Only one problem: *You need a name!*

Pali words such as *metta* (loving-kindness), *karuna* (compassion), *sunyata* (emptiness), and *bodhi* (enlightenment) seemed off-message for an American Buddhist magazine. Then came suggestions that elevated Buddhism to celestial remove or contained references to all things golden—threads, domes, rivers, bells, bowls, and mountains. Men who saw themselves as big fish in the little Buddhist pond argued for the most exalted titles, while women seemed to prefer names that were not English. Except for Lorraine, my suggestion of *Tricycle* was received happily by no one, placing it in equal running with other options. Buddhism in America was still in diapers, so even *Tricycle* was a stretch. Still, it's a training vehicle with associations to *Zen Mind, Beginner's Mind*, the book of Zen teachings by Shunryu Suzuki Roshi. Buddhist texts speak of turning the wheel of dharma, and Buddhist history includes three major vehicles—three turnings of the wheel. When I presented the Dalai Lama with a tiny gold tricycle and explained the various associations, he added, playing with the movable handlebars, *And relative and absolute!*

We would publicly debut *Tricycle* at the American Booksellers Association's annual trade show for ten thousand booksellers and publishers, serendipitously held that year in June at the Jacob K. Javits Convention Center in Manhattan. The day the magazine arrived from press, smelling of ink and looking shockingly gorgeous, I brought a copy to my mother at Mount Sinai Hospital. She had been diagnosed with lung cancer the previous fall, and contrary to all expectations, it was the last time I ever saw her.

The week between the press shipment and the book fair provided a break for a short vacation. For the past year, my long hours of work were often capped off with a visit to my mother, either at her apartment on Bank Street, less than a mile from my loft, or during one of her hospital stays. Clara and Richard Serra had suggested that I go with them to Iceland. Richard had completed his sculpture *Afangar* on Videy Island, off Reykjavik, and under the direction of Claude Picasso, a film crew would be making a documentary about the piece that very week, filming from boats and helicopters. My mother's condition had stabilized, and she was at home with a live-in caretaker. Two days before my departure she was admitted to Mount Sinai for excess fluid in her lungs. Her doctor encouraged me to go to Iceland, assuring me that she would be fine. To this day, I feel like a five-year-old when I think back to that conversation with the doctor. *He promised she would not die when I was away. He promised.*

I have always found it comforting that my mother died with a picture of the Dalai Lama by her side, for she loved him and had made a trip to Middlebury College years earlier to attend a conference in his presence. The weekend after she died, I joined a few volunteers at the Javits Center, all of us weighed down by shoulder sacks bulging with copies of *Tricycle*. When I wasn't hawking the magazine like a crackerjack vendor at the ballpark, I was hiding in a bathroom stall crying.

In addition to the Dalai Lama interview, the first issue featured exceptional pieces by Pema Chödrön, Lawrence Shainberg, Gary Snyder, and Thich Nhat Hanh. Yet a short excerpt from the Pali Canon—the teachings of the historical Buddha—received no notice at all. In my view, this was the most meaningful inclusion: the words of Shakyamuni Buddha on the racks of newsstands and bookstores and malls across America. In Penn Station!

A monk, when walking, knows that he is walking, when standing, knows that he is standing, when sitting, knows that he is sitting, when lying down, knows that he is lying down.

I savored the mix of contemporary poetry, art, photographs, and essays with traditional Buddhist teachings. But only this one passage from the *Mahasatipatthana Sutta* (Foundation of Mindfulness) suggested a modern version of stringing up prayer flags and calling the wind to disseminate the Buddha's good news of liberation. Maybe Buddhism really could help America become America. *A monk . . . when walking . . . knows . . . that . . . he is . . . walking. . . .*

The first issues of *Tricycle* appeared prominently displayed in the cycling sections of newsstand racks amid glossy covers of Hell's Angels on Harley-Davidsons, Tour de France champions in lizard suits, and biker porn that mixed leather, rubber, and naked women. This allowed for the thrilling possibility of a biker stumbling upon Shakyamuni Buddha describing a mind so liberated from conditioned reality that *he knows that is how it is. . . .*

For the second cover, Frank Olinsky chose an image by the artist Francesco Clemente: the left side of a flattened, androgynous face from the eyebrow to just under the lips. Inside the pupil of the enlarged eye are two crudely drawn naked figures in implied sexual union. Frank had strong opinions about using contemporary art and described the image as *tantric surrealism, simultaneously presenting the viewer and the viewed.*

Some critics decried the sexual reference to a tradition associated with monasticism. Others claimed that it promoted New York art aesthetics. Buddhists in the San Francisco Bay area were the first to complain: *Tricycle is an East Coast magazine.* When I told this to Philip Glass, who was on *Tricycle's* board of directors, he shrugged and said, *People in California always talk like that.*

In the early years of *Tricycle,* I struggled to find a still point to rest my mind between criticism and praise: *Tricycle* was the best thing that ever happened to Buddhism in America—or the worst. It upheld authentic Buddhist values brilliantly or denigrated them irresponsibly. A man who had been a close friend wrote to say how *sullied* he felt by the commercialism of the dharma. A co-director of a dharma community was incensed by the presence of ads, although he himself lived on donations and hadn't paid a light bill in twenty years. The look was too glitzy, too Madison Avenue, or not ready for prime time. The content was too intellectual or too sentimental, too Buddhist or not Buddhist enough. I remembered the up and down yo-yo teachings from Thinley Norbu: I was his smartest student and his dumbest; his most beautiful and his ugliest; up, down, up, down. *Watch your mind.* And from Bernie Glassman, another hard-learned motto: *No matter what you do, some people will like it and some people will not.*

Another lesson related to being *a difficult woman.* I wanted to *suffer fools gladly,* a virtue that I idealized precisely because it so eluded me. I could be a tough taskmaster, too often inhabiting my father's critical reactivity. I did not take kindly to missed deadlines, or errors in spacing, spelling, or shading. Each new issue astounded me, but the mistakes danced before my eyes like fireflies, illuminating every minor imperfection.

For several years I got very little sleep, either staying late at the office or staying awake trying to figure out how to make payroll. I often arrived at the office grouchy and feeling done in before the day started. One evening I had dinner with my friend Mark Epstein, the Buddhist psychiatrist, and I was speaking about the resistance to inhabiting my own authority; and that I just could not get how much affirmation my young staff needed. Mark said: *Get it, Helen. Just get it.* It was good advice, freely given. I made more of an effort to be friendlier, and I am still working on suffering fools.

At the same time, I have never known—or known of—a woman boss who was not called *difficult.* A male manager who walks through an office without smiling is considered strong, contained, concentrated, serious. For a woman boss, the mother projections demand more smiles and gestures of kindness—however insincere—than a workday could accommodate. Women with leadership histories in the workforce warned me never to hire anyone under thirty, especially men. But our salaries did not allow for an older, professional staff. Then, too, men of my generation in and out of the Buddhist world who considered themselves evolved, progressive, and sensitive were using *difficult* to describe the same women they had once labeled *bitches* and *cunts*: intelligent, strong, authoritative, independent, and outspoken—and often enough, smarter than they were. Women like me. *Bitch* sounded too plebian for these refined gentlemen; behind my back, they called me *mad barking dog. Ha, ha*—and with no inkling of what they were saying about themselves.

I got the reputation for never listening to anyone, criticism leveled by men who did not distinguish between making suggestions and telling me what to do. From a telephone message left by a prominent teacher that I had never met: *I really advise you not to name the magazine* Tricycle; an American Tibetan scholar beseeched me not to use Spalding Gray to interview the Dalai Lama; an executive in Buddhist publishing *advised* me not to use plastic sleeves for the mail orders. Another criticized the choice of a bound spine. Fine, except not taking the *advice* became tantamount to not obeying, to defying the authority, to challenging the accepted roles and rules.

In the beginning—1991, '92, '93—I had such a simple idea of what I wished to accomplish: disseminate the Buddhist teachings. Nothing esoteric. The basics. And this was happening issue after issue. There were still relatively few Buddhist books and no other Buddhist magazines, so this part was pretty straightforward, although it was never easy to get good material or to keep the content reflective of the kind of diversity we promoted. Even before *Tricycle* started, when Rick and I were constructing mock mastheads, Rick belittled my insistence on the ratio of women to men, same for Asians and Westerners. Exasperated, Rick had said, *We're not the United Nations.* Still, I counted, and once publication began, I kept tabs for every issue, compiling ratios for dead and living teachers, for excerpts and original material, for Theravada, Vajrayana, and Mahayana sources. Right from the start, *Tricycle* was perceived as being mostly Tibetan-oriented by some readers, too influenced by the Insight Meditation Society crowd by others, or *too Zen* by those who knew of my years in a Zen community. As long as that chorus stayed in harmonic balance, I figured we were on the right track. And even though the categories were often lopsided—especially with regard to gender—brilliant material filled the pages. Teachers got angry with views that contradicted their own, and academics deplored the removal of diacritics, but contrary to publishing conventions the readership continued to grow.

While the very fractures within the various communities had enabled a nonsectarian platform, they also led to a fracturing of views that had once been somewhat cohesive—if not sacrosanct. For example: the preeminent role that enlightenment played in the path of awakening. It's my understanding that the disillusionment with teachers became conflated with disillusionment about enlightenment itself. By the time *Tricycle* started, the very notion of enlightenment—the apex of the Buddha's story and what he called *the goal of this holy life*—was routinely disparaged by convert adherents. This was brought home by a particularly troubling incident that took place in the office.

Each day at noon there was a thirty-minute voluntary meditation. The numbers fluctuated and sometimes I sat alone. Any visitor to the office was invited to join, and if the visitor were a teacher, they would be asked to lead the meditation. It was not unusual for teachers to ask if they could stop by. Even those who were outspoken critics of the magazine wanted to be published in it. One day we were joined by a Zen teacher who had his own community in the Bay Area. About six of us sat on the floor in two rows facing each other in a cramped hallway area that divided the kitchen (my office) from the rest of the loft. After sitting together, a young volunteer who had been practicing at a Zen center with an elderly Korean master asked the American teacher a question about enlightenment. In response, he said, *I don't give a shit about enlightenment.*

The woman looked shocked, along with other staff members, who were mostly young and idealistic. I already knew something of the recent denigration of enlightenment, although I had never heard it expressed so crudely. I felt intensely embarrassed by him—and for him—and protective of my young staff. In my observation, he had used a current cool, hip dismissal of enlightenment as a way to disguise his own lack of awakening experiences—a trap that has caught a few tigers: after practicing for many years and having not had revelatory experiences that moved toward liberation, then best to conclude that those experiences simply do not exist; and that anyone who claims otherwise, such as those teachers who lied about sex, are defrauding the faithful.

Disparaging enlightenment also made a neat fit with a growing interest in Buddhist-oriented social activism. Helping others—personally or collectively, through volunteer work or sociopolitical networks—became a compelling path as Buddhism continued to spread within a society informed by Judeo-Christian values. It many cases, Buddhist social action programs became indistinguishable from their Christian counterparts; and rather than emphasizing the essential inseparability of helping one's self and helping others, the yearning for liberation was marginalized. Compassion became stuck in dualistic behavior, inseparable from charity, but not from emptiness—that essential ingredient that generates true altruism.

And what about Shakyamuni Buddha? To that inconvenient question, the answer from brash, unenlightened converts had become something like, *Who knows? He lived such a long time ago, and has been so mythologized, and spoke in the tongue and terms of his times that we have no idea what actually took place under the Bodhi Tree.*

Without doubt, among my own generation of convert Buddhists confusion about enlightenment ran rampant. Did it refer to an event, or a process; was it a verb or a noun; did it happen slowly and gradually or suddenly and abruptly; and what was the relationship between sudden versus gradual awakening? Was some degree of awakening the end goal of the eightfold path, or was it the necessary first step, without which the path simply became an exercise in religious dogma? What had it told us about the teachers who we felt had betrayed us? Had they not been enlightened in the first place, or did an enlightened mind rest within behavior that did not conform to conventions? These same questions still provoke heated discussions, disagreements, and conflicts—and, according to Buddhist historians, always have. My own current and personal understanding is that for those on a Buddhist path, if you are fortunate you will outgrow the questions, the concepts, and the elucidations, and place your faith in the experience of practice itself.

What sustained me throughout my years at *Tricycle* was the mission, which never, ever lost its appeal. I had no evangelical instincts and couldn't care less if someone became a Buddhist or not. I definitely enjoyed the entertaining arguments about enlightenment, but for America's first newsstand publication it was not necessary to double down on those experiences that both primed and affirmed what the Buddha called *this unshakable deliverance of mind.* Whatever doubts I had about myself, my abilities, my choices, my understanding, I never had any doubts about the benefits of introducing to a society gripped by materialism the radical idea that lasting happiness can never be attained by having more and more and more—money, cars, clothes, houses, stuff; that the mind is the source of suffering and the source of liberation; and that our daily lives can benefit from the Buddha's three foundational building blocks: investigating the reality of the so-called *self;* the suffering generated by mistaking permanence for impermanence; and misperceiving independence where none can be found. To participate in this dissemination was deeply moving, very rewarding, and I had confidence in my own integrity. I made many mistakes but still trusted my own moral compass.

When *Tricycle* began, the sociopolitical blueprint for the wave of convert Buddhism was informed by the legacy of the counterculture to the point where liberal causes became conflated with Buddhism itself, thus bolstering the incipient social action programs. Buddhism often got added to the mix of cures to fix all things: our minds, our attachments, and our society. Convert Buddhists were against racism and poverty, against apartheid in South Africa and nuclear arms, and for world peace and gender and race equality, gay rights, and protecting the environment—causes that were supported by progressives worldwide. For *Tricycle,* it made no sense to double down on views and values that were already part of the conversation when the most foundational views of dharma were truly radical and under the radar. No other magazine suggested that our very own minds were the source of suffering and the key to liberation; or offered practices as well as classical and contemporary material to work with the mind; or suggested that our minds are the *only* dependable source of refuge and contentment. In a relentlessly capitalist economy dependent on the excitation of greed and desire, nothing was more heretical than the claim that the material world would never provide reliable and lasting happiness.

Change Your Mind Day

Thinley Norbu Rinpoche used to repeat: *Useless is best*. I wanted *Tricycle* to be useful, as did everyone who contributed work, talent, and money. By the first year, the staff included Elizabeth Lees, a business administrator who had studied with Trungpa Rinpoche; and Carole Tonkinson, who had been working at the women's magazine *Mirabella*; and it would soon include James Shaheen, who had been working at *Forbes* magazine. No one earned fair-market wages, and Frank Olinsky still wasn't getting paid at all. The mission to spread the good news that suffering could actually be alleviated—and that we already had, at this very moment, exactly what we needed to realize this—was deeply felt by all of us and not considered useless.

I was thinking about *useful* versus *useless* one autumn day in 1993 as I drove east on the Massachusetts Turnpike to visit Joseph Goldstein at the Insight Meditation Society in Barre. It led to an idea about a public meditation program, not in front of the United Nations to demonstrate for peace or at a disarmament march or to protest apartheid in South Africa, but meditation without an agenda. Useless meditation.

Joseph laughed at Thinley Norbu's phrase. He also spoke of the distinction between *being, being useful,* and *using*—or *misusing*—meditation; meditation with or without a goal, with or without concern for results. We agreed that Thinley Norbu hadn't meant that meditation had no value, but that wanting anything, including spiritual aspirations, fosters grasping. I want, I want to be enlightened, to be free, to be rich and compassionate, to be kind, famous, and forgiving. Because striving for anything will entrap us in constructs, it's best to *just* meditate, without an agenda, without what some meditation teachers have called *gaining mind,* the mind that wants to add, to fix, to make things better. Yet like so much else in dharma teachings: easier said than done.

I had always wanted to fix everything, which is to say, I wished to change everything that I found objectionable, intolerable, or wrong—within or outside of myself. To enhance my image to myself and others, I could spew out advice on fixing just about anything: medical problems, romance problems, family relations. My lack of expertise didn't matter. What mattered was the need to insert myself into a conversation because the moment as it was, no matter what was going on, required my meddlesome interruption. The present moment always needed my—*useful*—help.

At the next *Tricycle* board meeting, held at Philip Glass's townhouse on the Lower East Side, I proposed a day of meditation in Central Park—free and outdoors, just like in the time of the Buddha. Teachers from different schools would present short talks and guided meditations. With a nod to Thinley Norbu, I suggested that we call it Meditation-for-the-Hell-of-It Day. The concept was enthusiastically received. But Lex Hixon emphatically argued against using the word *hell* in the name: *It's insulting! It's demeaning! It's offensive!*

Then came the debate about the budget. Central Park required fees for usage and security; we'd need a tent for speakers, money for travel expenses, and porta potties. We had no idea how many people would show up. Our Buddhist be-in might get rained out: an estimated $35,000 gone. The pragmatists were about to prevail when Philip asked, *If two people show up and one gets enlightened, what's that worth? A hundred thousand dollars? A million dollars?*

The event became Change Your Mind Day (CYM) and was a triumph. I remember the first year, introducing the speakers from a raised platform to the side of a lawn in Central Park, and looking out over a crowd of several hundred which, within a few years, grew to several thousand. I was amazed, as I had been with the first issues of *Tricycle,* to have played a critical role in bringing about anything this marvelous. I was still so unfamiliar with my own capacities and astonished by the success of any of my efforts. It was a glorious sunny day and the vibrations generated by meditations—led by, among others, Sharon Salzberg, Gelek Rinpoche, and Enkyo O'Hara Roshi, and chanting led by Lama Surya Das and Allen Ginsberg—felt strong enough to imbue the entire urban chaos of New York with a few moments of sanity. Was that in itself worth the money? Who knows. Perhaps another Hui Neng might pass by.

The sixth patriarch of Zen, Hui Neng, had been an illiterate woodcutter. One day at the market he passed a monk reciting the *Diamond Sutra,* and on hearing the reference to "the mind that abides nowhere," Hui Neng woke up. Just like that. Many Zen stories situate sudden awakening amid improbable circumstances. Whether or not these events ever took place doesn't really matter. Either way, they're a shot in the arm and energize the hidden potential for karmic connections, or for those so-called chance encounters that influence the course of our lives, even if they remain invisible. Who knows how the guided meditations impacted a young mother sitting on a blanket on the grass, her sleeping baby nearby, or a man in the throes of a life-altering decision; or how they might have inspired a person struggling to maintain their recent sobriety; or its effects on a Central Park wanderer who happened on a scene of such gentle tranquility as to carve out an oasis from the routine rhythms of urban velocity. Any one of them might be the next Hui Neng; or perhaps they were persons of more ordinary talents. Still, anyone's life might benefit by learning that the world of confusion that we take for granted is not the only world there is.

I loved that CYM was public and free, that it was so unscripted, that anything might happen, that we never knew who might stop by, and without ever knowing what might come of our efforts. No attachment to results. Within a few years, CYM was taken over by Rande Brown, an American woman who had returned to New York after living in Japan for many years, and had joined the *Tricycle* board. Under Rande's direction, CYM evolved into a multi-city, international event that continued for the following decade.

One Death After Another

The possibilities for connections to be made, even at their most invisible and unknowable, remained an uplifting dimension of Change Your Mind Day. This kind of serendipity must have come into play for Elizabeth Murray and her encounter with Zen from the retreat that she walked out of in 1980. Over the next twenty-five years she occasionally made dismissive comments about Buddhism. She could not tolerate references to reality beyond what she knew through her own senses. I loved Elizabeth, her bony, alley-cat toughness and obstinacy, her proclamations made in a soft voice with one hand on a twisted hip and her chin raised in defiance. I never tried to dissuade her from what I perceived to be her misguided blending of what she knew with all there was to know. Only after she was diagnosed with stage four lung cancer did a different relationship to Buddhism emerge. By then she and her husband, the poet Bob Holman, were living in a loft in Tribeca. Their two grown daughters had left behind empty bedrooms. I was mostly living upstate and often stayed with them when I came into the city.

Elizabeth's initial diagnosis was accompanied by emergency brain surgery. She came home from Mount Sinai Hospital with her head shaved and red crisscross incisions on her scalp that looked weirdly similar to marks made in her last paintings. On my first visit after her surgery, she asked me to join her in her daily morning meditation, bringing out from a hall closet a black meditation cushion and a black mat. And she quoted long passages from Buddhist writings that she had read in *Tricycle,* especially from a section on death and dying that had been published years earlier. At the end, I sat by her bed as she faded in and out, talking about heaven realms and black-tailed devils holding pitchforks. She asked about life after death and said that she wished to be cremated.

In May 1995, Maezumi Roshi died suddenly during a visit to Japan. He was sixty-four years old. I was in Cape Breton when I heard the news. A phone call. Then many phone calls. Then silence. Then a kind of paralysis which, sitting at the kitchen table, was easy to slide into, as nothing held together in that empty landscape. As the days went by, Maezumi's death had a disorienting impact, reminiscent of my mother's death a few years earlier. In both cases, their absence felt like the removal of a constellation in the night sky that had helped me navigate my way home. With my mother, I always knew how to thread my way back to her, whether from a distance of ten city blocks or from Asia. With Maezumi, my memories and projections of the best aspects of his mind had brought me back to my own. At some point, I understood that his death would not change that. And also, that his continued presence in my life did not lessen the sadness of his death. The day I learned that he died, I stared out the kitchen window without moving for hours, and only when it became too dark to see did tears stream forth.

Maezumi Roshi had been unequivocally supportive of my starting a Buddhist magazine. I don't believe that he ever questioned whether I was qualified or appropriate or knew enough. He simply supported the direction I was going in. If anyone put one foot forward, he was there to say, *keep going.* I spoke to him about difficulties at the magazine and my frustration with the recalcitrant, afflictive patterns of Buddhist practitioners, especially my own. Once, during a visit to Los Angeles, I spoke to him about a Zen poet who had taken offense to an article. This man already had a reputation for cranky opinions and picking small battles. Maezumi knew him quite well, but during our conversation, he said little. However, the day I arrived back in New York, Maezumi telephoned and, referring to the poet, said, *Try to remember: that's just who he is.*

Don't take it personally. Sometimes it was hard not to. Impossible. But there were also situations that made this lesson easier. Among my most vociferous adversaries were men I had known for decades—and had known well enough to be familiar with their own career challenges and disappointments. Now in our fifties, our trajectories were gliding in opposite directions. I had had no public achievements prior to publishing my book on the Zen teachers in my late forties, and after that I started *Tricycle*. Meanwhile, several of these old friends were in the throes of midlife meltdowns, just beginning to recognize that the ambitious goals they had set for themselves as self-assured young zealots were fading away. In my younger years, I had been too beset with doubt and self-deprecation to even imagine stepping into the smallest of public arenas. And then it took longer to stand by the virtues of being *a difficult woman*. By now, I had (more or less) outgrown my sense of failure while theirs was just settling in. Friendships fractured, and the anguish of these estrangements was exacerbated by the early deaths of Maezumi Roshi, Rick Fields, and Lex Hixon, three men whose reliable support had nourished me through some very rough times.

A few months after Maezumi's death, Lex Hixon died from cancer at age fifty-three. He was born on Christmas Day and died on All Souls' Day. Soon after his death, I dreamt that Lex was terminally ill and that he and Sheila had moved out of their spacious house in Riverdale with its spectacular views of the Palisades in order for Lex to live closer to the hospital. In the dream, I was with them in a large, dark, depressing apartment above an elevated train line in the Bronx. Cardboard boxes crowded the rooms. I was there to help them unpack and to arrange for doctors' appointments and transport services. Books, clothes, and dishes spilled out onto the floors, and in the midst of this chaos, the telephone rang. I answered. It was Maezumi Roshi calling to inquire about Lex. Overwhelmed, I told him, *Roshi, there are so many details.* And Roshi said, in his low growl, *It is all details. There is nothing but details!*

The following year my uncle Alain died in Paris at age ninety-three.

Although he had developed Alzheimer's and had lost his vision to glaucoma, he had remained at home. His impeccable manners served him well as his dementia increased. Years after my mother died, he would ask dozens of times in one hour, *How is your mother?* As each instance hit the same gracious note of genuine concern, I was happy to respond, even with my aunt Biala, grumpy and aggrieved, yelling, *Her mother is dead, mon cher!*

For the next three years, until her own death at ninety-six, Biala lived in her small house, increasingly depressed and debilitated by a stroke. In the fall of 2000, I flew from New York to Paris, after consulting with Pema Chödrön, who was staying at my house in Cape Breton. Throughout the 1990s Pema spent more time at my house than I did, often arriving from Gampo Abbey with an attendant for long stretches, and taking care of Moses while I stayed glued to my desk at the *Tricycle* office in New York.

I arrived in Paris on a gray Friday afternoon. Biala and I sat on the sofa in the dimming light. I took her hand and, following Pema's advice, told her that she did not have to stick around any longer than she wanted, that she had lived a wonderful life, an extraordinary life, that she had been blessed by loving relationships and had spent her days making beautiful art, that everything had been taken care of, that Hermine and I would carry out her wishes, and that she should feel free to leave this world. She remained mute and motionless.

Together we picked at dinner prepared by the housekeeper: frozen potato balls and other inedibles from the packaged food section of the local market. After the housekeeper prepared Biala for bed, I went into her room and lay down beside her in the dark. I repeated everything that I had said earlier, emphasizing that she had lived a wonderful life, that everything had been taken care of, and that she should feel free to leave whenever she wished. She fell asleep as I whispered on. The next morning at the breakfast table her heart gave out, and she collapsed against me.

9/11

After several years on the *Tricycle* publishing staff, James Shaheen took over my job as editor. The first time I met him, *Tricycle* was still located on Twenty-Second Street. I had already moved out, taking my pets with me, but Lorraine Kisly had just acquired a squirmy shepherd puppy, and the kitchen—which still doubled as my office—was swathed in wee-wee pads. James interrupted his workday in the editorial division of *Forbes* magazine to come for an interview. He wore a suit and tie and sat on a narrow wooden chair, his briefcase perched on his lap and his feet drawn in, away from the puppy's obsession with his shoelaces. His full face had an abundant sweetness, and his dress and polite demeanor suggested he had anticipated a *real* interview at a *real* office. Meanwhile, either Lorraine or I kept jumping up to clean a new mess, change a pad, wash the floor, find the spray deodorizer, wash our hands, and return to the table. All three of us pretended that this was a normal job interview. Presciently, I figured that anyone willing to leave their job at *Forbes* to work with us would be a good fit.

In the spring of 2001 James and I planned to work together through the following two issues, and then I would become executive director, code for fundraiser-in-chief. His first issue as editor was scheduled to go to press on October 6, 2001. I would be available to help—from Nova Scotia.

In Cape Breton I had a neighbor, Margaret MacDougal, a widow who lived four miles down the road, and who kept the television on day and night and liked nothing better than alarming news. I had no television, rarely listened to the radio, and Marge MacDougal made a mission of relaying news that she thought I needed to know. Over the years I had received warnings of two jailbirds in Michigan, heavily armed and heading east; hurricanes in the Bahamas that might head north; and an errant iceberg off Labrador capable of sinking our island. Her warning at 9 A.M. on September 11—*a plane that they're saying might be a terrorist attack*—sounded more Margaret MacDougal than Canadian Broadcasting.

Hermine and Bob had been drinking coffee at their house on the other side of town and had heard the news on the radio. Myles Kehoe, who pulled up in his pickup to help close my house for the season, had also been listening to the radio. The second tower had been hit. I called James. He and most of the *Tricycle* staff, walking toward the office on Vandam Street in Tribeca or emerging from the subway stations at Spring or Canal, had watched the plane hit the second tower and then watched the towers come down. Hermine called back to tell me that the Pentagon had been hit. Myles found a bottle of Scotch and sat near enough to wrap his arms around me. I talked to James once more before New York lost phone contact.

For the next three days, I watched television at Danny and Kathleen's. Danny was Margaret's son, a fisherman, and lived with his wife in the house adjacent to his mother. We were joined by an artist from New York who had been using Joan Jonas's house. None of us had met him before and didn't even know his name. It didn't matter. He was from New York City and was in Cape Breton and he didn't have a television. He and I sat weepy and speechless, watching the towers fall again and again while Danny and Kathleen cooked for us, brought pizza from town, served drinks, and made tea. At Hermine and Bob's, the neighbors arrived with casseroles, as they do for a death in the family, and platters of date squares.

After several days James called. *Tricycle* was in the barricaded zone. The office would remain in lockdown for another week. I asked how he was going to handle the terrorist attack in the magazine. He reminded me that our turnaround time from when the magazine went to the printers to when it arrived on newsstands and in mailboxes was a full six weeks. *By the time we come off press, it'll be old news,* he said. James had three weeks to close his first issue, and he sounded shell-shocked. I had my bags packed, but the borders had been closed, and at the St. Stephen-Calais crossing between New Brunswick and Maine, cars were backed up for miles. *James, it'll be with us until the day we die.* First silence, then a choked, muffled sound, and we agreed to talk later. By the time he called back he had mobilized a special 9/11 section and had invited teachers to comment. With harrowing prophetic vision, my brother-in-law, Bob Moskowitz, had made a series of paintings in the early 1980s of planes flying into the World Trade Center Towers. Bob arranged to get a print to the *Tricycle* office.

Buddhists filled online blogs with posts about compassion and loving the enemy, about emptiness and non-duality. Nothing sounded incorrect exactly, but not quite sincere either. Knee-jerk Hallmark platitudes, well-intentioned, professional Buddhism at its most hollow. Of course, nobody knew what to say. Pretending to be cool was one of my specialties, but in the aftermath of 9/11, I didn't wish to be anywhere but within my own fear and nausea. By the time I returned to the city, my friend Joan Oliver had already investigated volunteer options, and together we signed up through the Salvation Army to work at the site. Joan had been the editor of *New Age Journal* in Boston, and after she moved back to New York City in 1999 we worked together at *Tricycle*. Now, side by side, from within mobile kitchen trucks, we served enormous helpings of hot meat loaf, mashed potatoes, and spaghetti to lines of exhausted rescue teams. Altruism merged with judgment and pride. Volunteering even felt heroic, and I became annoyed by what I perceived to be the selfishness of friends who did nothing. I also found a genuine solace in placing my body close to the smoldering remains and was reminded of the angry American I had encountered in Cambodia some forty years earlier, who, in my imagination, felt compelled to cozy up to the horror.

It seemed unimaginable that a shred of benefit could emerge from the wreckage. Yet volunteering at Ground Zero confirmed that, as every Buddhist teacher had reiterated, goodness *is* our true nature. As often as

I had heard this, read this, tried to be this, only with 9/11 did this truth completely penetrate: that mind states defined as *normal,* such as anger, despair, desire, and greed, have been misidentified as immutable, inherent components of our identity, and this misperception obscures and distorts our essential, inherent altruism. This was my experience of 9/11, brought home with particular poignancy at the site: the contrast between the machinations of destruction and the spontaneous compassion that poured forth in response. The destruction had been carried out through laborious planning and strategizing; it required coordination, education, an ideology, and technology. Demolishing the Twin Towers verified a masterpiece of coordinated skills and calculations. In response, the empathetic heart burst open, prompting strangers to weep and embrace in public. I had placed a bouquet of flowers in front of the opened doors of the fire station on Tenth Street west of Greenwich Avenue and fell into the arms of a weeping fireman when he walked up to thank me. There was not enough time for this open heart to arrive from anywhere but from within. No agenda. No preconditions. It was so obviously already there, intact, fully matured, waiting to see the light of day. Just like the wish to help all sentient beings that started at the wishing well at the petting zoo when I was a little girl. How had I allowed the conventions of the confused world to obscure this dimension of being? How many times had I sat in Maezumi Roshi's interview room and listened to him repeat, with rasping insistence, as if trying to push this unyielding truth through my thick skull: *You are nothing but the Buddha, the Dharma, the Sangha.*

Taking a Different Seat

Breathe.
Breathe.
Push the breath down and hold it.
Sink your butt.
Straighten your back with the breath, not the shoulders.
Relax.
Keep your mind relaxed.
Focus.
Trust.
Body follows mind.
Mind follows breath.

I was the oldest and least experienced rider in the clinic. Some traditional instructors held to the emphasis on control and the alpha-beta dynamic between rider and horse. More often, a progressive generation of trainers sounded influenced by Eastern philosophies. I had bought Jupiter, an Icelandic gelding, from a farm in Nova Scotia named Mandala. One riding instructor also taught tai chi. Horse and rider were not one, not two. If you trusted the horse, the horse trusted you. Exercises proved that when your mind wandered, your horse became confused. If you spaced-out altogether, the horse might just stop and wait for you to collect yourself—collect your mind.

I had rented a small attic apartment in the hamlet of Rensselaerville, in southern Albany County in upstate New York. From here, I returned to the *Tricycle* office several days a week. I left Jupiter in Canada and bought another Icelandic, a blue dun named Joa, and was boarding her at a farm nearby. Early one morning I was riding through the woods when a deer darted in front of us. Joa reared and pivoted midair, and I came off in a torqued flip.

To a mind as wild as my own, dangerous circumstances helped keep my attention on the present. In a meditation session the mind wanders away, then comes back. The return to wherever you intended to place the mind—the breath, an image, or the mind itself—anchors the practice. That's when you awake to where you are. *Oh, I became distracted. I got lost. Come back.* But once you are thrown from a horse, with the breath punched out of your lungs, and you're no longer daydreaming even if you had been, you have already come back to this very moment, and you are nowhere else but gasping for air. That moment is always alive and terrifying, but my life with horses has never been more endangered than it was on that ledge in Nepal.

Nowadays I share my time in Cape Breton with two Icelandic horses. I have learned from them about the common fear that horses have of ground water. On occasion, I have dismounted to lead a horse through a wet patch, like the Tibetan who rescued me in Nepal. I have made miscalculations that put me and my horses in danger, but nothing close to that time near the refugee camp. I often go out to the field behind the barn at sunset to hang out with the horses, and I've told them the story of the ledge a hundred times, as if repetition might exorcise my fear.

For several years I paid more attention to a straight back and the movement of breath through horseback riding than through formal meditation. Sitting on a horse actually felt like a more potent way to release the self-preoccupied mind than sitting on my black cushion. I had continued to meditate every morning, but with more apathy than enthusiasm. My attempts to know spaciousness and to stay steady within vastness too often led to being spaced-out.

A woman at the Zen Community of New York had told me that she would be leaving Glassman to practice with another teacher. As if reading my biases, she explained, *Look, I know that the teacher I have chosen doesn't hold a candle to Glassman's understanding. But she can lead me through the baby steps in ways that he can't.* I wondered if I could have made the same decision. I wanted my teacher to be the most enlightened Buddhist on the block and did not know if I could trade this for a lesser version of greater value. I also had still been working too much to find out. But by 2002, I was spending less time in the office, and I signed up for a one-week retreat with Tsoknyi Rinpoche, a charismatic young Tibetan teacher.

PART EIGHT

WHERE IS YOUR MIND?

Return to Vajrayana

From upstate New York, I drove to Wisdom House, a former residence for Catholic nuns in Litchfield, Connecticut. It was my first retreat in several years. I had forgotten how relaxed the Tibetan atmosphere could be compared to Zen meditation halls. People moved and stretched amid pillows, colorful pashmina shawls, and notebooks that were scattered in disarray, and talked, with permission, during meals. I missed the security of rigid Zen rules; even breaking them meant I knew what they were. I was taken with Tsoknyi's warmth, his humor, and his accessible delivery of subtle wisdom, but in that particular retreat he mostly conjured the emptiness realms, and his teachings affirmed that diving into absolute reality was too spacious for what I needed at that time. Nonetheless, it reoriented me toward the Tibetan tradition.

The following year, I signed up for Gampo Abbey's winter retreat, a six-week program smack in the middle of severe Cape Breton winters, when full-time community members are joined by about thirty visiting participants. Pema Chödrön taught daily, and senior residents gave classes on the precepts and Buddhist monasticism. Visitors had the option of taking temporary ordination for the duration of the retreat. This included wearing the prescribed robes for novices, and abiding by the five primary precepts: to refrain from killing, stealing, lying, intoxicants, and sexual activity. (In lay precepts, the last vow translates into *sexual misconduct*.) The option of temporary ordination also included the head-shaving ceremony. Among women, aversion to being bald was the most dominant obstacle to temporary ordination. It's such a visceral affront to vanity—matched only by the pride that arises with doing it.

My attraction to the program specifically related to the ordination ritual, so there was no doubt about which mode to choose. I would be noting my sixtieth birthday during the retreat, and had vowed that when my hair grew in, I would no longer color it. I broke that vow at about an inch, just long enough for the dye to hold.

While this retreat had never been about testing the possibility of lifelong ordination, it fulfilled a longing to dip into this ancient ritual, a baptism of sorts, a submersion into the continuous stream of the Buddha's teachings. The emphasis on community encourages support for each other in an outrageously radical perception of reality, of self, of one's own mind as creator and destroyer, of the inseparability of compassion and emptiness. With ordination comes a ritualized invitation to be in communion with the millions who have gone before you in maroon robes, in black, blue, and gray robes, in ochre and white robes, men and women who, guided by the Buddha's teaching, have committed to edging toward sanity through layers of misperceptions and afflictions. It's a short ceremony of boundless dimensions and can be especially inspiring when the experience of living dharma practitioners disappoints with such regularity. But we are Buddhists, not Buddhas. *We are only human,* sighed Harold Talbott on a visit to Marion. Yet this ritualized obeisance to the Buddhist path can transform what it means to be human. Or what kind of human you wish to be.

Mingyur Rinpoche

During the retreat with Tsoknyi Rinpoche I learned that on several occasions he had been accompanied on his US tours by his brother, Yongey Mingyur Rinpoche, ten years younger. Students familiar with both brothers confided that Mingyur's teachings were by the book, undigested, perfunctory, not the real deal like his older brother's. Nonetheless, in the spring of 2005 I happily accepted an invitation to a dinner party in New York City for the younger brother. Through some combination of differences in training, schools, previous incarnations, karma, and what we might call *personality,* Tsoknyi's delightful social ease was not shared by his kid brother. Tsoknyi Rinpoche was a married lama with a wife and children and a head of thick black hair. Mingyur was a celibate monk with a shiny, shaved head, gold-wire-framed eyeglasses, and a stiff-backed formality. His manner was crisp. Even his robe looked more precisely pressed than that of the average lama. About twenty people attended the buffet dinner in an informal Soho loft. For much of the evening, the honored guest sat to the front of a couch, his knees close together, his hands folded primly on his lap like a British schoolboy. Quiet. Contained. Nothing felt consequential, but I took note when he mentioned plans to lead a retreat at Gampo Abbey in the coming summer.

Two months later, I once again made the sixty-mile drive along Cape

Breton's west coast and joined the abbey's resident community for five days. In the shrine room, with its windows facing the water, I listened as Mingyur Rinpoche asked one question in dozens of different ways: *Where is your mind?*

His hands, with their elongated elegant fingers, moved rapidly as if trying to keep pace with his quick, incisive sensibility. *Where is it now? Now? Show me where. Show me now.* His questions did not sound abstract but grounded, forceful, interactive, engaging. *You, where is your mind?* He led exercises that involved seeing, looking, feeling, hearing, touching, sending forth razor-sharp questions. Ping. Ping. *Say you have a pain in your knee. Place your mind on the pain. Now where is the pain? Where is your mind? Is your mind on your knee? Is your knee in your mind? Same or different?* Insistent. Assertive. Alert. Poking, pointing.

The precision felt like manna, exactly what I needed. The exercises pointed to the essential emptiness of all phenomena, but the questions felt substantial in their specificity and insistence and visceral impact. I concluded that this was the teacher I needed to keep me attuned to the difference between spaciousness and spacing out.

I was also attracted to what I knew of Mingyur's circumstances: the baby *rinpoche* (he was then thirty years old) relegated to the shadows of the magnetic older brother. I imagined a small scene, marginal, without the hoopla of guru theatrics. By the time I understood that I had gotten this part completely wrong, it no longer mattered. What did matter is that I had made this connection in Cape Breton, and this took on its own auspicious dimensions, as if my continued intimacy with this island had delivered this sacred bond, making it explicitly true and blessed. The following winter I began attending his annual retreats in Bodh Gaya, India.

Under Mingyur Rinpoche's guidance I resumed foundational practices that I had started with Dudjom Rinpoche, so that my entry into senior citizenship was accompanied by one hundred full prostrations each morning. Mingyur Rinpoche provided much more information about these practices than anything I had received thirty years earlier; or maybe I was ready to hear the same teachings in a different way. I had started prostration practice with a completely dualistic view: I, Helen, over here, was bowing to the Buddha on the pedestal over there. I had not understood the practice as a way of closing the illusory separation between here and there, between I and other, between me and Buddha. I had not understood that from the very beginning, practice could be undertaken from a non-dualistic starting point—that, for example, the Buddha that I was instructed to bow to was none other than the true nature of my own mind; and which is, in essence, no different from the mind of any sentient being, including the gurus and buddhas.

Once I returned to the Vajrayana tradition, with its numbers, and spheres, and complex logical systems, I concluded, as I had years earlier, that learning *about* Tibetan Buddhism was not my path. That made it even more important to keep asking: *Is this practice working? How do I know? How can I tell?* Full prostrations worked. They weren't *about* devotion and submission to the best of oneself, but rather embodied these states in ways that rendered texts and words irrelevant. It's hard to maintain habitual aggression and arrogance when you are stretched out flat on the floor. Later, perhaps on a tea break, I might become smug about my accomplishment—*Imagine, at my age! Full prostrations!* There were other, less athletic positions I could have used, but I was too proud. I secretly believed that full prostrations accumulated more points on some crackpot karmic scoreboard even though that was exactly the kind of magical thinking that I had expected to outgrow. I'm always shocked by the tenacity of beliefs that developed in elementary school. I can still see it: the poster with the names of my classmates, and beside the names little gold stars to reward good behavior. At PS 40, it was a foregone conclusion that my name would never appear on the poster of merit, but I would try to earn merit with full prostrations—until I came to accept that bowing uncovers the mind of humility and devotion carried out with arrogance and pride. As Mingyur Rinpoche said to me: *If you didn't have arrogance and pride, you would not need to do the practice. How else could you do it?*

Change I Could Believe In

Mingyur Rinpoche's 2009 winter retreat in Bodh Gaya started on January 20. I arrived a day late, after attending President Obama's inauguration. The previous fall I had signed up to canvass in a state too close to call and had been assigned to Ohio. At Cleveland headquarters a young woman flipped through a Rolodex of local residents who had offered to provide lodging for out-of-town volunteers. I moved into a modest house owned by a middle-aged man, divorced, with grown children. He had a girlfriend, but the house still had the trimmings of a bachelor pad: Chinese takeout containers toppling the garbage can, empty beer bottles staining the green felt of the pool table, a scuzzy bathtub, and the smell of marijuana. He did his best to make me comfortable in a small attic bedroom vacated by one of his kids and proved to be a companionable host.

Each morning I drove two miles to a campaign office in a white working-class neighborhood. It was run by young staffers with volunteers of every age. One man in his midthirties had returned to his hometown from a corporate job in China. Elderly women showed up at the office with casseroles, lasagnas, and pans of brownies. On every block, more than half of the small homes had *For Sale* signs in front or boards across the doors indicating that the mortgage holder had taken possession of the premises. With few exceptions, we were greeted with polite disinterest.

Obama had inspired me to give up an autumn in Nova Scotia, drive to Ohio, and move into the house of a man I had never met. Yet when confronted with a weary occupant residing among the foreclosures, the cheery words of electioneering sounded mealymouthed and insincere. Many of those who opened their doors on a midmorning weekday were men in their thirties and forties. Broken toys littered the narrow concrete walkways that let to their one-story homes. They wanted jobs and had no reason to trust *change we can believe in*. But the volunteers believed it, and when the votes were counted on election night we were gratified to learn that our district had gone Democratic.

When Clara Serra invited me to join her for the swearing-in ceremonies in Washington, I did not hesitate to delay my flight to India. Clara had tickets for a reserved section at the bottom of the west front of the Capitol, facing the National Mall. It was a glorious sunny day and bitterly cold. We took the train to Washington and walked among triumphant crowds to the Mall, past checkpoints that allowed us to enter the crowded grounds designated by her tickets. But we became separated when Clara, unbeknownst to me or to the legions of security guards, crawled under a fence to get closer to the swearing-in ceremony. When we met up again at Union Station, we shared our accounts of a jubilant day and, continuing the celebration, rode home in first class and drank champagne.

The next night I flew to Delhi and the following morning caught a flight to Gaya in the northeastern state of Bihar, the most impoverished district in all of India. From there, I took a taxi to Bodh Gaya thirty minutes away, arriving at Tergar Monastery tired and jet-lagged but still exhilarated from witnessing America's historic moment. I had left behind a country that I loved in hands that I trusted and felt energized to get on with the indispensable work of inner change. I had not acquired Harold Talbott's instinctual feel for the essential inseparability of the sacred and profane, but I had outgrown the disorientation of moving between the divergent spheres of my childhood. I had come to enjoy abrupt social dislocations and even, as on this occasion, to court them. And if many of the unemployed workers in the Ohio neighborhood where I had canvassed did not believe that Obama could change America for the better, I did, and that enthusiasm extended to thinking, as I had for decades, that Buddhism too could be an agent for change we could believe in.

Bodh Gaya, 2009

It wasn't just Washington, DC, that was particularly cold. The winter of 2009 was one of the coldest in Bihar's recorded history. The government ordered bonfires to be lit along the roadways to help the homeless, which did not prevent dozens of people throughout the northern regions from freezing to death. The retreatants gathered in the unheated main hall. None of us (or the resident monks) was mortally threatened by the weather, but we arrived for our sessions in layers of long johns and jackets and wrapped in blankets removed from our beds; even then, the dense wet fog that had settled over this area seeped deep into our bones. In the courtyard dining area, we huddled over the steam from noodle soups.

Dozens of students, including a contingent of Chinese speakers and another from Mexico, had made an annual pilgrimage to Bodh Gaya for the winter retreat, and despite the physical discomfort the reunions were warm, convivial, and sustained by mutual immersion in the study text for the retreat, *The Way of the Bodhisattva*. This classic manual for cultivating the mind of enlightenment was originally expounded by the Indian monk Shantideva in the eighth century at Nalanda, the renowned Buddhist university not far from where we were. To inspire young acolytes, Shantideva pivots between the fearsome consequences of ignorant self-preoccupation and the lasting benefits of a selfless path of wisdom and compassion. Yet it's Shantideva's graphic descriptions of everyday human behavior which harms oneself and others that makes this text so topical. Anger? Laziness? Greed? Despondency? *Shantideva, might you be talking about me? To me?* Fourteen hundred years after this teaching was first delivered, Shantideva was reaching into my heart and mind through layers of clothing, defenses, and recalcitrant habits.

During the retreat Mingyur Rinpoche asked for my help in putting together a chapbook on the foundational practices for his non-Tibetan students. This modest request became a 350-page book, *Turning Confusion into Clarity: A Guide to the Foundation Practices of Tibetan Buddhism*. My role as co-writer entailed translating Mingyur's broken English and maintaining his animated explanations while restructuring the grammar of every sentence.

Sherab Ling Monastery

The previous year, I had stopped working for *Tricycle* altogether, leaving me to wonder if any work would ever be as meaningful as my years with the magazine. From the moment Mingyur Rinpoche asked for my help, I never questioned that again. The following November I returned to India to work with him at Sherab Ling, a monastic complex in the northwestern state of Himachal Pradesh. He first came here at age eleven, and two years later began the traditional three-year retreat. In the fall of 2009, he was in residence to participate in teachings by the abbot, Tai Situ Rinpoche, the last of his four primary teachers still alive.

The monastery covers fifty to sixty acres of valley below the southern range of the Himalayan foothills. The paved road to the main area passes through a veritable forest of prayer flags. Thousands of small white and colored flags flutter from lines that crisscross the road and run through the forest for about a half a mile, creating a kind of tunnel of transformation.

At Sherab Ling I stayed in the old guesthouse, a modest three-story building opposite the main hall. Its cheerful, blue-painted exterior belied the crumbling state of its concrete frame. There was an internet café on the grounds that was often crowded with monks, and on occasion I sent out group emails. After my mother's death, I did not expect my letters to be saved, but I later discovered that Hermine had saved a few. Describing life at Sherab Ling in November and December 2009, I wrote:

> Every day that I have been here I have spent 1 to 2 hours doing interviews with Mingyur Rinpoche. His rooms are in the main monastery. This is a huge fortress of a building, four stories high, dark red with colorful Tibetan-style decorations around each of the many windows, doors, etc. There are about 800 people living on the grounds here and about 400 to 500 monks doing the annual three-month retreat inside this building.
>
> In order to get to Mingyur Rinpoche's rooms I have to go through the immense ground floor hall—a courtyard covered with a kind of white plastic dome, with temples and residences opening off the corridors on each level. My interviews are scheduled for either midday or 6 p.m., when the monks are not in formal sessions, but there are always dozens of industrious young monks doing full prostrations on the main floor. The light that filters through the dome gives the room a kind of smoky, sepia quality, which only adds to an already vibrant impression that I have walked into old Tibet.
>
> I feel totally privileged to be here and to be doing this work. There are days when I feel a little overwhelmed by the material or feel seriously handicapped by not knowing any Tibetan. I know the rudiments of the practice but cannot be flexible or playful or creative with the language. That will have to come later, because Mingyur Rinpoche's English, while becoming increasingly communicative, is still much too limited to apply in any way that approaches literal usage.

Between the monastery and the guesthouse there was a path through a gully that functioned as a shortcut alternative to the road that wound around the grounds. The grade was steep, and navigating it resembled walking down three or four flights of stairs and then up another five. From a letter to Hermine:

On some days, a troop of monkeys commandeer the bottom of the gully by the stream. I don't find them particularly cute or attractive and am a little afraid of them. There is also an amazing pack of large black dogs in front of the guesthouse. They look like Lab-Newfie mixes, common in Nova Scotia but very different from the average Indian dog. Perhaps they have some Tibetan Mastiff. They are quite beautiful. There is one that I am cultivating in hopes that he will walk with me to the monastery—especially on those times when I have to return in the dark.

The other evening, I came running up the last set of steps and arrived at the dining area of the guesthouse out of breath. A man from Canada who has come here over many years asked if I was OK. I said I was fine but that I was uncomfortable coming up from the gully after dark and had been running.

"Are you afraid of the leopards?" he asked.

"Leopards?" I had been thinking of monkeys.

He went on to say that he had not heard of any leopard sightings for a long time. But then a Danish woman who lives in nearby Dharamsala said that a leopard had been seen near the town last year.

After a few more evenings I asked the English-speaking custodian of the guesthouse if the shortcut from the monastery was safe at night. "Oh yes, completely safe," he said. Then he paused for a minute before adding, "Only one problem: the pig."

"The pig?"

"One pig."

"Is it a wild pig?"

"Wild pig, what means?"

"A pig with tusks, with horns that come out of its face."

"I don't know. I never saw. I only heard."

That made me laugh so much that I was less afraid to walk back to the guesthouse in the evenings. However, an update confirmed that the pigs were indeed wild, big, and no laughing matter. And a few days before I left

Sherab Ling, several people sighted a leopard on a hillside near the road to Dharamsala.

The guesthouse was freezing cold. I slept in a down jacket and fleece cap, under my quilt and the quilts from the two unoccupied beds in my room. From a letter to Hermine:

The past 10 days have been grey and cold. I miss the sun and the delicious (and only) warmth it provided. The attempt to have a heater in my room has turned into a saga. Tsultrim, the really adorable guesthouse manager, knocked on my door one evening with a small heater that blows hot air through electric coils. I had been particularly bundled up at dinner, wearing my fleece cap and mitts—and I'm never without my down coat. The heater was a lovely offering. Except that after about 6 minutes, the fuse blew in my room. On the second attempt, the fuse for the whole floor blew. Tsultrim said he would call the electricity man to fix the circuits. But the next day, electricity man was not around. Then electricity man had to go to a wedding. And then to a funeral. Finally, one day electricity man showed up and did some work on the outlets. But no heater materialized. Then yesterday, which was particularly overcast and dreary, Tsultrim arrived with a heater. He was very pleased and said, "Now, no problem."

I turned it on this morning when I got out of bed in the dark, and after about 30 minutes it came to a halt. The heater itself seems to have died. So that's it for now. Tsultrim left for Mussoorie for a few days. Some problem with his sister, who, I was told by local gossips, is pregnant and not married.

During this time, the monks were doing a particular practice that required them to remain in total silence. They were quite chatty by inclination, so the absence of sound around the main hall and on the paths felt both eerie and comical—as if the soundtrack of a movie had been turned off. I continued my daily meetings with Mingyur Rinpoche, but he explained that because of the special teachings we could only talk about dharma—which, the moment he said this, struck both of us as hilarious, as we only had one subject.

Those months at Sherab Ling remain among the best I have ever known. I was unusually relaxed and, despite the cold weather, unusually cheerful, and I went through my days free of worry. I loved the beehive thrum of monastic activity: the chanting, the gongs, the trumpets, the giggling and scurrying and adjusting of robes. I loved looking up into crystal clear skies and at shining white peaks, and my days were infused with a somewhat giddy disbelief in my good fortune to be doing this work.

In the summer of 2010, Mingyur Rinpoche announced his plan to enter a solitary retreat the following year, and he began making arrangements to be away for at least three years. That winter I spent several months in Nepal to continue interviews for the foundational practice book, and in April 2011, we completed our work together at his monastery in Bodh Gaya. By now, word of Rinpoche's plans for long-term retreat had spread, making him the most popular attraction in this holiest of towns. Everyone wanted his blessings before he disappeared.

Mingyur's house sat behind the main temple. We worked in a large room on the second floor, with shelves of cloth-wrapped books and gold statues; large *thangkas* (Tibetan Buddhist paintings) hung on the walls, and thick Tibetan carpets covered the floor. In this room, Mingyur received guests. Several hours each afternoon had been set aside for our meetings, yet throughout the day, every day, every few minutes, an attendant knocked on the door to announce a visitor. Or fifty or eighty visitors. Lamas from all over India or the northern regions came to see him, along with busloads of Bhutanese pilgrims, families from Sikkim and Ladakh, Westerners from North America and Europe, and students from Hong Kong, Taiwan, and Indonesia. Rinpoche always motioned for the newly arrived to enter. Each time, I gathered my computer, tape recorder, papers, pens, and walked thirty feet to the back of the room. Then watched.

What I saw was a young, small, bespectacled lama in maroon robes, seated cross-legged on a wide armchair. On a low table before him, trays of small clay Buddha figurines sat adjacent to a basket of blessed red strings. Very long lines might be waiting on the stairs and in the lower reception area.

Each person who entered prostrated to Rinpoche, either making the full flat-out bows, or bowing on their knees, or a standing bow from the waist. Each person presented him with a ceremonial scarf, each person lowered their head so that he could place the same scarf around their necks and touch his head to theirs, and then he gave each one their good-luck amulet and a red string to tie around their throats or wrists, all the while smiling. One afternoon I tallied over four hundred visitors and then lost count, but I never stopped watching from my post at the back of the room: Mingyur smiling, welcoming, receiving the scarf, replacing the scarf, touching the forehead. No signs of exertion. Not a flicker of resistance. Steady. Unflagging.

The limitations of my own stamina, especially when interacting with others, barely allowed me to believe what I was witnessing: all the ways that Mingyur Rinpoche was there—and not there. The transactional self that calculates giving and taking was nowhere in evidence. He became just the act of giving, dissolving the separation between giver and recipient. He seemed to function with no conflict, no eye on the exit, not one hint of wishing for these interminable lines to end—all of which I would have found *normal*. I have read accounts of devout followers whose faith had been forever sealed by divine revelations of their master, or guru, or patron saint, visions of light and rainbows and transcendent miracles. What I was watching struck me as most impressive, this display of the inseparability of compassion and emptiness, compassionate action rolling on unimpeded by self-protective concerns.

Shortly after I returned to New York, Rinpoche disappeared. Everyone around him, including students, monastery administrators, and family members had assumed that he would enter a monastery or hermitage for his retreat. It turned out that he had a secret plan: to wander alone in the manner of the Hindu sadhus, begging for food and sleeping outdoors. From June 2011 to October 2015 no one knew anything about Mingyur Rinpoche's whereabouts. Maybe I would see him again, maybe not. Meanwhile, he entered my mindscape frequently, intensified by working with his teachings as I wrapped up the book without him.

Vietnam

In 2014, I visited Vietnam for the first time since my fleeting stop at the Saigon airport in 1966. I started in Hanoi, the seat of government, and ended a month later in Ho Chi Minh City, formerly Saigon. Throughout much of the trip, I felt like one of those American children of immigrant parents from India or Ireland whose family had ardently kept the old country alive in the New World and who, only on finally visiting the motherland, comprehended that the old country had transformed, while their parents' memories of it had stood still. In Vietnam, I returned to a place that I had never been.

Prior to this visit, I reread fictional and journalistic accounts of the war, watched documentaries, and replayed *Apocalypse Now* and *Full Metal Jacket*. For months, the war plagued my dreams again. On the ground in Vietnam, the dead and the wounded appeared in my mind's eye—soldiers and children strewn by the roadside; languid sampans and rail stations foreshadowing explosions and flying limbs. Yet every chance encounter with a Vietnamese, especially younger ones, suggested that the war that was so vivid in my mind had long disappeared from theirs. They expressed fears about the economy and the control of water by the Chinese and grew particularly animated when talking about dance clubs.

On my first outing in Ho Chi Minh City, I went directly to the War

Remnants Museum, the city's most popular tourist attraction. Triumphant displays of captured American aircraft stand guard between the front gate and the marble steps. Some, like the CH-47 Chinook, look like ungainly prehistoric insects, incinerated, deactivated, yet still treacherous. Inside, the exhibits display every form of anguish caused by the Americans: torture, shooting, burning, the maiming of soldiers and villagers, old men, women, and children. Many photographs seem chosen to make the viewer gasp in disbelief, and if, like me, you are an American of a certain age and disposition, to again feel shame. They rarely miss their mark. Unabashed propaganda accompanies the signage and captions throughout. There is little reference to a civil conflict. Just the *aggressive American war* against the patriotic Vietnamese. Once again, I was horrified by *Napalm Girl*—the terrified nine-year-old child racing down the road naked to escape the explosions behind her.

I walked out of the museum weakened by flashbacks: my married life in Canada; my husband's battles with the war he refused to fight; my return to New York on my own. Half a century had passed since Thich Quang Duc's death. Moral certainties had lost their appeal. Purportedly the museum's mission is to promote peace, but this is compromised by its understandable glorification of Vietnam's victory. I felt nothing but sympathy with Vietnam's pride in defeating the United States. Small brown Vietnamese had brought big white imperialist America to its knees. Good for them. And yet the litany of dualities—good guys and bad, aggressors and victims, barbarians and heroes—reaffirmed the same old separation of self and other that fuels aggression. The museum educates the public about the atrocities of the American war and champions patriotic pride, but it's no endorsement for healing the divide between friend and foe. On a second visit to the museum, the battle cries sounded even louder and left me more disheartened.

Midafternoon one steaming day, I made my way along Cach Mang Thang, a wide avenue that heads toward the intersection where Thich Quang Duc set himself on fire. A small, unassuming memorial was erected soon after his death on the exact corner of his immolation. Across the six-lane avenue, set back on a rise, sits an enormous, gaudy golden sculpture of a monk in flames, erected in 2010. The monk being immortalized had sacrificed his life to defend the Buddhists of South Vietnam, who at the time had been estimated to comprise 90 percent of the population. The Buddhist population today has been officially reduced to 10 percent, and whether the communist authorities tolerate genuine religious freedom is a matter of whispered speculation. Similar to other commemorative sculptures around the city, this one has that distinct look of a government commission: utilitarian, unctuous, a sop to political propaganda.

Lined up on the ledge beneath the gold statue were an oil lamp, a cylinder filled with sticks of incense, a large incense holder, fresh flowers, and a glass jar for collecting money. I slipped some bills into the jar, lit incense, and stepped back, anticipating a solemn, wrenching moment. Perhaps I would cry. I recalled the photograph of Thich Quang Duc, tried to steady that image in my mind, but I could not avoid the flashy ugly monument, closer to Disneyland than to the dharma. There was nothing sacred about this site, and the attempt to glorify Thich Quang Duc with this garish public display struck me as absurd. Suddenly I found myself standing alone in Ho Chi Min City in front of a hideous statue, holding a stick of incense and laughing. I crossed the six lanes of traffic and returned to the original memorial.

Have you ever seen the photograph of Thich Quang Duc? I asked a young American man with whom I had dinner shortly before leaving New York for Vietnam. A graduate of an Ivy League university, he had recently spent a year in a Zen monastery in South Korea.

Of course, he replied.

What do you think that photograph is about?

I think it's a photograph of an enlightened mind.

I did not let on how much his answer meant to me and wondered if the idealism that I had shared with dharma friends from half a century ago had even allowed for such a wondrous possibility.

PART NINE

THE BARDOS

The Bardo of This Life

In the fall of 2015, after an absence of four and a half years, Mingyur Rinpoche returned from his wandering retreat. Six weeks later I went to visit him at Osel Ling, his monastery in Kathmandu, where a new residence had been built for him on a side of the steep mountain, below the main monastery buildings. On entering the reception room on the first floor I made three full prostrations and approached his chair, which was raised and draped with an embroidered cloth. I offered the ceremonial white silk *kata* (scarf), then took a seat to his left. His book on the foundational practices that I had worked on had been published while he was in retreat, and both an English and a Chinese edition sat on the table before his chair. I tried to overcome a tearful shyness on seeing him again. He then spoke—as he had been doing consistently since returning—about his near-death experience, which had occurred just three weeks after he secretively slipped through the gates of his monastery in Bodh Gaya. He had gone to a restaurant to beg for food and had been given rice and dal scooped from a bucket of leftovers scraped off the plates of paying customers. A stomach infection immediately took hold, and after five days of increasing weakness and extreme dehydration, his bodily systems began shutting down. Mingyur spoke of how much he had learned from almost dying and of his newly invigorated appreciation for bardo training. This refers to the cycle of teachings in the Tibetan curriculum that accustoms young novices to the reality of impermanence, the certainty of death, and the stages of dying. Mingyur said that he would like to write a book about the bardos for Buddhists and non-Buddhists and . . . *Would you be interested in helping me?*

You know the old saw: If something sounds too good to be true, it probably is. My hearing had been declining, a condition that he knew well from our previous work together. I remained immobile, dumbfounded. Speaking louder, he asked again.

Of course.

I floated back up the vertiginous stairs to the main buildings and more stairs to my room in the guest quarters. Sometimes clichés cannot be bested, like *walking on air*. Did my beloved spiritual friend really just ask me, now past seventy years old, to work on a book with him about death and dying? No one gets this lucky.

Yes, yes, of course. No, I do not need to think about it. There's nothing I would rather do. Fourteen-hour flights between Delhi and New York? No problem. I will learn how to die every day. I will learn how to live. *Yes, of course.*

We arranged to start working in Nepal the following March. I returned to New York still floating, still questioning whether I had gotten this quite right. Pema Chödrön telephoned from Colorado to inquire about Rinpoche's retreat. I shared the remarkable news that he had asked for my assistance with a book about the bardos that could be appreciated even by non-Buddhists.

You have found the perfect teacher, Pema said.

Why do you say that? I asked.

He has given you an impossible task.

For the next two to three years, we referred to our project as *the bardo book,* although in the end an introduction to this classic body of teaching—which first appeared some six hundred years ago—replaced the traditional detailed commentary, making the material basic and accessible. The bardos delineate six life stages. For conventional Tibetans, the first four correspond to a linear sequence from first to last breath; the following two come with the separation of mind and body after physical death. With their un-shakable belief in reincarnation, Tibetans typically connect *bardo* to phys-ical death and rebirth. The term *bardo* translates as in between two—in between this life and the next. In the formal map, *the bardo of becoming* describes the final stage: in between one body and the next—leaving be-hind the old physical body and becoming a new being. Inhabiting a new form starts the cycle of life and death once again.

What made these descriptions work for a general audience was Mingyur's explanation of bardos as states of mind. In this paradigm, each stage gathers together particular qualities that are not tied to a physical sequence. Inde-pendent of chronology, the dominant characteristics that shape living, dying, becoming, and rebirth reflect types of experience that we revisit throughout our days and nights during this lifetime. Expanding the bardo descriptions to include daily activities, ordinary trauma, and common psychological con-ditions allows anyone to engage in these teachings. This is not a modern, made-for-the-West interpretation. Placing the emphasis on states of mind—not physical stages—is how Mingyur was taught by his father and his main tutor. When rebirth is presented as a daily life experience that invites fresh-ness, encourages curiosity, embraces uncertainty, and supports openness and renewal, then the entire bardo cycle can transmit meaning regardless of any particular belief system. When the bardo of dying is experienced as the moment-to-moment letting go of this breath, this moment, this pleasant experience, this hateful impulse, this desire, this friendship, this thought, then the lurking, stalking projection of losing this physical body becomes a little less frightening. From our own awareness of letting go again and again, we can recognize the benefits of dying again and again, and learn that we are never too old to die.

The first effect that working on the book had on my own practice related to impermanence. For many years, my daily recitation has emphasized the importance of recognizing the fleeting, transient quality of all phenomena, no exceptions. Using the same mala that had been given to me by Tenzin on my first visit to Kathmandu, I often paused at this point, and holding the mala in my right hand, used my thumb to move each of the 108 beads as I identified impermanence within my immediate surroundings, starting with myself and moving out in concentric circles. In my house in Cape Breton, this might sound something like: *I am impermanent, and this incense is impermanent; this cushion, this text, this house is impermanent; this table, this chair, this horse, this cat, this barn, this neighbor, these relatives, these friends, this beloved teacher, and planet earth and the sun. . . .*

In one liturgy, the same reminder ups the ante: *All things are impermanent; death comes without warning; this body too will be a corpse.* My mala recitation became *I will die, and you will die, and this guru and this house, and this horse and this friend, and this tree, and . . .* Here, I visualized the dreamlike passing of all forms as crumbling, disintegrating, buildings falling, deathbed gasps, seas drying up.

With the bardo teachings, these strategies for recognizing and inhabiting impermanence came to feel inadequate, somewhat abridged. I had never gone beyond the ending of things as I knew them. I have repeated so many times that the barn is impermanent and that the barn will die, and in my mind's eye I have watched the barn falling down, collapsing, disintegrating without acknowledging that it will also continue, that it is right now dying, decaying, and at the same time becoming, turning into something else. The barn stands out as a particularly poignant example because about thirty-five years ago, the immense hand-hewn support beams were hauled from the wreckage of Margaret MacDougal's century-old barn down the road, which had collapsed years before. Looking around my house, I noted the previous use of things: a cow skull found in a field that has long served as a towel rack; potholders hanging on a five-pronged metal hook that was once a hoe. Tables, chairs, paper, books, blankets, pottery, sea glass—all once something else. I could not be the exception to the transformation of all things. I cannot claim clarity about what it means that the immateriality of consciousness reincarnates, but I am not speaking of such matters. Only that *everything* that can be seen, touched, known continues in one form or another, so that whatever exists is right now becoming something else. Sustainability-conscious funeral businesses now offer burial bags that transform human corpses into mushrooms and trees.

I am dying and becoming, and you are dying and becoming, and the barn is, and the teacher is, and the horse is . . . and the relationship is . . . If I let go of Helen and allow fixed ideas about Helen to die at this moment, what is born? What is reborn? If I let go of Helen, will I truly know what Dudjom Rinpoche meant when he implied the essential sameness between the man who was shot on the street and the man who was shot on TV? Will I comprehend that life and death are not separate—and not the same? I wonder if, at the time of physical death, when the container melts away and the conceptual mind is emptied, I will recognize the opportunity to join the passing clouds. When Elizabeth Murray was close to her last breath, she spoke about vast skies and wishing, as she put it, *to ride on clouds to find my death.*

To consciously acknowledge that we die every day encourages us to let go of recycling our constricted patterns, to let them dissolve and die, and then to go forward with a little less baggage, feeling a little less trapped by old explanations of who we are and why we can't change. If I had let go of habitual preconceptions, perhaps I could have seen fire coming from snow, as Mingyur Rinpoche did during the winter we worked together at Sherab Ling. His room, in the huge main monastic building, was up two flights of stairs. On the landing between them was a window that looked out onto mountains. At the end of one day, through that window I saw red flames leaping up from a crevice between two white peaks. Not knowing how fast or how far a fire like that could spread, I hurried to tell Rinpoche. He could not see the fire from his room so he came down to the landing. *A miracle! Fire coming from snow! I never saw before!* He ran back up to get his camera.

I missed the miracle. Faster than the sight of snow on fire registered, my mind filled the crevice between the peaks with leaves and brush deposited by wind. Even when I saw nothing but fire coming from snow, I could not see fire coming from snow. Click, click. Time to get to work. *But Rinpoche, is it dangerous?* He turned back to the window to look again, as if that possibility had never occurred to him.

The book that we had been working on, *In Love with the World: A Monk's Journey Through the Bardos of Living and Dying,* was published in May 2019. Mingyur's accessible approach got an unexpected lift from a serendipitous event in the spring of 2017, and soon after I returned to Kathmandu eager to tell him about a new best-selling novel, *Lincoln in the*

Bardo, by a famous American author, George Saunders. I enthusiastically described the curiosity in New York about this term *bardo*—what it meant, was it Tibetan, how did it relate to Lincoln, and . . . *Rinpoche, isn't it amazing that the word* bardo *is on everyone's lips, even though no one knows . . .*

Helen?

Yes, Rinpoche?

What's a Lincoln?

In the Bardo of Old Age

Dying every day. This day, in mid-August 2020, I am sitting at my desk in Cape Breton, watching my aging horses in the field off the back deck, their saddles yet to be carried from the house to the barn. A torn meniscus has kept me from riding, and I wonder if I ever will again. And if I will be able to discard the recently purchased first cane or find newfound comfort in rebirth as an airport wheelchair passenger. I watch Joa, with her fawn-colored coat divided by a chocolate stripe down the center of her back and her thick, long mane of various shades of blond, ash, and brown, for which the neighbors nicknamed her Tina Turner. When I used to dye my hair, I would bring photographs of Joa's mane and ask the colorist to match it. Now my hair is white like Freyja's who, this summer, lies down more frequently and her hind legs tremble when she first stands. After a few shaky steps, she's OK, and I watch, amused that I'm the same: unsteady, though for now, only at first. I wonder if they know that they will die. I wonder if I know.

In the market in Inverness, navigating my shopping cart and new cane, I ran into Lorette Feehan, a neighbor my age known for her sharp tongue and soft heart. She encouraged me to stop in for tea so that we could discuss our aches and pains.

Don't we have anything else to talk about? I asked.

Fuck no, she said. *Old age sucks.*

That same day an email from a high-school friend from Dalton questioned the wisdom of an eighty-year-old Buddhist teacher who had posted on Facebook that she could no longer ride her bicycle. In my friend's assessment, the teacher had declared defeat, especially, she insisted, as this decision could have been delayed with balance exercises. *But who knows? Old age sucks.*

Sections of the dirt road between the town of Inverness and my house are so narrow that vehicles need to slow and edge way over to one side when passing. This invites social exchanges, which is how I had recently learned of the fentanyl overdose of an adored twenty-year-old grandson, and about a black bear that had stolen a case of Coca-Cola from a neighbor's front porch. In June, I rolled down the car window to greet an old friend.

I'm not dead yet, he announced.

You certainly don't look dead.

Well, I worked the frigging mills fifty years, and some days hauling my ass out of bed is harder than hauling lumber. Old age . . .

I am listening for a different tune. Nothing in the bardo tradition includes a specific stage called *the bardo of old age.* Nonetheless, these years perfectly illuminate the bardo principle, which rests with the recognition of impermanence and in-between states. Acknowledgment of experience is the key here, as obviously every moment is an in-between moment, even as we get sucked into illusions of certainty and sameness and assume a seamless continuity where none actually exists. Yet old age so magnifies the transition of life into imminent death that recognition of the in-between comes with the territory.

My familiar life is slipping away. My injuries have left me using a chair for meditation, a position that does not offer the same support to my body-mind as sitting on the floor. Not riding horses marks a big shift. I can no longer drive at night. I don't always wear my hearing aids. I wonder if this decline will continue gradually or accelerate with illness. Either way, inescapable changes loom just ahead. Shakyamuni Buddha's mother died seven days after his birth, and in his search for meaning, he realized that one of the primary causes of suffering comes from not accepting the impermanence of all phenomena. No matter what our age or circumstance, the continuity of change never increases or decreases. What changes is our experience of it. Awareness of what is happening may become more or less clear and wakeful. Hobbling around with a cane was a definite boost to my own efforts to recognize inevitable change.

As my list of new doctors and medical tests grows, I am trying to hold the certainty of physical death with the uncertainty of how that will happen. Yet I am still in the bardo of this life and have not yet entered irreversible decline—the unwavering arc toward the final breath—that corresponds to the bardo stage of physically dying. In 1997, I did an interview with Rick Fields for *Tricycle*. Rick was then editor of *Yoga Journal* in Berkeley, California, and the interview took place near his office. A few years earlier he had been diagnosed with lung cancer. He had been walking a line between accepting death and fighting the disease and had recently published a poetry collection called *Fuck You, Cancer and Other Poems*. I asked him, *You have cancer and I don't, but we're both dying. What's the difference?* And he said, *I'm in the bardo of dying and you're not.*

The minute Rick said this, I understood that we were already far apart and immediately felt the loss of our friendship, as I still do. Old age is not the same as entering the zone of dying, but it edges close enough to consider the benefits of letting go while we can still think clearly—more or less. I have written a will and notes for deathbed wishes, if my dying should allow for that. In part, these notes were inspired by the circumstances of a Zen friend. In her final weeks, she was lovingly cared for by her daughter and sisters. With family in attendance, visitors were discouraged. Many of us regretted not being able to sit in meditation with her, and perhaps she regretted it too.

It was quite different when Allen Ginsberg died. For a number of years, Allen had been studying with the Tibetan teacher Gelek Rinpoche, who I had met through Philip Glass just as *Tricycle* was starting. Gelek, moon-faced and friendly, had playfully suggested a twist on the sacred Tibetan mantra *om mani padme hum*. To aid my fundraising efforts he advised that I cup my hands together in the prayer position and recite: *om money money come*. Carole Corcoran had also become Gelek's student, and one evening in April 1997, we were having dinner out when Gelek called and asked us to join him at Allen's. Allen was in his final hours, and he lay in a hospital bed at the far end of a block-long loft that stretched from Thirteenth to Fourteenth Streets. The dissolution had progressed, his inhale spasmodic with squeaky gasps. Friends sat on chairs encircling the bed at a distance, giving anyone the chance to pull a chair close and speak to him in private. At the other end of the loft, a group that included Allen's brother, Eugene, talked quietly. In between, Gelek had gathered students who read Tibetan texts and chanted prayers. People came and went, moved about, chatted and changed places, recreating the fluidity, openness, and welcoming availability in Allen's dying as it had been in his living.

I don't know whether Rick ever befriended his cancer. The afternoon before he died, I sat at his bedside in the small house in Fairfax, California, that he shared with Marcia Cohen, his wife of the past several years; and he appeared to have made peace with dying. John Giorno died in his loft on the Bowery in October 2019. His husband was out of town, and while their friends in the art and poetry worlds lamented his aloneness, Vivian said, *His death was perfect. He died alone, like a real yogi.*

A few months earlier, Harold Talbott had passed away after a debilitating illness. Photographs taken a week before show him sitting up in bed, smiling and at ease. On my last visit, Harold had reported that a friend had recently asked, *If you have been practicing Buddhism for so many decades and you're still a mess, why should I be interested in Buddhism?* Harold had explained that without Buddhism he would have been so much worse. Every Buddhist I know, and certainly myself, could say the same thing.

No one wants to care for old horses. I hope mine die before I do. I have been selecting holiday gifts from among my possessions to reduce what's left. I have taken care of the easy part, legal paperwork and *stuff*. Who knows what might snare my mind at the end—what voices might enter unbidden, perhaps of loves or regrets, of things said or unsaid. Perhaps the silence that I have come to treasure will erupt into screeching yowls of fear and remorse. I cannot recognize these shapes now—and know that this doesn't count for beans.

I was treated as an old woman long before I identified with being one. From middle age on, women in New York City become invisible, pushed to the margins by youth-oriented obsessions. At diner or bar counters, young patrons' orders are taken first, even though I have been sitting there trying to catch the waiter's eye. In clothing stores, a salesperson freed up to help a new customer will scan the room for a younger, more glamorous prospect. My morning greetings in the elevator to device-addicted neighbors going off to work in their Tod's loafers and stilettoes generally go unacknowledged.

Larry Shainberg recently spoke to me of the humor in growing old. I asked him: *What about growing old do you find so funny?*

The humiliation, he said.

A few years ago, I was in northern India, and a woman decidedly younger than I asked my age. *Seventy-six.* She was astonished. *No! I don't believe it! You have to be joking!* I was enjoying this, smiling broadly. Then she said, *Honestly, I didn't think you were older than seventy-five.* Inflation, dejection. *Watch your mind.*

Two years before, at a family holiday dinner at Hermine and Bob's loft in Tribeca, I had been describing the rhythms of the swimming pool use in my apartment building in Chelsea, how I like to slip in between the buff jocks and the old ladies who arrive midmorning. My sister cut in, *Ha, did you hear the way she said "old ladies" as if she's not one of them?* I was startled. It was true. I had not identified myself as *one of them* and was stunned that anyone else would. I was still in what Leonard Cohen called *the foothills of old age.*

That's changed. My determination to rid the barnyard of old hay, undeterred by cautionary twinges of pain and fueled by memories of Helen Boyd and habits of obstinacy, conspired to necessitate—some three months later—the surgical removal of an extruded globule of a spinal disk pressing on the sciatic nerve. A routine of stretches, ankle weights, and bands no longer promises to reset the clock. I have entered the bardo of old age.

Decades ago, with our long lives ahead of us, Clara Serra had told me about a great aunt of hers who had lived alone in the same small village in Germany where she herself had grown up. Every evening, the old woman sat in a rocking chair in the kitchen and sipped a cup of tea. When she finished, too tired to wash the cup and saucer, she routinely placed the dishes in the oven; should she die during the night, no one would discover dirty dishes in the sink. Initially, this story expanded my understanding of my friend, where she had come from, her world and its anxious attention to respectability. Now I am that old woman, doing the dishes before going to bed, just in case.

A conversation with my friend June Leaf reminds me that this bardo, like any other, has an expandable range. I recently visited her at her house in Cape Breton, which sits above the Mabou Mines harbor some fifteen miles south along the same coast as my own house. The kitchen looks the way it has for the past fifty years, and amidst the usual dishevelment of dishes, old mail, logs for the cook stove, books, pens, et cetera, we discussed options for her upcoming ninety-third birthday. She lives alone now, following the death of her husband, the photographer Robert Frank. They came to Cape Breton just about the same time as the other artists from New York, but independently. June continues to spend her summer days going into her studio and making art; she drives, swims, reads, and sees friends. Still, she told me wistfully, *I feel old for the first time in my life.* I did not tell her that she had told me the exact same thing last year. A few days later a dozen friends raised a glass and sang "Happy Birthday" to her on the deck of my house and wished her many happy returns. Perhaps she will return to this very conclusion that only now, for the first time, she feels old.

Vivian once cautioned me never to let go of vanity. At this stage I am willing to try. Maybe at this stage, she is too. In the spring of 2019, I undertook several one-year vows designed to push back at the habits of vanity. One was a renewal of an earlier vow inspired by the writer Ann Patchett. In an essay in *The New York Times,* published just before Christmas 2016, she wrote about the salutary benefits of vowing not to buy clothes for a year. Easing the commitment, just prior to reading Patchett's essay, I had purchased two dresses and a sweater. Additionally, I would soon return to Nepal, where residence in a Tibetan monastery with no hot water, hangers, closets, washing machines, or irons works best for clothes intended to be left behind. After maintaining the vow for a year, it became obvious that any purchases from here on out had nothing to do with need but only with a futile attempt to satisfy conceit and greed.

Another vow prohibits makeup. This has been the more interesting, seeing all the little ways the ego-self fidgets with reality, tries to placate it, please it, distort it with, say, just a tiny bit of lipstick, a smudge of eye shadow in order to . . . to what, exactly? Look a little prettier, younger, more likable? Without makeup, maybe I should smile more. Perhaps my age trivializes a vow to work with vanity. I wonder what others think, if they even notice . . . at my age. Mingyur Rinpoche assures me that I look fresh, bright. Of course. Everyone looks bright in his radiance.

In the fall of 2019, I was in San Francisco and visiting with my friend Cal Ferris. We first met through dharma some thirty years ago, and in all that time, her looks have not changed: still lithe, with shiny brown hair that hangs loose below her shoulders, and still gracious and glamorous in an utterly casual way. One afternoon we were sitting on the terrace of her house, which sits just below Coit Tower and looks out onto San Francisco Bay. We spoke of aging, and I gingerly stepped into an account of giving up buying clothes and wearing makeup. She listened thoughtfully, nodding, suggesting that I was making sense—for me. She then explained her attention to appearance as *holding up my end of the tent*. This reversal from getting—as in getting attention, praise, energy—to giving—as in giving energy, of uplifting even the most inconsequential of circumstances was such a singular approach, that with anyone else, I might have met it with distrust; but Cal always stays attuned to ways of giving, and so this made sense—for her.

On the occasion of her eighty-fifth birthday, I reached Pema in Colorado from my house in Cape Breton to ask how this milestone was landing. She told me about watching an interview that Oprah Winfrey had conducted with Toni Morrison. When asked about her advanced age, the writer reached out to touch Oprah's arm and said, *I hope you live long enough to find out.* I might live long enough. I am not so far behind.

Maintaining the vows has been made easier by accepting that my body is pulling into the terminal. At some point—seventy-five?—it seems that among friends my age, most of us are no longer climbing, dancing, bush-whacking our way up the mountain, wanting to get somewhere, be some-one, do something. Now, whether or not our dreams have come true, or our ambitions have been fulfilled or abandoned or corrupted, we have passed over the peak. With disfigured feet and arthritic joints, partly blind and going deaf, we are tumbling down the far side in a rollicking display of dysfunction. The constructed personas used for the upward journey are no longer needed. Gone are the days of trying to attract new partners or hold on to old ones, or impress potential bosses or outshine colleagues. The masks have been disintegrating through disuse and disinterest. Many of my closest women friends, Buddhists and not, will claim that aging would be harder without external enhancements. Still, with hubris and confi-dence, I use the royal *we*, with the assumption that they will agree—sooner or later. America, with its perilous materialism, treats its elderly like any other piece of junk that no longer works—cars, TVs, kitchen appliances. We no longer produce or manufacture. We have aged out of the workforce and the military. We are worthless, of no more value than the piles of refuse that blight the landscape. With or without lipstick, we wonder how we will die: Will our deaths be sudden or painful and prolonged; will we die before or after our partners, or be a burden to the children? Who will feed us and clean our soiled bums and change the dirty sheets?

At the beginning of 2020, I attended an event at which Mirabai Bush had been scheduled to read from *Walking Each Other Home,* the book she had just completed with Ram Dass. They had been close friends and collaborators since meeting in India in 1970. Two weeks before the event, Ram Dass, who had suffered a severe, debilitating stroke in 1997, died at his home in Maui. The reading turned into an impromptu memorial. Since the publication of his book *Be Here Now* in 1971, Ram Dass had been touted as the most awakened homegrown advocate for spiritual develop-ment. Yet those who knew him best recognized the truly salutary effects of his stroke, and the ways that he had become more amenable and sensitized to others. To start the event, Krishna Das, a singer of Hindu devotional songs, spoke of Ram Dass being a *saint.* So far, aging has not assuaged my cynical bent, and my first response was, *Ho hum, let the hagiography begin.*

KD then made a convincing case. He recounted that since the stroke—more than twenty years earlier—Ram Dass had known excruciating pain, that he could do nothing for himself, not move from his wheelchair to his bed, not put on a sweater or slippers, not go to the toilet, not wipe himself, and yet . . . *he never complained. Never once.*

Afterward, I asked Mirabai if not complaining came from transcending the complaining mind, or whether Ram Dass had made this a discipline. *A discipline,* she said. I thought, *There's a vow worth considering. I vow not to complain.* This virtue is definitely not specific to old age, yet aging bodies provide such ample excuses for complaint; and I can already hear that complaint itself—not pain or illness or even fear of dying—has the energetic force to consume us.

When asked, *Why do we meditate?* Zen master Shunryu Suzuki said, *To enjoy our old age.* In addition to Suzuki's sage—and perhaps somewhat humorous—response, an unexpected lesson came from James Brady, President Ronald Reagan's press secretary. Brady was with Reagan in 1981 when a deranged twenty-five-year-old opened fire, wounding the president and leaving Brady partially paralyzed. In a documentary about Brady, one scene takes place during a rehab session in a riding ring. Brady, strapped into a harness of his own, waits on an elevated platform to be mechanically hoisted onto a waiting horse. He had been asked about the effects of the attack on his young son. With his speech left high and halting and his words slurred, he said, *I . . . ha . . . ve to . . . pl . . . ay . . . my . . . ca . . . rds as . . . best I c . . . an. I have to play my cards as best as I can, and my boy has to play his cards as best as he can.* In its circumstances, this wisdom was so moving and surprising.

I believe that my namesake, Helen Boyd, played her cards as best she could. She grew into old age in a spacious apartment on the second floor of a building in the commercial section of the Ohio town where she had been born. By then, she had known various degrees of reconciliation with her three children but none lived close by. When she was diagnosed with cancer, they started to interrupt their busy lives to visit her. But she felt that she had interrupted their lives enough, and found it unconscionable to add to the difficulties she had caused them decades earlier, when she had abandoned them to live in New York City. One day she walked into the local firearms store and bought a pistol, explaining to the owner that she was being pestered by a rat. The owner did not hesitate. Shooting a rat was in perfect keeping with who everyone in this small farming community knew Helen Boyd to be. Then she sat upright in her polished brass bed and blew her brains out.

America in the Bardo of Dying

The 2016 presidential election felt like being swallowed by a whale and churning inside its slimy, repulsive, intestinal heaves. I thrashed about in horror, while trying to hold in mind the benefits of disruption. Bardo teachings underscore that fissures in the mind-stream—from personal loss or shock, or from extreme weather in the physical or political landscape—always contain the seeds of new possibilities and we can't know what those are. The potential for benefiting from disruption always exists, but for that potential to ripen we need to stay with the uncertainty, the upheaval, the fear, the unfamiliar, and not scurry away like crabs to hide under rocks. All good news, if, if, if we can rest within unknowable turbulence, allow it to permeate our interactions, stay open, and be curious about it. This has been a big *if. The world is falling apart; my world is falling apart. Sit with that,* I tell myself. *Try sitting inside the guts of a whale, far away from safe, cozy meditation halls. Try sitting still in the midst of motion, commotion, chaos.*

I was determined to watch the inauguration of the forty-fifth president. I felt I had an obligation, not as an American citizen but as a dharma practitioner who aspired to break patterns of avoiding anything that caused aversion or discomfort or disgust. Breathing in and out, trying to stay steady with *what is,* with whatever arises, including the filthy, legless beggar whose presence on the corner of my block in NYC is so dependable that when he misses a day I think he's dead; wealthy ladies dressed in animal furs; the oozing suppurating sores on the dogs in Kathmandu; the ugly, orange maniac about to be sworn in as president.

I could not persuade any friends to join me, and watched the inauguration alone, sitting close up to a small television. I tried compassion exercises, including a favorite of the Dalai Lama's: looking directly at a specific person on the street or the subway or the TV screen, seeing their face, their gait, their hair, their clothes, and remembering, *That person wants happiness and doesn't want suffering.* I tried meditations that generate empathy by looking at the longings and hurts and anger and fears of others and understanding that *they are just like me.* I was staring at a miserable human being, a bully and a coward who all his life wanted things to be different than they were and tried to bend the universe to his will. And I too had created untold misery for myself by wanting what I did not have, and not liking or appreciating what I did have. This moment was mostly never good enough for either one of us. I tried doing practices of exchanging self with other, practices that arouse compassion by dissolving the usual distinctions that define relationships. No matter what I did or told myself, or what mantra I repeated . . . I hated him. He was taking my country away from me, destroying the America I loved—the America that had liberated the death camps and that had welcomed desperate immigrants. For weeks afterward, I could barely meditate for two minutes before some news story about the dismantling of democracy entered my mind, and anger and despair caught fire.

Thinley Norbu Rinpoche used to repeat: *There is no perfect in this samsara.* Obviously, I didn't get it. Couldn't hear it. In my midthirties at the time and recently divorced, I dipped my toes into the Buddha's teachings while flirting with samsara in every which way, seduced by friendships, sex, food, and clothes, and still functioning as if more attention, praise, and popularity were sources of genuine happiness.

Growing up in the shadow of the Second World War meant learning that humankind had passed through the pinnacle of evil, never to be surpassed or repeated. Everything would get better from here on in. The ideology that promoted a progressive agenda as an inevitable trajectory was informed by family, professors, proponents of American exceptionalism, and finally, convert Buddhists who, like me, celebrated the marriage between American models of external political freedom and the Eastern wisdom of internal liberation. In keeping with the dictates of samsara, bad things would happen but never with the demonic appeal of the death camps. The dread of nuclear annihilation was offset by the air raid drills at PS 40. In case of an attack by the Russians, we were instructed to crouch under our wooden desks, open our soft-backed black-and-white composition notebooks, and place them over our heads—turning nuclear threat into a comic break from classroom boredom.

Back then, every problem had a solution: illnesses, poverty, discrimination. In 1952, when I was nine years old, my family took the Greyhound bus to North Carolina where my father had been invited to teach a summer session at Black Mountain College. We were not allowed to sit in the back of the bus, even when that area alone had four seats together. All the stops had separate water fountains and toilets for *whites* and *coloreds*. The separation felt mean and menacing, but it was not slavery. Like everything in America, it represented a direction away from something worse and toward something better. Americans were enjoying more prosperity, buying more stuff, more machines, cars, dishwashers. One time even my father came home from an out-of-town teaching job with a set of handwoven placemats. We were getting there. We were all going to get there.

The code used by the American Armed Forces radio station to implement the emergency evacuation of Saigon on April 29, 1975, was "White Christmas," sung by Bing Crosby: *I'm dreaming of a white Christmas, just like the ones I used to know. Where the tree tops glisten and children listen to hear sleigh bells in the snow. . . .*

Game over. I cheered America's defeat in Vietnam. As I saw it, only with the triumph of military dishonor could the United States straighten itself out, get back on track, and continue the founding mandate to evolve toward greater goodness. What's more, the merging of capitalism and technology, lauded for its modern advantages, threatened to imperil humankind in unprecedented ways, and enlightened new paradigms for *being* and *doing* were required to protect humanity from its destructive versions of success. Enter Buddhism—like a knight in shining armor, a new morning—and America's destiny to become America would now be realized with help from a new religious universe that had already put down stakes across the country. Amid the national bicentennial celebrations in 1976, the gala openings of prominent new centers in various Buddhist schools heralded an auspicious start to America's third century. Right around this time, Thinley Norbu arrived in New York and in his broken English repeated the lesson I have found so difficult: *There is no perfect in this samsara.*

I am still in the bardo of living while America itself has entered the bardo of dying, its vital signs diminishing as the last gasps of stage-four capitalism approach the death rattle. Yet perhaps never fully alive to begin with, for what appears to be dying is what never came to be. Like a stillbirth. The initial promises never matured. My naïveté and idealism are dissolving, dying, and transforming. I am trying to stay steady with uncertainty; trying to resist the comfort of outrage and opinions; trying to allow old fairytales to die; to steer clear of complaint and despair and especially nostalgia—that most pernicious enemy of ease. Some days I do this more effectively than others while reminding myself: falling in love with reality as it is remains just as much an option right now as it's always been. I repeat this, even as I feel newly born as a fugitive. Being outcasts now seems to be America's most shared experience. Cast out. Not from a country that we left, but from a country that left us. Every one of us. When white Christian Americans complain of feeling displaced and discriminated against, you know how bad it must be for everyone else.

I think back to my first time taking refuge with Dudjom Rinpoche, and all the subsequent times I have participated in this formal ceremony of leaving home to enter the Buddhist path, and to all the efforts I have made to release the false promises of the conventional world, both personal and political with all its mangled recipes for happiness and freedom. And never could I have anticipated such an impactful kick-in-the-ass shove out the door coming from a country that moved away.

One thing I know about my old age: I don't wish to spend it outraged. Maybe I cannot totally reign in the complaining mind, but the heat of outrage, with its glaring flames, invites a choice. And if I do catch fire, I still cannot say what will come from the ashes. Thich Quang Duc could not have known what might have risen from his ashes. The bardo descriptions of the dying process and the teachings on the transcendent mind— the mind that disidentifies with the body—propose that fire cannot burn space, that when you inhabit the spacious open nature of the liberated mind, nothing can hurt you, for the *you* who normally experiences hurt is no longer that same entity. In the aftermath of the 2016 election, millions of us felt scorched, and very few could sit still with the heat. Did the fourteenth-century Japanese nun Eshun feel the heat? When she was ready to die, she sat on top of a funeral pyre and lit it. As the flames licked closer, a brother monk yelled out to ask if she was feeling hot. Eshun answered, *Such a matter would concern only a stupid fellow like yourself.* I was among the stupid fellows, but I wasn't running for the water buckets either.

When Chögyam Trungpa told his students, *I want to talk about the aggression in this room,* it was at the height of American aggression in Indochina. By then, the late Vietnamese Zen monk Thich Nhat Hanh, whose dharma was also forged in the fires of Vietnam, had been advocating for the political urgencies of *being peace.* In 1967, Martin Luther King, Jr., nominated him for the Nobel Peace Prize, and he had been trying to show us by example, by words, through poetry and teachings that, as Mahatma Gandhi put it: *There is no path to peace. Peace is the path.*

Many years ago, I attended a talk by a middle-aged lama who had recently escaped from Tibet. He wore simple robes and his demeanor seemed similarly unadorned. In a soft, scratchy voice, he spoke movingly of his time in a Chinese prison camp and his compassion for the guards who had carried out orders to torture him. He explained that sooner or later their actions would cause them greater suffering than they had caused him. The entire audience was just about in tears. During the question-and-answer period, a sincere young man, better dressed in slacks and a button-down shirt than many of his scruffy peers, asked how those of us living in relative comfort could best help a world besieged by injustice. The American translator relayed the question. The lama seemed not to understand and questioned the translator. Their exchange went back and forth, until the translator explained to the young man, *The lama says that it seems you think you are something other than the world. Separate. Apart. What is this world but us? He says: You are this world. And every step, every breath, every intention can be directed toward the alleviation of suffering. Or not. Your choice. Do you understand?*

There's no perfect in samsara. And the dynamics of samsara have not changed since the beginning of time, and still we aspire to save all sentient beings. This will never make sense and that's OK. John Giorno used to say, *It will never get better than this.* The recognition that this moment is all we have does not automatically shape my days; my interpretive mind still functions as a conveyor belt that carries this truth through my head to my ears, my eyes, and my mouth, and I need to keep telling myself: *Stop wasting time wishing it were some other way. Everything that was is now. Everything that will be is now.*

I used to rely on dharma to constantly remind me that change, uncertainty, and death are all we can count on. These days everyone talks about uncertainty, change, fear of dying. Newscasters, journalists, columnists use uncertainty to add dread and fear—about democracy, the planet, warming oceans and drying land, migrations, race relations, nuclear war, wealth inequality—delivered as if uncertainty itself were a new plague, as if there were a time before when certainty prevailed and now it does not. During the pandemic, uncertainty and death were spoken about as to give the impression that in the good old days sentient beings were not afraid to die. Tell me when.

In times of crises, slow down: the traditional Yoruba message, proclaimed for the world today by Bayo Akomolafe, the Nigerian philosopher. I take solace in remembering that slowing down and staying with the discomfort will prove to be more helpful than panicking, running away, or hiding within smoky plumes of horror and fury. It also helps that the escape routes have been cut off. The leafy streets of small towns no longer provide protection; nor do the commemorative parades, the university campuses, or elementary schools; not the malls, the supermarkets, or the Capitol.

Sales are up for drugs, guns, and bunkers. At the very same time, in this world that looks bleak and getting bleaker: *You are* still *nothing but the buddha, the dharma, the sangha.* The message from the lama: *You are the world.* You are the home of anonymous spontaneous compassion that is capable of continuously arising, again and again. *Slow down.* From this home, this slowed-down home, we can emerge from fragile and illusive shells, and engage with this desperate world, protected by accepting that we will die, that everything will, sooner or later; protected by compassion for ourselves and others; armed with confidence and resilience. From this home, we have a chance to slip through the residual scum of fear and madness to some sort of sanity, and then to look around and figure out how to help.

What feels newly born is recognizing the benefits of my current situation; appreciating the multiple opportunities for intensifying awareness of things as they are; and of connecting to a state of mind, to an open heart, to a diamond core with the intrinsic capacity to survive being a stranger, even to myself, or living exiled within my native country. To steady myself on the path of awakening, I could not ask for more favorable conditions than being in the bardo of old age, in a country that is falling apart, and in a world on fire. I have been dealt an extraordinary hand. The rest is up to me.

Acknowledgments

For reading early drafts, for encouragement and enduring friendship, thank you to Mirabai Bush, Carole Corcoran, Sheila Hixon, Vivian Kurz, and Larry Shainberg. For reading later drafts with an eye for accuracy, thank you to Nancy Mujo Baker, Benjamin Bogin, Pema Chödrön, Donald S. Lopez, Jr., and Roshi Enkyo O'Hara. Thank you to Toni Burbank for astute observations at the beginning; to Sharon Salzberg for help at the end; to Jared Bland for expert publishing insights; and to James Shaheen for wise and loving counsel over the long haul.

I owe a special debt of gratitude to Joan Duncan Oliver. No one played a greater role in shaping unruly pages into this book; and no one offered more criticism with greater dedication to getting it right.

I wish to acknowledge my sister, Hermine Ford. Although we had the same parents and grew up together, we came away with different experiences of our family. Yet Hermine never faltered in her support for telling my story as I saw it; for this, I am so grateful.

Many thanks to Kim Witherspoon and her team at InkWell Management for championing *Lotus Girl*, and in particular to Maria Whelan.

At St. Martin's Press, thank you to Emily Anderson for careful attention to the finishing details; and to Joel Fotinos, for collaboratively guiding this story into the world.

Helen Tworkov
Cape Breton, Nova Scotia
Summer, 2023